D0042311

Answering the Ultimate Question

Answering the Ultimate Question

How Net Promoter Can Transform Your Business

Laura L. Brooks, Ph.D.
Richard Owen

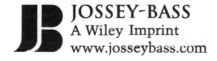
JOSSEY-BASS
A Wiley Imprint
www.josseybass.com

Published by Jossey-Bass
A Wiley Imprint
989 Market Street, San Francisco, CA 94103-1741—www.josseybass.com

Jossey-Bass books and products are available through most bookstores. To contact Jossey-Bass directly call our Customer Care Department within the U.S. at 800-956-7739, outside the U.S. at 317-572-3986, or fax 317-572-4002.

Jossey-Bass also publishes its books in a variety of electronic formats. Some content that appears in print may not be available in electronic books.

Library of Congress Cataloging-in-Publication Data

Owen, Richard, 1965-
    Answering the ultimate question : how Net Promoter can transform your business / Richard Owen, Laura L. Brooks.
        p.   cm.
    Includes bibliographical references and index.
    ISBN 978-0-470-26069-2 (cloth)
        1. Customer relations.   2. Customer loyalty.   3. Consumer satisfaction.
4. Success in business.   I. Brooks, Laura L., 1963-   II. Title.
    HF5415.5.O93   2009
    658.8'12—dc22

                                                                2008032858

Printed in the United States of America
FIRST EDITION
HB Printing   10 9 8 7 6 5 4 3 2 1

Contents

Introduction

"How likely is it that you would recommend this company to a friend or colleague?" That's *the ultimate question*. Fred Reichheld's book of the same name started a transformation in how businesses think about their customers. Published in 2006, it challenged the conventional wisdom of customer satisfaction thinking and coined the terms *bad profits* and *good profits*—a distinction between profits gained at the expense of customer loyalty and those that were not. Reichheld's book took a critical look at many of the existing practices around customer satisfaction survey-and-analysis research practices, finding much of it to be ineffective at driving business outcomes. The book inspired business leaders to put customer loyalty at the front of their agenda, not just because it was the right thing to do but because it was the best way for their businesses to increase retention and growth. As you have probably guessed, we are fans of Fred Reichheld's work, but it horrified many in the traditional market research community who saw it as an assault on their science. We think they missed the point.

One Powerful Question, Many Powerful Insights

In 2000, we began a journey to understand the linkage between customer loyalty and profitable growth. Frustrated by our observation that few corporate leaders took the topic of customer loyalty seriously, we sought a model that would convince them, using data, of something we all intuitively understood: customer loyalty drives financial performance. In a research project between Fred Reichheld and Satmetrix (our technology company focused on automating customer loyalty programs), we tested potential loyalty predictors. Based on a database that Satmetrix had developed, Reichheld and Laura Brooks generated a series of insights around buying behavior, resulting in Reichheld's breakthrough 2003 *Harvard Business Review* article, "The One Number You Need to Grow." The Net Promoter Score (NPS) was born.

At its inception, NPS represented an important advance in measuring the relationship between companies and their customers. NPS is based on one simple question: "How likely is it that you would recommend Company X to a friend or colleague?" It helped articulate what many businesses understood intuitively but were unable to easily capture and represent: that within their customer base, there are individuals who contribute to growth through their purchasing and referral behaviors (*Promoters*), impede growth due to their negative referrals and high cost to serve (*Detractors*), and represent unrealized opportunity (*Passives*).

Measuring and tracking NPS—the percentage of Promoters minus the percentage of Detractors—serves as both a measure of the success a company has achieved in building a positive customer experience and a leading indicator of its prospects for growth. We asked a simple question that cut to the heart of loyalty and found compelling data that correlates NPS with business growth.

That was then. Today Net Promoter is more than a metric. It is a discipline by which companies profitably grow by focusing on their customers. A successful Net Promoter program is multidimensional, including NPS measurement, leadership practices that instill customer focus, organizational strategies to ensure program adoption, and integration with core business processes and operational systems to support information collection, analysis and distribution. The Net Promoter discipline has become integrated in the operations of organizations around the world.

This simple, but powerful, concept gained momentum due in equal measure to its intuitive nature and its potential for fostering change on behalf of customers. However, it became apparent that companies needed a strategy to use the score to create effective change. We found that many organizations that had made investments in Net Promoter programs achieved mixed results. All too often they discovered that harnessing a powerful yet simple idea requires sophisticated approaches and many choices along the way. Business transformation is never an easy task, and it should come as no surprise that decisions made regarding the implementation of Net Promoter can mean the difference between business impact and just another metric to post on the wall.

Our delight at the rapid adoption of Net Promoter was tempered by anxiety. We were alarmed by the number of companies that were publicly declaring their commitment to Net Promoter but, by their own standards, were making unsatisfactory progress toward driving business success with those programs. At the same time, no one could fail to be impressed by some of the innovations fostered by the use of Net Promoter by leading companies. We felt an urgent need to share the best practices of the companies achieving success.

What Did Companies Do with Net Promoter?

Our challenge, and the motivation for this book, was identifying the actions that companies take to achieve Net Promoter success. Put simply, what has worked? We believed that if we could build a Net Promoter Operating Model based on the answers to that question, we could create a practical how-to guide targeted at practitioners who seek to implement a program themselves.

Since the original research, we have had the opportunity to examine hundreds of companies that have implemented, with varied approaches and equally varied degrees of success, Net Promoter within their businesses. We talked with CEOs, line managers, executives, and employees and did our best to capture their wisdom. Through the website netpromoter.com, we have seen thousands of participants exchange ideas on what worked for their business and what did not. We developed a measurement framework that we used to gather data across many of these companies. We then examined the multitude of programs that we had been involved in, as well as interviewed many great companies with which we had no involvement. In short, we believe we developed the most comprehensive perspective on Net Promoter success that exists today.

Pivotal Practices Make or Break Programs

From these studies, we learned that while 68 percent of companies rated themselves as highly customer focused, only 15 percent would claim they are executing their Net Promoter programs effectively. Digging deeper, we identified critical practices that influenced their progress and we share them in detail in the following chapters.

The most significant insight we hope you take away from this book can be summarized as this: thinking about Net Promoter as only a score trivializes the implementation of a major corporate transformation and is a sure recipe for disappointment. If you learn nothing more from this book, you are starting to move in the right direction. Thinking of Net Promoter as an enterprise-wide program—applying management disciplines and techniques with appropriate leadership and investment throughout the organization—is what gets results.

A How-To Manual for Net Promoter Success

Many readers are already familiar with Net Promoter. A visit to netpromoter.com and reading Fred Reichheld's *The Ultimate Question* will fill in the blanks. This book begins from Net Promoter conceptualization, represented by these sources, and proceeds to

Net Promoter actualization. Along the way, we look at the elements that make up a successful Net Promoter program and share the experiences of a number of companies that have made Net Promoter an integral part of their organizational processes.

By its nature, a Net Promoter program pervades the organization. Risking a cliché, it becomes part of a company's DNA. That said, employees' participation is very much role based. Customer-facing frontline employees and their managers will naturally have different perspectives from those of executives, but each one's role and perspective is critical to program success. We explore these various roles and responsibilities.

This book is written for those interested in improving the customer experience and increasing loyalty. We believe that everyone in an organization can have a positive impact on customers. The chapters are designed to reflect our Net Promoter Operating Model and provide insights to help in constructing a successful program and avoiding pitfalls. The chapters are largely self-contained, and although we think they are best read in sequence, the nature of the material does not always lend itself to a sequential storyline. It turns out that programs evolve in many ways, and key concepts often apply to multiple areas. Feel free to read the index and dip into specific areas of interest.

True Stories from Real Businesses

We had the good fortune to look under the hood of many great companies and their programs. We selected examples and case studies with the principal goal of illustrating success or validating our conclusions. We also sought diversity, large and small companies, U.S.–based and European, so you can find examples that you can relate to. Not all of these companies are famous yet, but if they keep doing what they're doing, many of them will be.

We believe that everything you need to know to create a successful Net Promoter program is described in this book, along with proven ways to implement it. If you apply these learnings, you will have a consistent measure of customer loyalty and a quantitative process for tracking changes over time. You will be able to take action on data, close the loop with customers, and tie loyalty directly to financial results. You will create a program that includes everyone in your company in the pursuit of customer-centric excellence.

October 2008   Laura L. Brooks, Ph.D.
                                                    Richard Owen

Answering the
Ultimate Question

Net Promoter Fundamentals and Operating Model

We have driven, since early 2000, the notion that to be customer centered is a very important part of the value system of our company and we have to keep that ever present in our minds.

John W. Thompson,
chairman and CEO, Symantec

This chapter lays out the basic elements of the Net Promoter Operating Model and sets the context for much of the rest of the book. You may think this is an obvious task, but when posed with the question, "What is Net Promoter?" we found that beyond the metric, no consensus seemed to exist. We start with the metric, summarizing the underlying concepts that support it, and draw a distinction between it and more traditional approaches. Finally, we propose a model to build a Net Promoter program and drive a customer-centric culture.

A Net Promoter Primer

Is Net Promoter a metric or a way of doing business? The answer is "both." Net Promoter is a discipline that has progressed well beyond the computation and into a series of best practices that drive positive financial results for the organizations that adopt it. This chapter goes beyond the simple mathematics required to calculate the metric and into the discipline that makes Net Promoter work. Applying Net Promoter as a management discipline separates successful programs from those that fail. However, before we elaborate, let's review Net Promoter the metric.

Net Promoter is the most progressive methodology in loyalty measurement. When people refer to "the Net Promoter question" or "the Recommend question," they are referring to the *ultimate question* from Fred Reichheld's book of that title: How likely is it that you would recommend Company X to a friend or colleague? The response to this question has proven to be an effective means for measuring customer loyalty and ultimately long-term growth.

In order to calculate the Net Promoter Score (NPS), the Recommend question should be asked using a scale from 0 to 10, in which 10 is extremely likely and 0 is not at all likely. The calculation then takes the percentage of respondents that select a rating of 9 or 10 minus the percentage of respondents that select a rating of 0 through 6 (see Figure 1.1).

NPS captures two key behaviors: buyer economics (the value of the customer) and referral economics (their potential value through referral). The first deals with an individual's own choices and the second with how those choices influence others. The difference—the *net*—is the metric of interest. It takes into account the positive impact of Promoters (higher repurchase rates and referrals) and the negative impact of Detractors (negative comments, lower repurchase rates) to yield a summary metric. This is

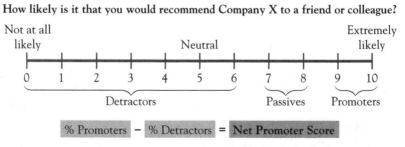

Figure 1.1   Calculating the Net Promoter Score

particularly critical in today's connected world, where word of mouth can spread more quickly and positive or negative sentiments can remain on the Internet for a long time.

NPS's compelling benefit lies in its ability to capture the net effect of customers who promote over customers who detract. By taking into account the increased growth achieved through positive buyer purchase and referral economic behavior, as well as the impediment to growth caused by the effects of reduced customer purchase and negative referral behavior, NPS provides an accurate assessment of customer loyalty and its impact on growth.

The payoff for a company with an improving NPS is reduced customer churn, decreased cost to serve, increased lifetime value, and improved cross- and up-sell opportunities. NPS also reflects the reality of word of mouth since Promoters provide positive word of mouth, and Detractors engage in negative word of mouth about the company and its products or services.

Some have argued that Detractors don't matter—that they don't actually have a negative impact on a business. Based on three years of data comparing NPS and publicly disclosed financial results, it is clear that there is a direct correlation between increased scores and increased revenue growth. Similarly, higher percentages of Detractors also link to reduced growth rates (see Figure 1.2). This evidence shows that it is not just Promoters but the absence of Detractors that create a positive growth engine.

Why Traditional Approaches Fail

Successful Net Promoter programs are not traditional customer satisfaction programs with the Recommend question added for convenience. Before Net Promoter, many customer satisfaction programs yielded management reports that lacked credibility. Perhaps more important, they didn't deliver business results. Before we lay out what makes an effective program, it's worth considering the contrast with prior approaches. We have boiled

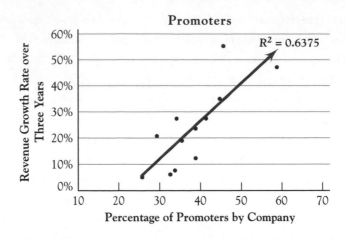

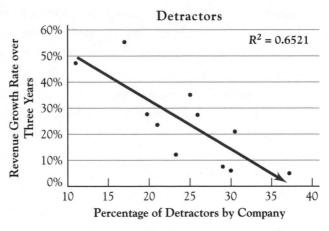

Figure 1.2   Revenue Growth Rates by Promoters and Detractors

Source: Satmetrix client data. Average international NPS from 2002–2004 (N = 12, n = 80,000); public financial data 2003–2005 or 2004–2006 depending on fiscal year.

this down to the distinction between research studies and operational programs.

An Operational Approach, Not a Research Project

Research-based approaches to customer satisfaction have not been tremendously successful in terms of improving satisfaction.

Customer satisfaction scores for the majority of large corporations have not historically shown significant improvement. Although annual reports highlight the importance of customers (usually accompanied by glossy photos and glowing tributes), many CEOs, when interviewed, have expressed a lack of confidence in their customer satisfaction efforts or a disregard for the programs that exist. Billions of dollars a year are spent on customer satisfaction surveys and market research, and outcomes seldom seem to result in any real changes to the business. Consider your own experiences as a consumer. When you fill in a customer satisfaction survey, do you believe that something will happen as a result?

Research can be valuable for the organization, but viewing your investment in customer loyalty as a research project is setting your efforts up for failure. We unfortunately continue to witness the stereotypical annual customer satisfaction report, presented to a suspicious executive team that invests just enough time to argue its validity before consigning it to the corporate bookshelf for another year. This is the classic outcome of a program that is driven from the needs of research rather than the needs of the business.

By contrast, an operational approach starts by understanding which customer data and internal processes will create change across the organization and how to use that information effectively. Whereas a research approach focuses on creating an insightful report for a handful of executives, an operational approach is concerned with building a program that engages the entire organization in improving customer relationships. Your operational program quickly becomes part of the ongoing management processes and touches line employees in their everyday jobs.

Creating a new research project that simply uses and measures NPS won't change your business; no miracle will occur simply from adding the Recommend question. Instead, success will come from grounding your program in an operational approach and applying Net Promoter principles one customer at a time.

Satisfaction Versus Loyalty

It's worth clarifying the difference between satisfaction and loyalty. Simply put, satisfied customers still defect. The fact is that satisfaction is a standard that had great meaning in the postwar industrial growth of Europe and the United States but falls short against the standards of global hypercompetition today. Worse, it provides a false standard that undermines the impact that leadership could obtain by applying a higher standard to their businesses.

If you turn on your TV and see a company claiming to have 90 percent customer satisfaction, what does it tell you? It certainly indicates that the company's basic products or services seem to work as advertised. It might also suggest the company is able to handle inevitable problems in a reasonable and timely fashion. You might even suppose that this business' help desk phones are not clogged with customers calling in to complain about the company. But does any of this sound like a basis for competitive advantage or an engine for growth?

Net Promoter programs establish a higher standard than simple satisfaction, one worth holding your business to. There is no false sense of comfort, just a real focus on the drivers of growth and competitive advantage.

Dell, the world's largest direct-sale computer manufacturer, runs a global customer experience program and understands the distinction between satisfaction and true loyalty. Dick Hunter, who heads the global consumer support program, told us:

> The thing I was struck by is that we were all hung up about customer satisfaction, and I frankly didn't think that was the right goal. It's one thing to have a customer call us with a problem. We solve their problem, and they're satisfied with the fact that we solved the problem. It's an entirely different matter if, after a customer

calls us, they're much more loyal to us and say, "I'm going to buy from Dell forever because I really get great service and that's part of the overall experience that is great and I couldn't imagine buying from anybody else." There's a huge difference between those two. And my view was that we had to go toward loyalty and move away from satisfaction.

We couldn't agree more.

Loyalty Metrics Held to the Standards of Financial Reporting

If you have heard Fred Reichheld speak, you may have heard him refer to his goal of having the NPS achieve the same standards of rigor and "auditability" as accounting based on Generally Accepted Accounting Principles. Most companies take financial reporting seriously. They hire outside auditors to confirm that their representations of the facts are accurate. Standards exist and evolve to meet the needs of current business practices. The repercussions of misrepresenting the numbers can be very serious under law, including jail time.

Another way to look at financial reporting is to understand that the most important output of good reporting is quality data given to management on which they can base important decisions with confidence. In other words, this is information for running the business. In the same way, a Net Promoter program should provide quality customer data that enables strategic decision making.

Now picture the way most companies review customer satisfaction data and imagine for a minute using the same method for reviewing financial information. Board meetings would consist of lengthy sessions where the accounting team seek to explain the meaning of the organization's performance in statistical terms that only they could understand. Executives would debate the validity of the numbers. There would be a refusal to take action because the board relentlessly questions whether those are "real numbers" or even "realistic scenarios." Department heads would claim to understand the true picture around actual and projected revenue without this and would argue they don't need accounting telling them what they already know about their business. Why spend money on this kind of data anyway?

This scenario is a bit absurd, yet it's exactly what happens with customer data when it fails to achieve a standard we reserve for critical information about our business. Net Promoter differs from traditional satisfaction metrics in that it focuses on customer data as an instrument for general business management, not just customer research, and because it is simple for everyone to understand and is actionable by employees. Moreover, the emphasis on obtaining high response rates, census approaches in business-to-business markets, antigaming focus, and methodical goal setting are all part of what makes the Net Promoter approach more trustworthy. Boards and management can use Net Promoter data just as they do financial data to make decisions that grow the company.

Bad Profits

The concept of bad profits is critical to Net Promoter. We were recently challenged by an executive to explain why the term *bad profits* is not an oxymoron in the business world. Well, that's exactly the problem many companies face. The simplest way of looking at bad profits is to consider them profits that come at the expense of long-term growth because of the Net Promoter penalty they incur. They are short-term profit and cost friendly, but long-term customer and profit unfriendly.

There does seem to be a lot of confusion around this issue, so we illustrate it with our favorite example of a CEO who understands the difference, Rupert Soames from Aggreko. He nailed it for us:

The disadvantage of financial reporting is that it is a lagging indicator, not a leading indicator, and the lag can often be quite long and quite severe. Managers are confronted daily with the opportunity to make more profit in the short term and give poor customer service at the expense of irritating their customers in the long term. What I have always been looking for is a way of squaring the circle that will enable us to say to employees, "Yes, you are to make as much profit as you can, but in so doing, we want to judge your operational effectiveness in terms of the way you're delivering service."

The first of the month, we map NPS to revenues and costs, and we can quickly relate financial performance to operational excellence and to delivering new customer service.

Tackling bad profits does not, in our opinion, mean that you are in business to be altruistic. Nor does it mean that every customer has a vote on what should be good or bad profits. Many customers have their own ideas that may not be right for your business. You might personally think that it's outrageous that your public relations agency charges you a rush fee to amend copy at the last instant, but it may fully reflect the agency's costs and the increased value that you receive. Instead, bad profits often rely on some form of trap—a business process that is perfectly legal but clearly designed to charge abnormal profits to take advantage of a customer in the short term. The vast majority of customers would recognize this behavior as being bad profits and penalize the organization with lost future business.

Companies that believe in Net Promoter are sensitive to the issue of bad profits and actively find ways, as in the Aggreko case, to safeguard against these types of business practices. It's often the case that root cause analysis of Net Promoter results will point directly to the underlying source of those bad profits and present a clear business choice of current versus future costs.

Net Promoter: Key Tenets

A successful Net Promoter program includes several factors that work together. Although NPS is useful, the most prevalent cause of failure in Net Promoter programs is the inability of the organization to go beyond the metric and build out a complete operational model with NPS as its centerpiece. The breakthrough in Net Promoter comes from shifting the entire program from a research model to an operational model and embedding it in the business. To help you get started on this, we have built a framework that captures all of the elements necessary for a successful program, which we outline in the next few pages. For now, we start with the key concepts behind the framework.

What makes Net Promoter programs unique are five key tenets: methodology, philosophy, action and accountability, emotionality, and linkage to financial outcomes.

Methodology

"NPS is the metric we use to say we are making progress or not. We like it, it is simple, easy to understand, our team gets it," noted Enrique Salem, chief operating officer (COO) of Symantec. A Net Promoter program is based on a simple metric. There has been some debate as to the strength of this metric relative to proprietary metrics. Needless to say, companies whose economic fortunes are tied to their promise of superior mathematics are not happy with the idea of standardizing on a simple, open standard that doesn't require a doctorate to understand it.

Simon Lyons from Aggreko said it best: "The beautiful thing about NPS is that it's simple. Each layer of complexity which other research metrics add move them further and further away from being adopted by our management teams and the employees at the customer-face." The challenge for the "more complex is better" camp is not whether they could construct a metric that is in some way a better indicator of some business outcome; the challenge is whether the costs of complexity are outweighed by the benefits. In most of the practical cases we see, the answer is a resounding no. The potential benefits of measuring loyalty across a long series of complex questions are rarely significant in the practical business world. Worse, the added cost of a lack of openness around the metric's calculation and the difficulty of helping the organization to understand it are significant.

A simple single metric wins advocates and converts skeptical employees and executives who would otherwise not support such a program, enabling the alignment of an entire company. When eBay first learned about Net Promoter, it also questioned the metric and program. When Kip Knight, vice president of marketing, learned about Net Promoter, he admitted, "I was a bit skeptical because coming from market research, NPS seemed too simple to be valid." After implementing the program, he remarked, "Net Promoter was like religion: the more I understood and practiced it, the more of a believer I became." Simple is good if your goal is to persuade thousands of employees all over the world that they should track a number in their daily routines.

There is a difference, however, between a single metric and a single question. We spend ample time later discussing data and survey design, but let's go on record as saying that we don't see an automatic prescription for one-, two-, or three-question survey length in your data collection efforts. More on that later.

Philosophy

Net Promoter has a built-in, unique, and compelling philosophy that engages employees at all levels in the company and across all functions. Its basis is the Golden Rule. The Golden Rule and the ethic of reciprocity is a fundamental principle that simply means treat others as you would like to be treated. Throughout history, philosophers and religious figures have stated the principle in similar ways. For an esoteric example the ancient Greek philosopher Pythagoras offered his theorem: "What you wish your neighbors to be to you, such be also to them."

The idea of the Golden Rule and *good profits* provides an underlying business approach that has demonstrated its appeal across all sizes of business and geographies. It's a positive approach to business that everyone can relate to because for most people, it simply summarizes the right thing to do. The most frequent comment we hear when we talk about Net Promoter is, "Of course, that's true!" Just because something is intuitively sensible and aligns with most people's view of the universe does not mean that it will automatically be put into practice. However, it's a lot easier to implement a program that aligns naturally with the culture and values of a company and its employees.

Orange Business Services subscribes to the Golden Rule. Even when the company was under strong competitive pressure, Orange held firm to *good profits* to drive revenues. Axel Haentjens, vice president of marketing, brand, and external communications, remarks:

> It was quite a challenging time for the company—our margins were under pressure. Delivering good quality to our customers and good customer experience was seen by all of the employees as a very good way to restore the trust in our company. Because if we were doing so much for the customer it would surely pay off; it would surely translate into increased revenue or increased margin. As a result, I think everybody embarked on the program. And we reached all our goals at the same time: it increased customer loyalty, boosted revenue growth, and established Orange as the reference worldwide brand for services to Multinational Corporations.

Action and Accountability

Net Promoter programs are not simply about giving an annual presentation about customer metrics to a handful of executives and persuading them to take action on the data. Net Promoter programs challenge all levels of the organization and thousands of employees to take action every day to improve interactions with customers.

Obtaining aggregate customer data is not sufficient for a successful Net Promoter program, although it is often what customer loyalty programs consider their end goal. Rather, successful programs are about taking action many times a day across the entire organization in a highly focused and outcome-optimized approach. A closed-loop process where customer feedback is acted on and communicated back to the customer is the heartbeat of a Net Promoter program and should be tailored to the needs of the organization. This means that employees receive data, understand it, have the skills to perform the necessary root cause analysis, and know their role in closing the issue with the customer. Although the process can be as simple as a choreographed follow-up phone call with a customer, organizations usually experiment to find the right approach for integrating action into existing processes for maximum effect.

As a leader in information services, Experian knows how important integrating relevant information can be. Laura DeSoto, senior vice president of strategic initiatives, Credit Services Decision Analytics, and Julia Fegel, senior manager of client experience, lend their reflections. DeSoto said:

> A key enabler of success is getting client feedback and loyalty information to people in ways that reflect their regular workflows. We struggled with this at first; we would send out numerous e-mails or spreadsheets, and that just was not working. So it was a learning process for us. However, we've made great strides, especially with our sales organization. We ask our sales team, "What is the best way for us to provide client loyalty data so that it is easily understood and actionable?"

Actions prescribed by the closed-loop process design need to be married to accountability for customer experience across the entire organization. Once NPS is well understood, made visible, and communicated across the organization, the Net Promoter program should be operationalized, ensuring that employees feel accountable for their impact on NPS.

Net Promoter programs drive cross-functional problem solving as a core activity. Many of the issues identified by root cause analysis will be resolved through cross-functional teams aligned with a common understanding of the ideal outcome: how to create Promoters and minimize Detractors.

The employees at LEGO Company, the global toy manufacturer headquartered in Denmark, certainly get the idea. Conny Kalcher, vice president of consumer experiences, says:

> We use the NPS in all of our consumer-facing divisions. The employees can see the NPS and the comments and the activities that are being suggested to improve the consumer experience every month. We review each touch point to dig even deeper into the issues that our consumers are not happy with. Since we are all measured on the NPS as part of our KPIs [key performance indicators], we all work together constructively to improve the score, reach our shared targets and to create the ultimate LEGO experience.

LEGO's CEO chose NPS and stands behind the program, tying every employee's bonus to an NPS key performance indicator to drive focus and accountability across the organization. Every month the leadership team reviews NPS results for each key customer interaction point, known as a touch point. Touch points are those critical interactions customers have with your organization that define their experience. Different business areas have monthly dialogue about the actions that should be taken in order to improve the experience or address performance gaps. A monthly newsletter highlights NPS and shares with everyone what loyalty issues exist and what people are doing to address them. Incidentally, LEGO has recently experienced the best growth rate in its history and is gaining market share in a tough market. We believe Net Promoter was a "building block" for LEGO's success!

Emotionality

One reason Net Promoter has caught on is its natural appeal to emotions. Just the fact that we have Promoters (people who think well of us) and Detractors (people who think poorly of us) tugs at our emotions. Customers don't view most organizations unemotionally, and employees shouldn't treat customers like numbers. Net Promoter translates the customer's perspective into terms that employees, who have the power to fix problems, can relate to. Many companies with an exclusive focus on process control or Six Sigma–type approaches run the risk of losing sight of the fact that they are not just identifying root causes of process, but also of behaviors.

The very term *Detractor* creates a negative feeling; no one wants to have disgruntled Detractors actively voicing their negative opinions. Everyone feels good about Promoters who are raving fans. An executive at an airline once told us that Net Promoter held appeal because everyone could understand what *Promoter* meant and *Detractor* meant, from the executive to the baggage handler. This broad understanding and attraction to Net Promoter is a key differentiator compared to traditional customer satisfaction and loyalty programs.

Laurie Schultz, senior vice president and general manager of Sage Software's Accpac and Simply Accounting division, agrees wholeheartedly:

> We have quarterly all-hands meetings and always talk about Net Promoter. People are clamoring to be recognized as involved in this effort; it has become a status symbol. Can you name me one other organization where people want to call Detractors? It is a badge of honor

for those teams. As leaders, we need to make sure that people see it as one of the critical focus areas.

Linkage to Financial Outcomes

"It's as plain as day—the economic benefits of having Promoters versus Detractors. . . . The Net Promoter concept is a powerful, powerful tool to get the culture focused," says Larry Hyett, vice president of retail sales and customer experience at TD Canada Trust (TDCT). TDCT evaluates the financial linkage of NPS and its business of 10 million customers, but this company is hardly alone. In our studies of business-to-business companies adopting the Net Promoter discipline, successful companies saw an average of 23 percent increased revenue growth. To get this result, we gathered the NPS data from more than a dozen business-to-business companies between 2002 and 2004 and compared that information to their financial results over the period 2003 to 2005. The one-year difference between the data sets takes into account the delay between a change in NPS and an impact on the bottom line. This study shows that as NPS increased, revenue followed suit, and therefore demonstrates that NPS provides a leading indicator for revenue growth.

Industry-level analysis is interesting and goes a long way to proving the theory of linkage between NPS and growth, but it's a company's individual circumstances that count. The success of Net Promoter is that it continues to demonstrate financial linkages at the individual company level. However, Net Promoter economics can be taken much further. Successful programs apply sophisticated segmentation of data that organizations use to develop growth strategies to facilitate the creation of Promoters, the elimination of Detractors, and perhaps the upgrading of Passives. They apply these strategies across their business or selected segments of their customers to link NPS to profitability, growth, and other economic performance indicators such as churn.

Top executives aspire to incorporate economic analysis as a cornerstone of their business. Neil Berkett, CEO of Virgin Media, says:

> I have always believed in the fundamentals behind NPS. We are in the process of linking Net Promoter directly to customer churn. It is our intention to show in our budget a direct relationship between NPS improvement and customer churn on a monthly and quarterly basis. We will include both NPS and a range of financials that are impacted by churn in our balance scorecard providing a direct linkage.

Chapter Two discusses the underlying approach to creating these economics.

Now that we have described the five key tenets that make Net Promoter unique, we will explain the Net Promoter Operating Model in detail.

The Net Promoter Operating Model

It's one thing to identify all the attractive characteristics of successful Net Promoter programs; it's another to build one. Our goal is to provide an operating model that will enable practitioners to implement a Net Promoter program with a high confidence of success. This section outlines the components of the Operating Model that will be referred to in the rest of the book.

Although the idea of Net Promoter is simple, making it work isn't simple. One of the greatest sources of program failure has been management's trivializing the program's undertaking. Many companies assume that implementing Net Promoter will be simple because it looks simple and forget that any business transformation effort takes significant investment.

We are not suggesting that Net Promoter takes more work than any other corporate initiative with a highly leveraged outcome. But it is optimistic for a multibillion-dollar organization to think that it can resource a major initiative with a small budget and a small staff and expect it to deliver great outcomes. We are not trying to discourage you from building a program, but we are trying to discourage you from doing it without adequate infrastructure. We do believe that a well-developed Net Promoter program will return a higher payback for dollars invested than the majority of investments organizations make.

The Net Promoter Operating Model is organized with a sequence in mind. The model provides a checklist of critical components, which will be expanded upon throughout the book and supported with case studies and data describing successful implementations. However, as we explore in Chapter Four, program roadmaps don't necessarily mature in a linear fashion. There are circular elements to the process that require repetition rather than straight-line progress.

Figure 1.3 illustrates the six elements of the Net Promoter Operating Model. The first critical element at the core of your program is the creation of a customer-centric culture, or DNA. Next is a well-thought-through plan—an enterprise roadmap for your program to continuously evolve. Building trustworthy data is the keystone of the Net Promoter Score and the basis on which strategic business decisions can be made. To improve your score, you must identify the root causes of promotion and detraction, as well as drivers of loyalty. Taking action and holding your organization accountable will show customers that their feedback matters and will enable operational and structural improvements. These elements will drive innovation and transformation across products, employee engagement, business processes, and the customer experience, to name a few. Incorporating all six elements of this model will ensure greater Net Promoter program success.

Figure 1.3   The Net Promoter Operating Model

Element 1: Create Customer-Centric DNA

No successful program for transformation starts without creating the environment for it to flourish. We have identified two key components to building a customer-centric DNA: executive sponsorship and organizational alignment.

Executive sponsorship is a founding principle of success. As we will see in Chapter Three, programs typically don't succeed without the right sponsorship from the top of the organization. This does not prevent many companies from trying to implement Net Promoter without the right level of executive support, and data from the Net Promoter community suggests that over a third of companies try to do so. However, without executive support, programs may lack the financial investments, human resources, and focus on customers that is needed to make big changes. In these instances, our experience is that Net Promoter becomes simply a different slant on a classic research project, and the results fall short of being transformative.

Beyond the senior leadership, you must get the rest of the organization aligned behind the program. This affects compensation and incentive plans, internal culture, and communication strategies, and Chapter Three discusses these in some depth. We believe that customer focus should be at the core of the organization and permeate all decisions. Setting up a program governance structure will ensure that employees know their roles and responsibilities and the organization stays focused on improving loyalty.

Element 2: Develop an Enterprise Roadmap

It is striking how many programs are started without a plan for evolving them over time. Even more common is a plan that lacks a complete understanding of the elements outlined in the Operating Model.

In Chapter Four, we discuss various approaches to building a program roadmap, with the explicit understanding that programs evolve at different paces to suit the needs of different organizations. Net Promoter programs don't stand still; if they do, they run out of steam and die. The best programs are refreshed based on the evolution of the customer relationship, ideally driven by constant improvements and learning from the program. Programs can be both evolutionary and revolutionary over time, depending on the nature of the corporate environment.

Net Promoter economics are a valuable element to incorporate in the planning process. Chapter Two discusses the economics and segmentation strategy of Net Promoter. At the very least, you should be building an understanding of the value of Promoters and Detractors as a fundamental underpinning of the choices you will make to change your business over the coming months and years.

Planning should take into account the critical customer touch points for your customers' experience. We are not suggesting that all touch points are equally important or should be measured immediately. However, it makes sense to understand how the different touch points affect the overall customer experience, which ones have the greatest impact on loyalty, and in what sequence they should be addressed. Most important, we want to avoid a situation where data is collected and analyzed based on an internal view of the universe rather than a customer-driven view. You will learn more about these techniques in Chapters Four and Five.

Finally, planning should include regular review meetings with the program, executive, and cross-functional teams to analyze data, create prioritized action plans based on feasibility and impact, and share learning and train employees across the organization.

Element 3: Build Trustworthy Data

Many programs perish from poor data quality. The quality of data means everything to the success of a Net Promoter program; in fact, it is the lifeblood. Many programs start with poor data rather than trustworthy data. Data is trustworthy when it has been collected in a manner that ensures it is an accurate and reliable representation of your customers and their perceptions and behaviors. If not, it provides a false sense of security.

Even the choice of metrics can be a challenge. With multiple touch points, NPS may not be the right metric under every circumstance; other metrics may need to be integrated. How will these different metrics overlap and work in congruence?

Trustworthy data requires you to measure the right customers. Although this may also seem self-evident, not all companies understand who to target. We call this *measuring who matters*. Finally, you need to decide *when* to ask the Recommend question: at transactional touch points or at the overall relationship level. Chapter Five discusses these elements in detail. Having achieved the goal of trustworthy data, you can start to set realistic goals for improvements and benefits. Goal setting is part science and part art, and Chapter Eight explores these nuances.

Element 4: Identify Root Cause

Analyzing the data to determine root causes for customer behavior is a critical part of the Operating Model. Several useful techniques around root cause analysis, including inferential driver analysis—based on regression—and stated driver analysis from follow-up interviews are covered in Chapter Six.

Companies often think they know what drives customer behavior, but sometimes the data reveals vastly different loyalty drivers. Using a combination of analysis tools to identify root causes enables employees to address the real and relevant loyalty drivers for their customers. Reading transcripts from follow-up interviews is eye-opening and motivates employees to take action, especially if the comments are very positive or very negative. A good mix of quantitative and comment analysis increases the likelihood that you will make the optimal customer-focused decisions.

Element 5: Drive Action and Accountability

Good data and good analysis are prerequisites, but they are of no use if you don't take action. NPS should not be like watching television; it's a participation sport. At the heart of the Net Promoter program is the ability to put understandable, actionable, and timely information in front of employees who can use it. Aisling Hassell, Symantec's vice president of customer experience, agrees:

> It's not about the score. It's about the actions around the score. The score is just a metric. We are trying to change the behaviors of our employees around customer loyalty. . . . There has to be some cadence around communication to employees about customer centricity. We tell our employees that it's not just the CEO who is responsible for tackling customer loyalty; it's everyone's role.

To achieve this goal, the data needs to make sense in the context of the job an employee performs and line up with their processes and incentives. An accountability framework needs to be in place so that it's clear who has responsibility for taking action and changing the score. Experience suggests that this should be driven across the entire organization and not just rest in the hands of a central group. There must be closed-loop processes where data is understood, root cause is analyzed, and actions are completed, resulting in direct improvement of the customer experience. Chapter Seven covers these topics in detail.

Element 6: Innovation and Transformation

The goal of a Net Promoter program is transformation, both within the corporate culture and in the marketplace. Net Promoter leaders experience product innovation and improvements through the iterative process of listening to customer feedback and making improvements. They use increasingly sophisticated techniques, including the use of Net Promoter segmentation, feedback from communities, and root cause probing for strategic planning, overall go-to-market approaches, product strategy, and customer cocreation of products, services, and business processes.

The payoff from a successful Net Promoter program is the ability to make the right strategic decisions and foster innovations that ultimately improve your market position. This is where the advantages of superior Net Promoter execution convert into competitive advantage. Chapter Nine presents case studies from companies that have applied advanced Net Promoter techniques to their business and have experienced NPS leadership.

Putting It Together: Implementing the Operating Model

The Operating Model is the product of extensive work looking into the factors behind success and failure in Net Promoter programs. Some organizations are at the initial stages of their Net Promoter programs, while others are running mature programs and are applying advanced techniques. Organizations that outperform the competition tend to be strong in many of the Operating Model elements. We are not suggesting it's impossible to enjoy program success without addressing all these factors; in fact, very few companies are outstanding at all of these elements. You should consider the experience of others, reviewing what worked well and what did not, in order to avoid pitfalls. We hope you can draw parallels to your industry, product, culture, operations, and organizational structure and infuse new techniques into your program.

2

Using Customer Economics and Segmentation to Maximize Loyalty

Dell switched from being too cost focused and went back to our roots of being customer focused. Part of this change was reversing the myth that a good customer experience costs a lot of money.

Laura Bosworth,
director of global customer experience strategy, Dell

Truly loyal customers do more than simply appreciate you; they express their loyalty in ways that make them an incredible asset to your business. According to the research that Satmetrix conducted with Fred Reichheld and Bain & Company, loyal customers exhibit specific behaviors that help to drive growth. As discussed in Fred Reichheld's book, *The Ultimate Question* (2006), we found four primary customer behaviors that link to growth and profitability:

1. *Repurchase.* Loyal customers continue to buy goods and services from you not because they have to or because they feel trapped, but because their experiences have led them to want to patronize your business.

2. *Increased purchase.* For many businesses, the total spend of loyal customers tends to increase over time, as does their share of wallet relative to their spending with your competitors. Companies are more likely to up-sell and cross-sell additional goods and services to loyal customers.

3. *Referral.* Loyal customers tend to refer their friends and colleagues. This word-of-mouth advertising is a powerful economic benefit in that it drives new business growth while simultaneously reducing your acquisition costs.

4. *Feedback.* Loyal customers spend more time with you, providing valuable feedback and giving you insights into their thoughts as well as ideas for improvements. They do so not simply to benefit themselves but because they want your business to succeed.

Collectively these behaviors facilitate financial growth by increasing revenue, providing some relief from pricing pressure, driving new business, reducing acquisition and service costs, and identifying opportunities for the business to innovate. NPS, as an indicator of the behaviors that result in these outcomes, is a powerful tool to use to predict growth.

In this chapter, we explore the economics that underpin a Net Promoter program. We examine how a good segmentation strategy enables organizations to maximize loyalty and profits. How can focusing on specific segments improve sales? We know instinctively that Promoters are valued, but what is a Promoter really worth? We provide examples that show the value of moving an additional one percent of customers into the Promoter loyalty segment. Also, we discuss the value derived from referrals, and what word of mouth is worth. You can use these financial calculations to determine the value of Promoters, Passives, and Detractors as you build a business case to quantify the value of your program and secure budget and support.

Quest for Customer Intimacy

Knowing your customers helps support growth. Understanding customer needs and motivations enables you to make smarter, more customer-centric business decisions and to build a more distinctive customer experience that motivates profitable customer behaviors. For instance, popular consumer companies such as Amazon.com and Tivo drive purchases and use by interpreting buying habits and making recommendations based on customer desires. Casino hotels may use behavioral data from card swipes and campaign response to identify high-value and high-priority customers and deliver a differentiated experience to these customers across all key touch points.

In each of these cases, careful customer segmentation is the key to building this competence. Segmentation helps to both integrate and differentiate customers based on their characteristics, behaviors, attitudes, and needs across the customer lifecycle. A deep understanding of your customer segments, including what makes them unique, what they are seeking, and how they feel about your business, is necessary if you hope to influence their buying, retention, and referral habits.

Segmenting for Optimal Results

Most competitive companies use some form of customer segmentation, though in many cases it is retroactive. Information based on customer characteristics (for example, demographics), behaviors (for example, responses to campaigns, purchases), or aspects of the business (for example, product line, sales region), is typically accumulated in a customer relationship management (CRM) system. In the context of a loyalty program, customer segmentation should be employed proactively as a means for collecting and organizing insights about specific customer groups in order to create greater customer intimacy. For example, using NPS to learn which segment is the most loyal and lucrative can provide direction for prioritizing and focusing limited resources on delighting that segment. In the long term, this approach enables you to target customer segments with products and services that provide distinctive value to each group. We know that customers who feel you want to know them and provide superior value to them will become more loyal.

There is no one-size-fits-all approach to segmentation. As you will see in Chapter Five, we recommend that you target customers in a way that is tailored to your business—taking into consideration your market, your organization's current approach to segmentation, and the strategic value of different types of customers. Segmentation strategies tend to be quite different for businesses in the business-to-consumer (B2C) versus business-to-business (B2B) markets. In B2C environments, segmentation typically focuses on customer behaviors, such as recency and frequency of purchase, and demographics. Strategic customers are those who tend to buy more, and buy more frequently.

B2B businesses that sell to large enterprise accounts add a layer of complexity in that different individuals within the account perform different roles and have potentially diverse needs. Segmentation may be based on account characteristics such as account size, account type, region, or business unit, as well as on individual customer characteristics, such as job role or purchase influence. Consider a typical technology sales scenario in the B2B arena. These complex transactions could involve individuals from across the organization, including the chief information officer, technical experts, implementation managers, and end users, each varying in influence and decision-making power. A successful customer segmentation strategy for this type of business should integrate the needs and experiences of decision makers, influencers, and end users.

LEGO's Brick-by-Brick Segmentation

A customer for a B2C organization may encompass multiple roles, including being the decision maker, influencer, and end user. That said, the resulting segmentation may still be complex, with the customer experience being both multifaceted and multidimensional. LEGO understands how complex segmentation can be. After mapping out its customers' touch points, Conny Kalcher, vice president of consumer experiences at LEGO, helped build the company's consumer segmentation model "one brick at a time."

LEGO measures specific experiences at the point of contact with the customer and has analyzed NPS by segment, point of contact, and market, resulting in a three-dimensional segmentation model. Its core segmentation breaks consumers into four segments: parents, children, adult fans, and teachers. These are further subdivided by purchase mechanism: direct purchase, club, website, retail brick-and-mortar, and school. Finally, each of these groups is subdivided by geography: United States, Germany, United Kingdom, and others (see Figure 2.1).

"Segmentation is a big part of LEGO's business strategy and how we think about consumers," says Kalcher:

> We talk about customer segmentations in different ways. We can look at segmentation on a rough or granular level. A rough cut at segmentation would be kids, adult fans, parents, and teachers. Kids are our

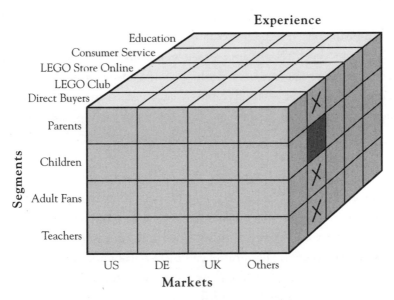

Figure 2.1 LEGO Company's Segmentation Model
Note: Measures are not needed for each cell; for example, the club is only for children, as illustrated by the shaded box.

main target group, but within kids we segment as well. We segment by age: five- to nine-year-old boys are our core segment that we aim at when we develop new products. Then, within that boy age-group segment, we have different play patterns and "need states" with play.

Some kids are more role-play oriented so we would do play themes like LEGO City or LEGO Space for them. Meanwhile, other kids are more action oriented, and LEGO Company developed BIONICLE products for them. There are some kids who are more build-to-display oriented, so LEGO developed the Creator line and the LEGO Technic line for them.

Regarding purchase influence, LEGO has an interesting business because both parents and children are involved in the buying process, and their roles change based on age and stage. Clearly there are both decision makers and influencers at work over the customer lifecycle, although reasonable people might debate which is which. LEGO understands that within the segment from birth to two years, parents decide on which LEGO products to buy. In the three- to four-year-old segment, parents direct the children, but the children influence the decision-making process. Says Kalcher, "The five-plus year segment is where the kids decide, even if the parents are still paying the bill. Categories of influencer, decision maker, and buyer change with age."

Of key importance is that LEGO cares about the dynamics behind each unique segment and understands the intersection of its core segments in a way that permits it to create a targeted customer experience for each. Through its Net Promoter program, the company can compare drivers of loyalty for parents who buy via retail outlets in the United States to those in Germany. After compensating for cultural differences, LEGO may decide to take certain actions in all geographies according to what will provide the greatest return on the investment in each region. LEGO can also focus on understanding the behavioral needs of five- to nine-year-old boys and develop targeted offerings and programs for that group, or tailor sales channels, such as in-store or online ordering, to different purchaser segments.

What is instructive about the LEGO approach is that it integrates Net Promoter dynamics by segment into its overall segmentation strategy for growth. It's wise to choose segments where your business will most benefit from increased loyalty because you can't necessarily delight all customers all the time. LEGO works actively to create specific products, channels, and communication strategies for just those segments.

Segmenting for Good Profits

LEGO is an interesting example of aligning NPS with customer segmentation. However, even simply grouping customers into Promoters, Passives, and Detractors can be a simple and effective way to identify customers with similar needs, attitudes, and characteristics. Looking closely at your Promoters will help you understand what drives customers who are excited about your products and services, unearth strategies for differentiating your business from that of your competitors, and develop effective strategies for customer retention. Profiling Detractors will quickly identify what processes need fixing and help you formulate strategies for reducing churn. By integrating NPS into your ongoing segmentation strategy, your business can focus on developing mutually beneficial relationships with the right customers.

Net Promoter data, segmented by loyalty category, can also provide insights for making operational decisions and trade-offs. Businesses often link operational and financial metrics to loyalty and customer satisfaction data. One technique we recommend for identifying customers who represent good profits (customers who are both highly profitable and highly loyal) is to analyze the data along multiple dimensions: customer segment, operational metrics such as revenue, and the NPS categories of Promoter, Passive, and Detractor. The quadrant chart in Figure 2.2 shows accounts mapped along three dimensions: (1) NPS along the x-axis, (2) revenue along the y-axis, and (3) margin, as represented by the bubble size.

Which accounts are performing well, are primed for growth, or are at risk of defection? Based on the location of the bubbles within the business position map, accounts can be classified into one of four quadrants: Fix, Move, Grow, and Model. The ideal quadrant is "Model," where accounts are characterized by both high loyalty and high financial value. These accounts represent a relatively stable, ongoing stream of revenue. The accounts in the Grow quadrant show high loyalty but low financial value. These accounts represent a true growth opportunity: their loyalty

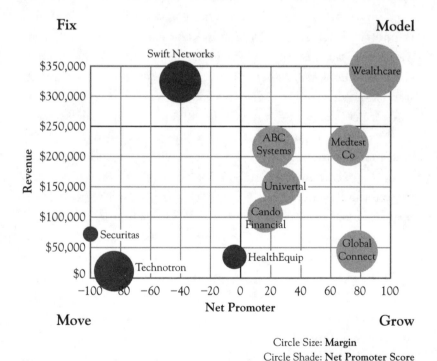

Figure 2.2   Business Position Map of Top Accounts by Revenue and NPS

will make them more receptive to up-sell and cross-sell offers. Accounts in the Fix quadrant represent significant risk: they carry high financial value but are characterized by low NPS. Immediate follow-up to understand their issues and address concerns is warranted. We revisit this analysis in Chapter Seven with possible actions account managers and frontline employees might take depending on the quadrant. Finally, accounts in the Move quadrant require considering whether their limited financial value warrants the investment of additional resources to improve NPS. Is it worth the time and effort to salvage the relationship, or would it be wiser to divest based on the ratio of investment relative to return? Mapping customers into segments according to their loyalty and value in this manner helps organizations to fine-tune their strategies and to maximize return on investment.

Other financial and operational metrics that may be linked for analysis in this manner include pipeline, margin, share of wallet, cost of service, and quality indexes. For instance, a B2B company might compare data based on revenue or pipeline by Passive versus Promoter customers. A B2C company may have extensive call center operations and wish to compare loyalty against call resolution time and call volume. Where can the call center optimize average hold time and loyalty? As with our example business position map in Figure 2.2, what's important is that you select the metrics and segments that reflect your business objectives.

These segmentation exercises can yield nonintuitive insights about your customers. A favorite story comes from a financial services leader who saw NPS improvements in one segment of buyers directly correlate to negative financial returns. The problem was that these customers were unprofitable for the company, and investments made to improve their loyalty scores fostered a financially poor result. A better strategy would have been to (1) avoid recruiting the wrong type of customer in the first place, (2) concentrate on understanding and nurturing those customers who represent the intersection of financial value and loyalty, and

(3) make smart investments to move other valuable customers up the loyalty chain. Reviewing each segment-based loyalty disposition will help formulate strategies for where to focus resources to achieve the greatest return.

Calculating Return on Promoters

Organizations that don't achieve superior customer loyalty face a difficult battle if they are to succeed. With the exception of organizations that operate in less competitive markets, usually due to a natural or regulatory monopoly, our research indicates that very few companies with inferior NPS will succeed in achieving significant growth. In most industries, the profit pool is fully absorbed by just a few industry participants—typically the ones with the most loyal customers.

As we've discussed, sorting customers by their degree of loyalty helps to reveal basic problems and potential opportunities. In conjunction with internally supplied segmentation data, customer data can point to issues requiring immediate attention as well as required structural improvements. With a little more detailed data, it becomes feasible to estimate the financial impact of moving customers from one loyalty segment to another. Used in conjunction with internal estimates on the costs of undertaking process improvements to improve loyalty, financial impact data can provide excellent first-pass analysis of return on investment.

Analysis of Strategic Customers

Many programs in B2B environments adopt a top-account or strategic-account orientation. These accounts may be channel partners or enterprise accounts. Concentrating on strategic accounts is sensible because early-stage programs often need to focus their initial investments and demonstrate the ability to produce tangible results. Concentrating on top account segments minimizes the customer population while maximizing the potential impact. In this section, we examine several approaches to demonstrating value in these types of programs. We begin with an example that requires only the Net Promoter question and verbatim comments.

Let's consider the case of ABC, Inc., a company that provides large-scale data-processing services and applications. ABC grew rapidly through acquisition of similar businesses, which continued to operate as relatively independent subsidiaries. A downturn in the economy required the company to cut back expenses, including some used for customer service and product development. With costs under control, management's attention returned to growth, and a customer-experience program covering the two hundred largest customers was implemented. Responses from 406 key influencers and decision makers across 161 of its top accounts were obtained.

The company's overall NPS was computed at −11.9 percent (see Figure 2.3) with 23.9% Promoters and 35.8% Detractors. Compared with competitors in the industry, ABC's NPS was ranked in the bottom quartile of the Satmetrix Net Promoter benchmark database, which has an industry average NPS of 4.5 percent.

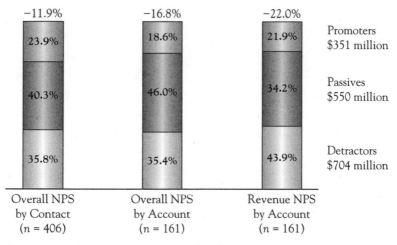

Figure 2.3   ABC's Revenue-Weighted NPS

This was not much of a surprise given the customer service cost-containment measures from the preceding few years.

Delving deeper into the Detractor segment, the company discovered a large concentration of customers with extremely low recommend scores of 0 and 1. Scores of 0 and 1 are indicators of significant problems that often present powerful challenges. Nevertheless, these customers were still engaged with ABC, spending their time providing valuable feedback and therefore giving ABC an opportunity to turn the tide. Effective management intervention at this stage may be required to reverse an otherwise inevitable loss.

To diagnose the issues, ABC carefully reviewed the comments from these low-scoring accounts. Many expressed frustration over a specific problem of an administrative nature that had never been resolved and required immediate attention. Some Detractors stated their intention of dropping their relationship at the first opportunity unless the problems were resolved.

Although senior management was generally aware of problems and dissatisfied customers, this level of information and detailed comments was eye opening. Senior management and sales executives combed through the comments, quickly sorting out accounts at risk and planning appropriate interventions. Executive management believes these efforts, although they were not effective in every case, averted the loss of a significant portion of contracts up for renewal.

In addition to this tactical follow-up, they reviewed the feedback for strategic insights. First, the company analyzed the Net Promoter categories with two years of total revenue and revenue by region. A revenue-weighted, account-level NPS was calculated. As seen in Figure 2.3, account-level scores were weighted by the account revenue to calculate an adjusted NPS.

The NPS of -16.8% calculated from the account-level averages was lower than the initial respondent-level NPS, given the high number of low Recommend scores. Worse, the calculation of the revenue-weighted NPS produced another substantial decrease to −22 percent. The decrease in the revenue weighted score meant that the largest accounts were also the least loyal accounts. This was a seemingly counterintuitive (and undesirable) result since loyal accounts tend to buy more over time and become larger customers.

ABC reviewed the comments of the largest accounts and found that newly installed products and major product upgrades were not functioning properly, which pointed to a lack of internal quality control processes. Poor product quality, coupled with the cutbacks in support and service staff, meant that customers whose share of wallet had increased were experiencing more problems from the latest product upgrades than those who were not spending more with ABC. As you might expect, the segment that spent more money on product upgrades had expectations that their greater investments would result in more value, and these customers were the most underserved. This analysis led ABC to immediately launch a companywide task force to develop and implement more stringent quality control procedures.

Next, ABC segmented its data by region. It became obvious that Detractor customers were heavily concentrated in a few geographical business units. EMEA and APAC (both multimillion-dollar regions) had large Detractor segments relative to other regions (see Figure 2.4). Reviewing customer comments, one business unit stood out from the rest. The support group in EMEA had been offshored shortly before the survey deployment, creating a sudden and severe negative impact on customer experience. Management, aware of the offshore move, had little idea of its consequences on customer experience and took immediate action to rectify the situation, including training for offshore customer support.

These uses of NPS data can be applied in almost every situation to better understand the loyalty of strategic customer segments. Often the same techniques can also be used to identify up-sell and cross-sell opportunities. Chapter Seven provides additional detail on how to use this type of information.

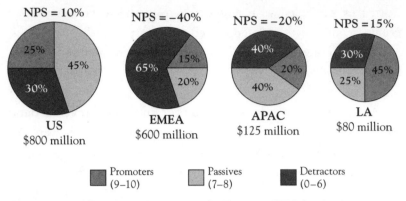

Figure 2.4   Identifying Detractors by Region: NPS by Account Revenue

Estimating the Value of Moving Customers Between NPS Segments

Many practitioners are asked to provide a business case for proposed investments, or at the very least to support the idea that investments in a Net Promoter program will yield financial benefits. Although there are many ways to demonstrate value, including computationally complex approaches to predict the impact of specific investments, the most effective approach is sometimes the simplest. Often all that is required is reliable internal financial data and a few specific survey questions.

Estimating the Value Using Financial Data

If you have financial data that can be linked directly to customer segments, or B2B accounts, the simplest approach is to build an economic model that shows the association between NPS and growth. The model will likely illustrate that growth lags NPS. This lagged model is based on two suppositions: (1) Net Promoter functions as a leading indicator of growth, and (2) higher Net Promoter scores are associated with greater financial value (for example, greater share of wallet).

In this example, we examine the relationship between NPS and financial growth for a large B2B software provider. The model calculates the revenue growth of each loyalty segment. Our process was as follows:

1. We compiled roughly five quarters of loyalty and revenue data for each of the top accounts. It is necessary to be able to track both loyalty and revenue contributions at the account level to support the model.

2. It became clear from the analysis of revenue data that the bulk of revenue for each account accrues at the time of license renewal (incremental spending had a meaningful but small contribution by comparison). For most of the accounts, license renewal occurred on an annual basis. To keep our approach simple, we analyzed the same four quarters of financial data for each account, assuming that most would experience a renewal event sometime during that period.

3. For our financial metric, we settled on revenue growth over the period of a single year (for example, measured as the change in spending between the first quarter of the first year and the first quarter of the following year). Using growth rather than absolute revenue ensured that the contributions of a relatively few large accounts would not skew the results. Outliers, for example customers whose revenue grew at greater than two times the standard deviation of the mean growth score, were excluded for much the same reason.

4. We used NPS as the loyalty metric. Each account was assigned to a Net Promoter category of Promoter, Passive, or Detractor based on the average Recommend score of the individual respondents. This permitted us to calculate the proportion of accounts in each loyalty segment and link loyalty and revenue at the account level.

5. We introduced a lag between loyalty and financial growth. In our previous studies, we have typically found anywhere from a

three-month to one-year lag between NPS and growth. As a result, we used the NPS for each account one quarter prior to the time period used to calculate annual growth.

———

Results are presented in Figure 2.5. As we expected, Promoter accounts tend to buy more. At 11 percent annual growth, they represent the engine that drives the most growth. The Passive segment is 38 percent of the account base but contributes only modestly to corporate growth, falling far short of the positive economic impact of Promoter accounts. Detractor accounts, few though they are (12 percent), exert a negative impact on revenue growth of −6 percent. Together, the proportion of accounts that fall into each loyalty segment, when weighted by their average growth, approximates the overall growth rate reported by the company for the time period reported (roughly 5.3 percent). The model clearly illustrates that accounts with higher NPS yield higher revenue growth, and Detractors do the opposite.

While these results are interesting in their own right, they also present an opportunity to model the value of moving accounts (or customer segments) between the various loyalty segments.

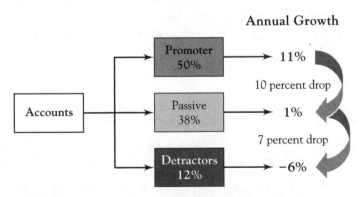

Figure 2.5   Effect of Drop in NPS: Lower Economic Value

Figure 2.6 presents two scenarios for improving loyalty and the expected impact on growth over time. The growth rate of 5.3 percent is associated with the current breakdown of accounts into Promoter, Passive, and Detractor categories at the growth rates calculated for each. Holding these growth rates constant, we are then able to project possible scenarios for revenue growth based on moving some accounts up the loyalty chain. In scenario 1, we arbitrarily move 6 percent of the accounts into the Promoter category, 4 percent from the Detractor category, and an additional 2 percent from the Passive category. This has the net effect of raising the expected corporate growth rate to 6.1 percent overall. We created a more aggressive second scenario. Moving an additional 6 percent of accounts into the Promoter category yields an additional increase to overall revenue growth of 7.0 percent.

Note that this approach permits the estimation of revenue impact as well. In this example, if the company's annual revenues are approximately $1 billion per year, the impact of increasing growth by 0.8 of 1 percent would be $8 million per year; increasing growth

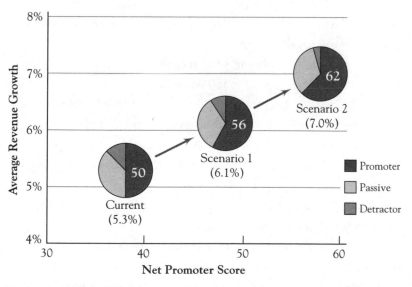

Figure 2.6   Economic Impact of Improving Loyalty

by 1.7 percent overall would represent an expected gain of $17 million year over year. These figures could then be used as a basis for building a business case for investments to improve loyalty, comparing the cost of investment against the projected gain in revenue.

With financial data and NPS, you can build a business case with models that calculate the value of each loyalty segment, as well as the value of moving customers from the Passive and Detractor segments to the Promoter segment. In addition, you can project revenue growth based on estimated growth rate increases.

Estimating the Value Without Financial Data:
Using Proxy Measures

When financial data is not available at the customer level, calculating the potential gains associated with moving customers from one Net Promoter category to another requires different means. One question that often appears on loyalty surveys is, "How likely are you to continue purchasing?" Using this measure, it is a relatively straightforward exercise to calculate the propensity to continue purchasing for each loyalty segment and to use this as a basis for projecting the financial impact of moving customers up the loyalty chain.

Another client example of a medical device company, XYZ, with annual revenues of $360 million, will help to illustrate this process. We begin by cross-tabulating responses from the Recommend question with responses to the "continue to purchase" question. To be conservative, we decided to bucket scores of 9 and 10 on the "continue to purchase" question as highly likely to make a future purchase and grouped 0 through 8 scores as unlikely to continue purchasing. The results of our investigation are presented in Figure 2.7.

Our findings reveal that approximately 90 percent of Promoters are likely to continue purchasing as compared with only 4 percent of Detractors. Overall, Promoters are four times more likely to continue purchasing than Passives and twenty times more likely than Detractors.

Net Promoter Segment	Likelihood of Continuing to Purchase	
	0 to 8 (Not Likely)	9 and 10 (Likely)
Promoter	10%	90%
Passive	78%	22%
Detractor	96%	4%

4× } 20×

Figure 2.7   Likelihood of Continuing to Purchase by Net Promoter Segment

We can now use this information in a simulation model to calculate the impact of moving 1 percent of customers up the loyalty chain. In Figure 2.8, we estimate the impact of moving 1 percent of Passives to the Promoter segment using the following steps:

1. We represented the distribution of customers across the loyalty segments (column 2) for the current and the projected states (increasing Promoters by 1 percent and decreasing Passives by 1 percent).

2. We multiplied those proportions by the likelihood to continue to purchase (column 3) to produce a weighted contribution to revenue (column 4).

3. We combined the weighted probabilities to create a total weighted average for each scenario (current and projected). The averages themselves do not mean anything; it is the relationship between them that we will examine.

4. We took the two weighted averages and calculated the degree of difference between them (0.58206 − 0.57526/0.57526 = 1.18 percent).

The difference between the weighted averages is 1.18 percent. If we assume that our continue-to-purchase data represents the likely contribution of current customers to revenue, this suggests that each 1 percent shift in NPS (from Passives to Promoters) will increase the revenue from current customers by 1.18 percent.

Current

	Net Promoter Segment	Continue to Purchase	Weighted Average
Promoter	56.4%	90%	0.50760
Passive	27.9%	22%	0.06138
Detractor	15.7%	4%	0.00628
Total (weighted average)	NPS = 40.7%		**0.57526**

Projected

	Net Promoter Segment	Continue to Purchase	Weighted Average
Promoter	57.4%	90%	0.51660
Passive	26.9%	22%	0.05918
Detractor	15.7%	4%	0.00628
Total (weighted average)	NPS = 41.7%		**0.58206**

Figure 2.8   Impact of Moving 1 Percent of Customers from Passive to Promoter

Companies that can separate revenue contributions for existing customers versus new business can calculate the actual revenue impact of this change by multiplying revenues from existing customers by 1.18 percent.

In this example, increasing NPS by shifting 1 percent from Detractors to Passives increases revenue by only 0.3 percent. For this company, a strategy focused on moving Passives to Promoters will have a substantially higher payoff than moving Detractors to Passives. This exercise can help identify where to focus efforts and resources in order to make the greatest impact on financial growth.

Estimating the Impact of Word of Mouth

"Half the money I spend on advertising is wasted; the trouble is I don't know which half," is the famous maxim attributed to

John Wanamaker, considered by some to be the father of modern advertising. Many marketers might agree when they look at the low response and conversion rates for traditional advertising.

At the beginning of the chapter, we referred to the four positive behaviors of loyal customers. One of these is the propensity to refer your organization to others. This positive word of mouth is more effective than traditional advertising because it comes from a trusted and valued source of information: peers. These advocates and vocal Promoters are a marketer's dream.

Thus far, the simple techniques we've discussed for assessing the value of loyal customers focus on direct purchase benefits—in other words, the propensity of a given customer to continue to purchase, increase spending, and do business with you over a longer period of time. With word of mouth, we direct our attention instead to the indirect benefits that accrue from customer loyalty, the most significant of which is the likelihood of acquisition of new customers through referral. After all, Net Promoter is based on the stated likelihood to recommend friends and colleagues; it's reasonable to assume that some proportion of customers follow through on this stated intention and that some proportion of these referred individuals become customers themselves.

In this section, we discuss two approaches for calculating the financial value associated with word of mouth. The first approach is based on the incidence of positive referrals. It requires the addition of two simple questions to your survey:

1. Did you select COMPANY primarily on the basis of a referral from a friend or colleague? (Y/N)

2. Have you positively referred friends or colleagues to COMPANY in the past twelve months? (Y/N)

In the example of the medical device company, we explored how to use reported likelihood to continue to purchase to assess the financial benefits accrued from moving Passives to Promoters. We could also leverage customers' answers to the positive referral question ("Have you positively referred friends or colleagues to COMPANY in the past twelve months?") as well.

For instance, the company reported that roughly 18.2 percent of its revenues were obtained from new accounts. To estimate the percentage of revenue associated with new accounts that were obtained through referral, we leveraged the *were you referred* question ("Did you select COMPANY primarily on the basis of a referral from a friend or colleague?").

Roughly 34.6 percent of all accounts indicated that they had been referred, so this proportion was assumed to extend to new accounts as well. As such, the total revenues from referral would be 6.3 percent (34.6 percent of the 18.2 percent of revenues from new business).

We can then use the responses to the *have you positively referred friends or colleagues to COMPANY in the past 12 months* question in the same way we used the responses to the *continue to purchase* question demonstrated in Figure 2.8. By calculating the percentage change in referrals associated with moving Passives to Promoters, we can estimate the increase in new accounts that are referred. When we combine that estimate with the increase in revenue associated with accounts that will continue to do business, we can gauge the overall impact of improving the NPS. The calculation for the total value of the change in the Net Promoter mix is $(0.818 \times 1.0118) + (0.063 \times 1.0042) + 0.119 = 1.0099$, rounding off to 1.01, or 1 percent. The first term is the proportion of revenue from current accounts times the change in continue to do business. The second term is the proportion of new business from referrals times the change in referrals, and the third term is unattributed new business, which is left unchanged. For our medical device company with annual revenues of $360 million, the impact of spend-and-referral behavior from moving 1 percent of customers from the Passive to Promoter category totaled $3.6 million (see Figure 2.9).

Current

	Percent	Referred Others	Weighted Average
Promoter	56.4%	38.9%	0.21940
Passive	27.9%	25.6%	0.07142
Detractor	15.7%	15.1%	0.02371
Total (weighted average)	NPS = 40.7%		0.31453

Projected

	Percent	Referred Others	Weighted Average
Promoter	57.4%	38.9%	0.22329
Passive	26.9%	25.6%	0.06886
Detractor	15.7%	15.1%	0.02371
Total (weighted average)	NPS = 41.7%		0.31586

Figure 2.9   Value of Moving 1 Percent of Passives to Promoters

While this approach helps to estimate the impact of recommendation or referral, it doesn't really capture the full impact of word of mouth. Loyal customers will indeed recommend you, but disgruntled customers may likewise dissuade others from doing business with you. Word of mouth entails both positive and negative messages regarding your organization and brand. In the following example, we explore an approach for estimating the impact of word of mouth that integrates the behaviors of both Promoters *and* Detractors.

A Case Study in Valuing Word of Mouth

In 2007, we compiled a benchmark of ten enterprise software companies. Based on the average self-reported spend of their customers, we were able to quantify the impact of word of mourh behaviors as capturing, on average, an additional $565,000 per Promoter, as well as a loss of $701,000 per Detractor. This value was obtained over and above the differences between these and other customers in terms of purchase patterns and customer tenure.

It is simplest to begin with an estimate for the referral value of Promoters. This calculation requires the addition of one more survey question to the two previously discussed:

1. Did you select COMPANY primarily on the basis of a referral from a friend or colleague? (Y/N)

2. Have you positively referred friends or colleagues to COMPANY in the past twelve months? (Y/N)

3. How many friends or colleagues did you positively refer to COMPANY in the last twelve months? (1, 2, 3, . . . , 10 or more)

In addition to this information, you will need financial data to estimate the financial impact of word of mouth captured in questions 2 and 3. Our example will calculate the impact of referral behaviors on the basis of average spend per customer, but variations of this model could be created on the basis of total and net revenue, profitability, total revenue associated with new customers, or lifetime value.

To arrive at the figure for Promoters, we began by looking at the percentage of Promoters who have referred others (question 2) in the previous twelve months. For this industry, that proportion is quite high at 81 percent. Data collected from question 3 indicated that each of these actively referring Promoters referred, on average, 4.2 individuals over that period of time.

The final step is to determine the "batting average" for these positive referrals—in other words, how many referrals, on average, are necessary to convert a potential customer into an actual customer. We took a straightforward approach, dividing the total number of customers who had been obtained through referral (question 1) by the total number of positive referrals issued by Promoters, Passives, and Detractors. This represents the total number of referrals being made, compared against the total number of referred customers.

On this basis, we estimated that for every six positive referrals made, roughly one new customer is gained (a conversion rate of 16 percent). Based on this conversion rate, each Promoter can be expected to generate, on average, about one-half of a new customer. As the average customer spend within this industry was $1.05 million, this represents additional revenues of 0.54 × $1.05 million = $565,000 per Promoter (see Figure 2.10).

We also estimated that the negative word of mouth from Detractors cost this group of companies an average of $701,000 per Detractor. To arrive at that figure, we leveraged two additional survey questions:

1. Have you advised friends or colleagues *against* doing business with COMPANY in the last twelve months? (Y/N)

2. How many friends or colleagues did you advise *against* doing business with COMPANY in the last twelve months? (1, 2, 3, . . . , 10 or more)

As with Promoters, these questions permit us to assess the volume of negative word of mouth associated with Detractors and how many potential consumers are affected by those behaviors. In

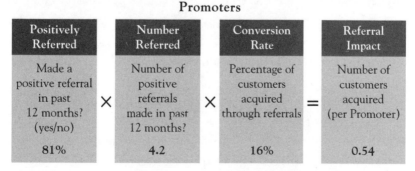

Promoters

Positively Referred		Number Referred		Conversion Rate		Referral Impact
Made a positive referral in past 12 months? (yes/no)	×	Number of positive referrals made in past 12 months?	×	Percentage of customers acquired through referrals	=	Number of customers acquired (per Promoter)
81%		4.2		16%		0.54

Figure 2.10   **Estimated Value of Promoters' Positive Word of Mouth**

this instance, 26 percent of Detractors reported actively dissuading others from doing business with their vendor on the basis of their poor experiences. On average, these unhappy customers spoke to four other individuals.

Calculating the impact of these negative referrals requires making some additional assumptions. After all, it is not possible to directly determine the number of customers who would be current customers of a particular company if not for the influence of negative word of mouth. To estimate a defensible conversion rate—the number of potential customers exposed to negative word of mouth who purchased from other providers as a result—we must depend on the limited available empirical findings regarding the impact of negative referrals.

Several sources describe the disproportionate influence of negative information relative to positive information (Anderson, 1965; Mizerski, 1982; Laczniak, DeCarlo, and Ramaswami, 2001) including its influence in customer contexts (Arndt, 1967; Dillon and Weinberger, 1980; Wilson and Peterson, 1989; Herr, Kardes, and Kim, 1991). However, there are relatively few studies that specifically try to quantify the degree of difference between the two. The best of these tend to suggest that negative information is four times (Kroloff, 1988) to five times (Richey, Koenigs, Richey, and Fortin, 1975; Reichheld, 2006) more influential than positive information.

On this basis, we opted to take the positive conversion rate for this industry, 16 percent, and apply a factor of 4 to produce a likely conversion rate for negative word of mouth of 68 percent. With this established, we were able to estimate that each Detractor can be said to cost two-thirds of a potential new customer (see Figure 2.11).

Our findings in this and other industries have been corroborated by one of the few studies of the impact of negative word of mouth on consumer decision making. The Verde group, in conjunction with the Baker Retailing Initiative at the Wharton School of Business, found that 31 percent of dissatisfied customers

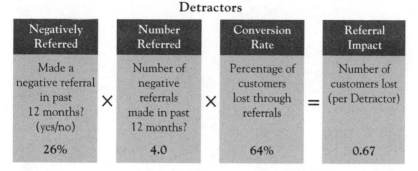

Figure 2.11   Estimated Cost of Detractors' Negative Word of Mouth

will tell others about their problems (compared to our 26 percent) and that they tell on average four others (identical to our 4.0). They also found that roughly 64 percent of customers who are recipients of negative word of mouth about a specific vendor choose to shop elsewhere (identical to our 68 percent).

Calculating Total Customer Value

Thus far, we've looked at techniques for estimating the economic value and costs associated with spending and referral behaviors of Promoters, Passives, and Detractors. To understand the integrated impact of these behaviors, we created the Net Promoter word-of-mouth economic model, which provides a more complete and sometimes surprising picture of the financial impact of NPS. For instance, in our examination of the enterprise software business, we found that Detractors spend less—an average of $665,000 in comparison with Promoters' $1.49 million. This also understates the true difference between these customers. It is only when the different referral economics for Promoters and Detractors are factored in that an accurate picture emerges. The actual total customer value of Promoters exceeds $2 million, a gain of 38 percent. Detractors, by contrast, have no real long-term value at all; they represent a net cost to financial growth once their negative word of mouth is taken into account (see Figure 2.12).

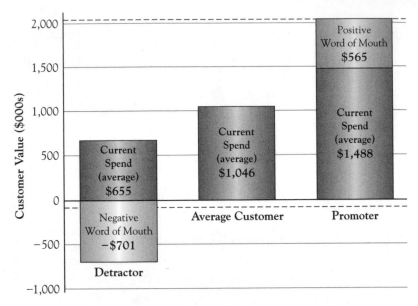

Figure 2.12   Total Customer Worth for Promoters and Detractors Based on Average Spending and Word-of-Mouth Behaviors

Apple's Word-of-Mouth Success

Apple is a particularly interesting example of loyalty leadership. Although Apple's market share in the personal computer marketplace does not compare to that of industry leaders, its strategy of cultivating a distinct brand image and delivering value to Apple devotees has resulted in strong, ongoing brand loyalty. In fact, almost from the outset of Satmetrix's industry benchmark efforts, and well before Apple's recent explosion into the digital music and communication markets, the rest of the personal computer industry has run a clear second to Apple's loyalty leader status.

For this reason, we became interested in applying the economic framework to Apple and its peers in the industry. Most businesses and consumers alike are aware that Apple enjoys a reputation for loyalty leadership, but exactly how much is it worth to them? To answer the question, we compiled data from our Net

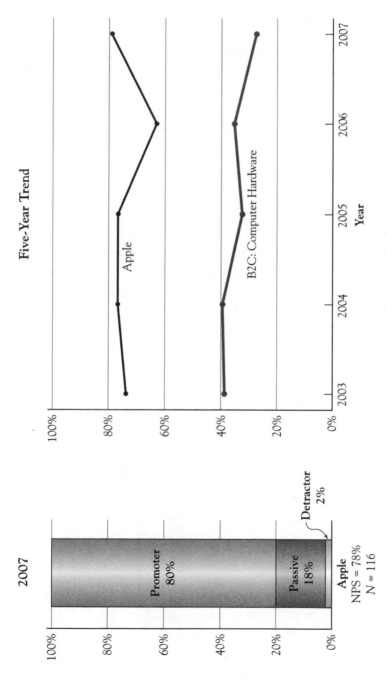

Figure 2.13 Apple Net Promoter Performance Versus Overall B2C High-Tech Computer Hardware

Promoter benchmark database to compare Apple with other computer manufacturers.

The gap between Apple and its collective competitors is clear in Figure 2.13. The vast majority of Apple respondents are Promoters, while the remaining few are Passives. Less than 2 percent are Detractors, an enviable position for any company. In general, Apple has maintained this impressive performance—with minor variance—since the inception of the Satmetrix benchmarking program in 2001.

Apple's Net Promoter Economics

The advantage that Apple's loyalty leadership confers in terms of customer self-reported spend is impressive; average spending for Apple buyers is $2,344 as compared to $1,615 for general computer hardware consumers—a gain of 45 percent (see Figure 2.14). The limited sample size available for Apple Detractors prevented us from calculating their average spending, an omission whose impact is likely to be minimal considering their overall contribution to Apple revenue stands at roughly 2 percent of their overall customer base in 2007.

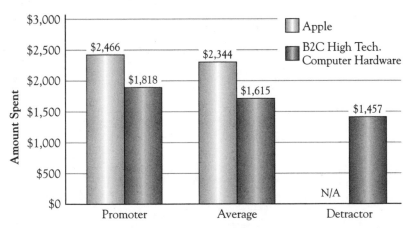

Figure 2.14   Economics for Apple Promoters and Detractors Versus Overall B2C Computer Hardware Manufacturers

Apple's high Net Promoter score is also a strong indicator of referral behavior. In fact, Apple Promoters are among the most passionate we've found about sharing their experiences. Over 90 percent of Apple Promoters report having positively referred Apple to a friend or colleague in the past twelve months, compared with 75 percent for the computer hardware industry. What's more, each Apple Promoter will share these positive sentiments

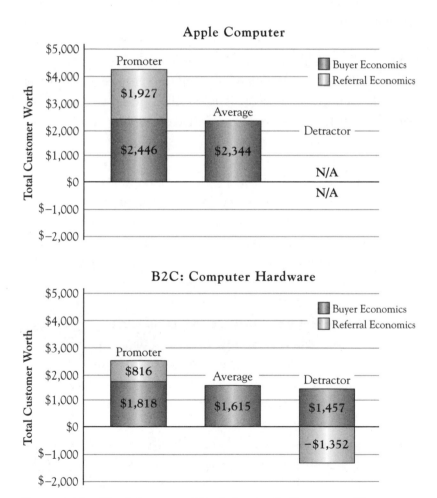

Figure 2.15   Total Customer Worth for Apple Computers Versus Overall B2C Computer Hardware

with over five people in that period of time as compared to the industry average of a little less than four per Promoter.

The strong positive referrals and lack of negative word of mouth due to few Detractors results in a strongly positive picture of total customer worth for Apple. In fact, total customer worth of Promoters is almost 1.7 times greater than that of Promoters for other computer providers (approximately $4,400 as compared to $2,600). Apple Promoters, who spend significantly more than general Promoters within the computer hardware segment, also benefit Apple by securing almost two and a half times the referral value attributable to positive word of mouth ($1,927 as compared to $816). Lastly, Apple incurs very little opportunity cost at the hands of Detractors while negative word of mouth costs its competitors roughly $1,350 per Detractor (see Figure 2.15).

Conclusion

In this chapter, we have reviewed a number of methods, from the simple to the complex, for establishing the economic value of your NPS. These methods can be used for building a business case, demonstrating return on investment, and estimating the economic impact of strategic investments designed to move customers along the Net Promoter continuum.

Establishing the value of your Net Promoter program begins with a good segmentation strategy, financial data, and NPS. This intersection allows you to start understanding the economic impact of a Net Promoter program and the strategies for creating more Promoters and fewer Detractors. For Detractors, who in many cases represent a net loss for companies even when acquisition and support costs are not factored in, the obvious imperative is to understand the source of unhappiness and how it can be remedied so as to minimize unfavorable economics. For Promoters, there is also the very real possibility of opportunity. Creating Promoters is the goal, but leveraging existing Promoters to maximize their referral value will also yield dividends.

3

Driving Change
Instill Customer-Centric DNA

It is one thing to dictate the use of NPS, but the real success comes when employees want to use it.
                    Neil Berkett, CEO, *Virgin Media*

Net Promoter programs are about transformation, but it is hard to define specifically what that means for a given organization. When we met with the leadership of organizations that are implementing programs, a disproportionate part of the conversation centered on the topics of change management, culture, or DNA. Programs that do not achieve results seem either to ignore or fail to adequately address the organizational issues required to achieve successful transformation.

Why Discuss Change Management?

Let us be clear: there will not be a simple answer to the question of how to drive organizational change. Generally the solution is unique to each organization, so you will almost certainly have to develop your own approach. Because this is a make-or-break issue for your program, in this chapter we give some pointers based on what we have observed in Net Promoter programs that are successful and, well, not so successful.

You would think that every organization, regardless of product or industry, desires increased customer loyalty and tries in a variety of ways to attain it. It would be a reasonable expectation that increased loyalty translates into myriad business benefits, including increased sales and profits. Yet the data does not support the idea that simply making investments in customer loyalty yields business improvements. On average, Net Promoter scores have barely improved over the past six years, despite major investments. Absent measurable improvements, organizations struggle to find a return on investment for their program and may give up, or they underinvest to the point where the outcome is effectively the same.

Challenges in NPS-Driven Change

If NPS feels like the right thing to do, consider some of the roadblocks that prevent its immediate success:

- *Skepticism.* Employees simply do not believe that loyal customers drive results for their business. For example, the organization may be seen as being in a commodity business where price is the dominant factor, so how could improving loyalty make a difference? Or it may be that most employees think that the company is only as good as its last product, so customer-related improvements will have no impact. Even with a program in place, employees may be skeptical over the data's credibility.

- *Execution:* Employees may believe loyal customers matter but don't think the organization can execute. Previous actions have led them to think that the organization is not serious or is incapable of change. Perhaps previous large-scale initiatives have not stuck, or the company has experienced failure with similar efforts, such as enterprise resource planning (ERP), Six

Sigma, or customer relationship management (CRM) implementations.

- *Diffusion:* Although the strategy might be initially clear, the original purpose becomes confused or reprioritized as it traverses the organization, and the message is lost.

- *Resistance to new methods:* Traditionalists in market research may see the Net Promoter program as an erosion of their span of control, job, or skills.

- *Misalignment of goals:* Incentives and goals are in conflict across business units and functions. The focus of increasing customer loyalty is at odds with competing goals such as cost controls or employee productivity.

The Net Promoter Operating Model addresses some of these change management issues. For example, one way to contend with skepticism is by getting relevant customer feedback directly to employees to help them engage with customers and make a difference. Making the program personal to employees encourages increased accountability and action. Also, creating goals and incentives that align with customer centricity will rally employees to drive effective change.

One area we want to highlight is misalignment, a common theme in challenged programs. It is important for standard operating procedures, quality assurance measures, investments, and rewards to align with the direction the organization wants to go. When it comes to customer loyalty, conflicting goals may reinforce or reward behavior that's counterproductive to good customer decisions.

The Tale of Two Companies That Create Alignment

The first company is Virgin Media. CEO Neil Berkett shares a story about Virgin Media's fault management center that highlights the challenge that can result from misalignment of goals with standard operating procedures:

> Our agent takes the customer through the process, does really well, and gets to the end of the call and the customer is starting to become pacified. Then the agent said, "By the way, the engineer is going to come on Tuesday, and if you are not at your home, we will charge you ten pounds." So the customer got angry again. I asked the agent afterward, "I knew you were uncomfortable saying that. Why did you say it?" The agent told me that if he had changed what he said, he would have failed his quality check.

This is an example of standard operating procedures trumping employee empowerment and meeting customer needs. Virgin Media's Net Promoter program now helps focus the organization on the right goals: outcomes rather than outputs. Virgin Media changed the metrics it used to measure agent performance as a result of the program (dropping agent handling time and focusing on first contact resolution) based on a belief that focusing on the outcome with the customer will completely change the organization and customer relationships. As you will read later, Virgin Media's NPS has increased due to refocusing on customer experience.

Dick Hunter at Dell has a story with parallels:

> I've been in manufacturing for thirty years, and nothing that you say will just immediately resonate with people; when you try to change fundamental culture, it takes a while to do that. And it takes a lot of repetition showing people that I mean what I say I'm going to do. I remember vividly the first few meetings where I was thinking that our measurement system is off. What are we doing measuring handle time on an agent? That

doesn't make any sense to tell an agent, that they had a certain amount of minutes to solve a problem. That's crazy and doesn't map to customer goals.

So Hunter removed that measurement and announced that they were no longer measuring the team on handle time. Some of the four hundred people attending the meeting started immediately clapping, but others were skeptical. Some (brave) people spoke up to say, "We don't believe you. You know, you've been measuring us on handle time for years. We don't believe you that you're going to change that." Today, no one on Hunter's team talks about or worries about handle time. They worry about solving the customer's problems because their mantra is resolving the issue on the first call. Although they do track how long it takes to resolve problems, they don't measure agents on handle time. Making structural decisions that will change the culture and the customer's experience at critical call center touch points was part of Dell's strategy to align the organization to focus on customer needs.

Aligning the Organization

Is your organization aligned so that your customers' perceptions of seamless service are borne out in day-to-day transactions and overall customer experience? Here are some characteristics of an aligned organization:

- Senior leadership is committed.
- Line management drives activities based on customer feedback in every line of business and region.
- Employee programs are in place to establish meaningful goals tied to customer experience.
- A customer loyalty strategy has been developed, communicated, and embraced by the entire organization.

- Exceptional customer experience is a core value that is emphasized throughout the entire organization.

Symantec has a well-aligned organization, especially given its 17,500 employees and multiple acquisitions. We asked the chief operating officer, Enrique Salem, what worked. He said:

> It starts with visibility. You've got to make what you are doing very visible, and people have to understand the direct correlation between customer loyalty and business results. You've got to make sure that every executive staff member, every manager in the organization, and ultimately every employee understand that they are directly linked. Through some of our own experiences, we can definitely see that there is absolutely a direct impact—as customer loyalty improves, the business improves. We have also focused on what behaviors we want to reward.

Getting Senior Leadership Committed

There are virtually no case studies of successful Net Promoter programs without a high level of buy-in from leadership. Our research suggests that this does not deter firms from trying, just from succeeding. Leadership is needed at an appropriate level. This doesn't always mean the CEO. For instance, in an organization with independent strategic business units, a general manager might be the right person to act as the pivotal leader. Ultimately it comes down to individuals who are empowered to create change at a sufficient level for program success. Empowerment encompasses financial resources, the ability to control incentives and goals, and the individual's credibility within the organization.

Our data gathered in 2007 from companies using NPS found a gap between what executives say about customer loyalty and the actions they take to create a customer-centric culture and operation. Whereas 68 percent of executives stated that their companies were highly customer focused, only 15 percent of those same companies practiced behaviors that define a customer-centric culture. In other words, the belief is there, but execution falters. Only 47 percent of these firms rated themselves as strong performers with respect to an executive underpinning. In addition, when you compare the commitment to actual investment, there is often a significant gap in aligning organization resources to a customer-centric vision.

So how do you close this gap? We know that investment alone won't solve the problem because there may be perceived shortcomings in execution capability. Leadership needs to be convinced that these investments will yield a positive return: they want proof points. This is where the Net Promoter economics come in, putting future outcomes in the context of current financials. Leadership may understand intuitively that short-term costs will lead to longer-term gains, but may doubt their ability to realize the benefits. Our research shows that the time between investment being made and financial returns being harvested represents one of the biggest impediments for program success. Even if management understands the lag effects, they are forced to risk uncertain future returns for certain current costs; this takes a lot of confidence and foresight from the organization's leadership.

Techniques for Cementing Leadership Alignment

We have seen several methods work in a wide array of environments to overcome these challenges. These leadership alignment strategies include "show-and-tell" Net Promoter program and NPS wins, finding surprising insights, drawing on emotions or culture, and building a case around Net Promoter economics.

• *Show-and-Tell Net Promoter Program Wins.* In this approach, an organization may launch a mini–Net Promoter program, with the goal to have results to show leaders and other departments.

This program should demonstrate a complete cycle of issue identification, resolution, and business benefit. In B2B situations, the simple path is to focus on a specific segment (such as several top accounts) and put in place a cycle of NPS feedback, action, and resolution. Saving a major account that would have been lost without follow-up action grabs everyone's attention. Up-selling an account due to uncovering client needs also demonstrates value. Showing the success and telling the organization how the Net Promoter program helped save and improve accounts can win over skeptical executives.

• *Find Surprising Insights.* Another way to get people to focus on the program is to find insights that surprise them. Often the first round of data from the program will provide some surprising findings. Typically companies uncover these revelations while reading and categorizing customer comments into key areas that drive loyalty; the insights found in the comments and root cause analysis could surprise people. Focus on the conclusions that are less obvious, and take immediate actions to address these areas and demonstrate value.

• *Draw on Emotions.* In some organizational cultures, one method is to win over the executive team on an emotional level, although this comes with risks. In an ideal world, everyone's support is based on rational decisions. Many successful programs, however, start with finding members of the executive team who intuitively align with Net Promoter thinking. The Net Promoter philosophy of both the golden rule and the emotionality around Detractors and Promoters may draw out more program supporters.

Symantec has engaged senior leadership with both insights and emotionality. The top twenty-five leaders in the company get together for two days at the CEO's quarterly leadership meeting for one standing topic: How are they doing on customer loyalty, as tracked by NPS? They review it across all lines of business and then discuss what actions they are going to take over the next 90 to 180 days to make sure that they are driving and executing against the necessary investments. Salem, the COO, shares specific actions the organization took to increase alignment:

> One action that has made a big difference in galvanizing Symantec around the fact that everybody needs to be a part of this was sharing what we did around Symantec's partners. Our program team gave each of our executives twenty Detractor partners to call and then report back to say how we were doing. It was an incredible, eye-opening experience to have the leadership team of the corporation hearing firsthand—not filtered, not summaries, but first-hand from our partners—what were the things that were blocking them or having them move to other vendors.

A word of warning around this approach is warranted. Programs based on iconic senior leadership appealing to the core culture of the company often get off to a quick start. Sometimes they also discover that without eventually building a strong economic argument, the rest of the organization is saluting the flag but not really buying in. The risks here are going through the motions or loss of traction if the leader gets distracted or replaced.

• *Build a Case Around Net Promoter Economics.* In many organizations, Net Promoter economics drive successful program adoption. By building a comprehensive understanding of the economic value of Promoters, you build a case for action linked to financial impact. Managers may be skeptical around claims of future sales growth, so presenting a business case around customer economics of increased up-sell opportunities, reduced churn, and customer lifetime value can be more effective. A solid business case calculating customer lifetime value will help prove the economic benefits of running a Net Promoter program. For marketers, word-of-mouth economics are increasingly seen as a viable way to measure program impact. Ultimately economics is the most effective and persuasive way to get leadership on board. Ignoring the need to build a solid financial case will put your program at long-term risk.

Getting the Front Line Aligned

One of the most exciting, and daunting, elements of Net Promoter is its strong call for frontline employee involvement. For purposes of definition, let's just say that the front line is the employees who touch the customer—the principal point of contact. These can range from highly paid sales account managers, to contact center employees, to staff working the checkout at a supermarket. We know that these people deliver the customer experience in every business, and we know it's incredibly hard to move this group in the same direction. Persuading half a dozen executives in a room to take action is one challenge; getting six thousand employees around the world to do so is another task altogether. In this section, we examine approaches to getting the front line aligned with the Net Promoter program.

Virgin Media shared its experience aligning employees. Berkett told us:

> Every single level of our organization has embraced NPS. The first step in aligning the organization around Net Promoter is to achieve real buy-in from key influencers within the company. . . . I've been out in the field and have seen NPS on walls and in call centers. I've spoken with team leaders about their use of NPS and see that it is being driven right down to the engineer level. There is not a day that goes by where NPS is not used in some conversation I hear.

The lesson here is to never forget the importance of leadership attitude and constant communication to the front line. If the leadership is not behind the Net Promoter program, the front line won't be either. The commitment of executive and first-line management is highly significant in influencing employees' behavior.

We believe that frontline employees generally want to do the right thing. Few people sign up for a job as a customer care representative so that they can thwart customers from getting value from their products and later listen to negative feedback on the phone. Who wants to spend their workday dealing with frustrated customers? Frontline employees live in a world defined generally by:

- Skills and level of training
- Standard operating procedures and rules
- Metrics and compensation

As with all other efforts to manage performance, these are the levers that can be adjusted to increase the impact of employee performance.

Clearly, training is a major component of behavior. If you want to influence the behavior of frontline employees, improve their training programs. Within the Net Promoter program, frontline training for closed-loop follow-up with customers is critical, as we discuss in Chapter Seven, as is root cause analysis, which we discuss in Chapter Six.

Standard operating procedures form the basis of repetitive jobs at the front line. Think of an airline: the employees' actions and roles are highly defined around formal Federal Aviation Administration regulations and corporate airline policies and operating procedures. The typical contact center has dozens of rules, phone scripts, and escalation procedures defining how to handle customer concerns. These procedures are theoretically designed for both customer service and efficiency, but sometimes they miss the mark because not all customer experiences fall neatly into prewritten rules. Nevertheless, standard operating procedures can align frontline employees with the Net Promoter philosophy. Create flexibility in your operating procedures to allow your frontline employees to address customer issues while they maintain critical business procedures.

And then there are metrics. What gets measured usually gets managed. For example, in many environments, there are quality metrics that tell us about defects and output. In a contact center, the metrics are lit up on the wall, and key performance indicators are posted on bulletin boards. At the very least, you will want to ensure that your choice of operating metrics doesn't misalign with the goals of your Net Promoter program.

Employees are trained to believe that there is both a carrot and a stick. Execute the standard operating procedures, follow training, hit the metrics, and it's all good. There may be bonuses and incentives, or at the very least psychological rewards such as peer recognition. Either way, usually there is a combination of financial and nonfinancial incentives aligned around the goals.

Techniques for Cementing Front Line Alignment

Here are more tips and guidelines on what has worked for companies to get the front line on board:

- *Enlist.* Employees know the truth. They understand the issues better than you do. You can't fool the collective knowledge of thousands of people, so enlist them.
- *Educate.* Share business goals and policy decisions with the front line. For example, frontline employees may view business policy to maximize efficiency as inconsistent with the goal of providing superior customer service. It is important to explain to these employees that not all customers get the same service levels but there is an underlying level of service for all customers. Choosing different service levels based on your segmentation strategy should not undermine the Net Promoter program.
- *Align goals, procedures, and metrics.* If standard operating procedures and metrics don't align with the NPS goals in a

logical fashion, the program won't gain adoption. And if goals are unachievable, employees will quickly give up. Set up standard procedures to support goals and metrics that challenge employees yet remain achievable.

• *Customize.* Information really does drive behavior, and the time span between these is short. Make information relevant to people in their tasks. This could be at the team or the individual level, depending on your culture. Whichever you decide, make certain that the information is trustworthy at the level you choose (see Chapter Five).

• *Relevant reporting.* Keep reporting frequency in line with the nature of the job. If you measure people weekly on key performance indicators, make sure the frequency of the Net Promoter data is consistent. If it's out of sync or the frequency is less, it will be seen as less important. Reporting NPS data along with other key performance indicators in a relevant time frame will make the link to metrics more apparent.

• *Reward.* Let the front line know that they make a difference and their contributions are valued. This can take the form of non-financial recognition and reward. Verbal affirmation and organization-wide recognition play key roles. Enrique Salem tells us that Symantec rewards behaviors that make the customer's experience pleasant and effective: "We make the loyalty program visible. We highlight individuals who are being customer driven and putting the customer first. Every quarter, we highlight four or five individuals who have done something that is clearly above and beyond in making sure we are taking care of customers." Recognizing and rewarding model behavior will reinforce program goals.

Building a Fanatical Employee Culture

Net Promoter can integrate into an overall strategy to build employee culture, as we saw at Rackspace Hosting, an IT hosting company based in Texas whose mission statement is "to become one of the world's great service companies." The common definition of a host is someone who receives and entertains guests, and Rackspace has built its company and culture around an idea called "Fanatical Support." Although the concept of Fanatical Support can be hard to define, Rackspace's customers and employees (called Rackers) know what it is. Rackers have a sense of urgency and accountability about serving customers and genuinely caring about them, investing in the success of its customers' businesses, and making it personal.

To deliver on the promise of Fanatical Support, Rackspace has created a unique culture that encourages and enables Rackers to give their best every day. In 2008, *Fortune* magazine ranked Rackspace thirty-second on its list of "100 Best Companies to Work For." The company spends a great amount of time selecting and training the best people to become Rackers, helping them develop their strengths rather than asking them to change who they are. This approach creates happier, more engaged Rackers who look forward to coming to work every day.

Lanham Napier, CEO, shared his thoughts on employee culture:

> Fanatical Support underpins Rackspace's philosophy and transcends the entire business. Often customer roadblocks are cleared by a single person who steps in and handles a situation well. We know that this desire to take full responsibility in challenging customer situations cannot be mandated; Rackers have to volunteer to make this extra effort. They must instinctively know and actively want to do what it takes to build lasting trust with customers. The most coveted award in the company is the Straightjacket Award. The winners are the company heroes, whose actions are celebrated and who exemplify Racker culture.
>
> The company believes investments in Rackers and the work on our Net Promoter program will lead to greater employee engagement, which will in turn create

higher customer loyalty. Although some may consider this approach an expensive way to do business, we respectfully disagree. Our Fanatical Support culture, coupled with our new NPS-driven operational investments, will help us achieve our goal of maintaining customers for life.

Focusing on employees as a key component of the program and instilling a fanatical customer-centric culture throughout the organization lays an excellent foundation for Net Promoter program success.

Goal Setting in the Context of Change Management

Goals are inherent to how organizations create change and therefore offer one of the major levers for moving the organization. You might not initially use them, but over time they become essential. Chapter Eight covers details around goal-setting techniques, but there is a more existential question: Is formal goal setting a good idea? By way of definition, we will use the terms *goal setting* and *target setting* interchangeably. However, typically *goals* refer to objectives, while *targets* are the actual measurement or score an organization is trying to achieve.

An entire generation of managers has been trained to believe that goal setting is the basis for driving results. For these people, the absence of formal goals represents a signal that a measure is not important. For others, formal goals and measurement systems may run counter to existing organizational and cultural norms. They run the risk of alienating employees, damaging enthusiasm for the program, and even undermining the cultural values the Net Promoter program sought to create.

An interview with John W. Thompson, the chairman and CEO of Symantec, supports the view that formal goal setting helps focus his organization on improving results:

> I've always believed that nothing helps alignment better than a situation where everyone must focus. And we

needed to focus here as our revenue performance had not met our expectations because we made significant changes in our systems infrastructure that impacted customer and partner relationships. One of the beauties of the Net Promoter process is that we were able to see, within a short period of time, how those changes had a negative effect on customer and partner satisfaction. As our leadership team saw the NPS start to decline, it became easier to galvanize the team around the set of actions that we needed to take. We set fairly aggressive targets and socialized them to gain momentum. As a result, Net Promoter scores continue to improve, as it has over the last couple of quarters.

Thompson pushed the team with target setting in order to focus everyone's attention on revenue performance and customer experience. If your culture is based around formal goals and metrics, the basic steps outlined here can help your efforts:

• *Make goals visible.* The best techniques are the old manufacturing ones—post goals everywhere. We like Experian's way of doing this: post the goals in the corridor on a board opposite the elevators to get everyone's attention.

• *Make goals personal.* The aggregate corporate NPS goal might be interesting to the CEO and maybe the board and executive staff, but what about Sally from accounting? How does she affect it? Make the goals personal and relevant to empower individuals to affect change.

• *Recognize NPS improvements and stability.* NPS can be a volatile metric because it is an amplification of your customer's loyalty. Some volatility is good because scores can change quickly and get people taking action. Employees rally as the score improves. However, at the same time, you should understand the volatility of your metric before you set formal goals. It might take a full year or more to get response rates up from customers who matter and have stable and trustworthy data. If you set the goals too soon, expect organizational backlash when you have to reset goals or hold people accountable to an unstable score. This can undermine your efforts in change management.

Let's say your CEO wants an NPS program and charges you with making it happen. You design a survey and ask the ultimate question, then sit back to enjoy the results. The quality of your initial data wasn't quite what you had hoped for, but you're not worried because you can improve the information over time. So what if the initial response rate was only 5 percent? You have heard of worse! And a 20 percent NPS doesn't sound quite so bad.

The CEO is happy with the progress, but she wants to see the score improve and wants to set an aggressive goal. Heck, let's improve the score to 30 percent in a year! Why not? But wait! We still don't have everyone's attention. Let's link 20 percent of everyone's bonus to the score. That will keep them focused.

One year later, the response rate is up to 10 percent. It's not great perhaps, but still an improvement. The NPS is down to 15 percent, however, and the organization is ready to chase the program team out of the village with pitchforks and torches. Bonuses will not be paid. The organization just got "net demoted" and they aren't going to take it.

This is clearly a bit of tongue in cheek, but we have seen organizations lose alignment because of premature or incorrect goal setting. Use proper goal-setting techniques, examined in Chapter Eight, and understand data stability issues (see Chapter Five) to ensure alignment rather than possible dissension.

Incentives

Few topics provoke quite as much discussion as that of incentives. Financial and nonfinancial incentives can move people toward the same goal. Regardless of your beliefs around their pros and cons, the one thing we can say for sure is that you should have a clear strategy around their use in your program. We think incentives matter.

First, as a group, people respond to incentives. The economic behavior of groups is highly influenced by their incentives structure (including likely cheating behavior). Individuals may vary in their behavior, but across your entire organization, you will see the connection. Second, they are a form of signaling. People look for direction as to what is expected of them. Incentives create alignment from the shareholders to every individual.

Finally, incentives will take on a life of their own. They will drive behavior in often nonoptimal ways, including cheating or gaming, as we refer to in Chapter Five. Expect and manage cheating in a system where incentives are meaningful.

What's all this about cheating? You might feel we are being overly cynical at this point, but that is not our goal. Many economists regard their science as a study of incentives, and our favorite perspective on this comes from Stephen D. Levitt and Stephen J. Dubner in their book *Freakonomics* (2006). Levitt and Dubner look extensively at the issue of cheating in economic systems ranging from sumo wrestling to high school testing. From our own observations, we concluded that incentives and cheating have an unnerving habit of standing side by side. In a large enough population of participants, you can expect someone to game the system. This does not conflict with our premise that people want to do the right thing. This is about the behavior of groups and the effectiveness of incentives coupled to the law of unintended consequences.

It is sometimes a fine line between cheating and optimization. Ask a sales rep to provide a list of contacts for your program and say that he or she will be paid based on the percentage of Promoters. What are the odds the list is focused on known happy customers? Will the sales reps be more encouraging or persistent with known Promoters? Are they cheating or just optimizing a metric with which you are measuring them? Providing an incentive based on the percentage of Promoters may encourage behavior that does not match your goals. Perhaps you want team members to increase participant response rates, which would both expand the pool of customers providing comments and would be more representative of what is truly happening in the business. You might want to establish a policy that the omission of known Detractors could have serious consequences for them as evidence of cheating. By the way, we believe that overt cheating, such as false data entry, should result in significant penalties.

Ultimately we are seeking truth in data. Behavior that reduces the quality of data is a program killer and should be fought. Incentives *will* change behavior. Our advice is to take great care and anticipate the unintended consequences of your policies. With this in mind, leverage both monetary and nonmonetary incentives, and consider other short-term goals (such as improvements in data quality or response rates) to get the organization aligned.

Cross-Functional Integration Through Ownership

Let us bring these organization issues to a point with an example of FileNet, now called IBM Enterprise Content Management. Prior to IBM's acquisition in 2006, FileNet created a commercially successful document-imaging solution for businesses. It rounded out its offerings over twenty-four years through development and acquisition. In 2002 FileNet evaluated its operations and found it had the following issues:

- A fragmented client relationship model
- Limited visibility into customers' enterprises
- A fragmented customer-centric culture
- No concise measurement of satisfaction levels

- No concrete data for driving customer-centric programs
- No understanding of key drivers of customer loyalty
- No formal way of gathering product requirements

FileNet is far from alone in these regards. Against this backdrop, the program team embarked on several initiatives, including one called the "Customer loyalty initiative." FileNet's preparations followed a classic Net Promoter Operating Model. One of its key objectives was to ensure that accountability and actions were well distributed and understood throughout the organization by both customer-facing and noncustomer-facing departments (see Figure 3.1).

	Manage Expectations	Product Knowledge and Improvement	Build Relationships	Understands Needs
Sales	●	●	●	●
Field marketing	●	●	●	●
Engineering	●	●	●	●
Product development	●	●	●	●
Information technology	●	●	●	●
Finance	●		●	●
CS&S	●	●	●	●
Legal	●		●	●
PS	●	●	●	●

Figure 3.1   IBM FileNet's Cross-Functional Commitment on Key Priorities

Note that all organizational groups are accountable for managing expectations, product knowledge, building relationships, and understanding needs. The only exceptions are finance and legal with regard to product knowledge, which makes sense. Otherwise accountability and action are present throughout both customer- and noncustomer-facing groups. In other words, everyone had a role in improving the customer's experience. They made every department a stakeholder in the program's overall success.

Accountability and action were spread throughout the organization, which enabled it to resolve many of the initial problems. Then FileNet developed an NPS-based program that gave it the unified customer-centric environment it required.

FileNet has had impressive results. When it began in 2002, its NPS was in negative territory (−6.37 percent). By 2006, prior to its IBM acquisition, it had pushed those metrics well into the positive (+20 percent), a net positive shift of 26 percent. By the standards of B2B software, the level of NPS improvement is approaching best in class. The program also was directly linked to increased revenues and profits from its existing base, from 72 to over 80 percent.

Program Governance Model

When we ask companies, "What has been your greatest challenge in establishing the foundation for a customer-centric culture?" the common response has been, "We know the right things to do; we just don't invest in the infrastructure, processes, and people to establish the tools and capability to support and maintain them."

A missing ingredient here is often proper program governance. Governance is the glue that holds together the key components of a Net Promoter program. Governance helps define:

- Who keeps the organization focused on customer loyalty
- Who is responsible for running the program smoothly
- Who is responsible for acting on the information and driving accountability

When programs lack coordinated leadership, they tend to form silos. A program in a silo is easier to manage because there is less cross-functional coordination. For example, a vice president of one business line has control over the entire customer loyalty program, including collecting data, root cause analysis, driving outcomes, and setting targets. Such programs tend to be more operationally than strategically focused (they fix tactical issues within that line of business), which limits the program's overall value. If the program methodology is not consistent with that of other business units or information is not shared throughout the organization, the program cannot achieve full potential.

In contrast, a coordinated, organizationwide program can provide greater value and return on investment, but it requires more effort. It demands that multiple business units contribute and act on data. When you integrate enterprise technology systems and cross-functional information sharing into the global governance program, you can quickly develop strategic planning and tactical remedies.

Creating Roles and Responsibilities for Governance

Figure 3.2 shows a typical governance framework and flow between different departments and individuals as well as interdependencies. Figure 3.3, at the end of this section, displays a detailed checklist of typical responsibilities.

We like to start with a steering committee, which usually includes the senior leadership backing the program (the CEO, for example), the executive sponsor, and the functional executives who are internal program stakeholders. The steering committee works to send the message that business functions (lines of business) are responsible for understanding their data and developing action plans to improve loyalty and act on the results.

The CEO's Governance Role

The CEO's involvement is important to keeping the organization focused on customer loyalty. In large businesses, this role may be

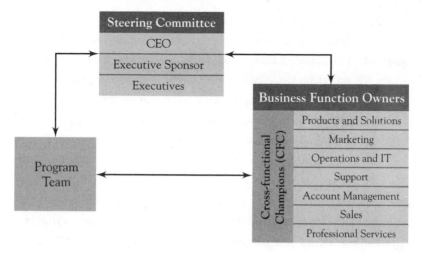

Figure 3.2   Program Governance Model

performed by a group president of some form; the key element here is the level of authority, capabilities of the individual, and, of course, the bully pulpit.

Executive Sponsors

The executive sponsor has arguably the most important role in aiding the program's visibility and viability. He or she must be passionate about customer centricity and display strong communication skills up the line to the board of directors, across the lines to other executives, and down the line to all employees.

Executive sponsors are the first line of attack or defense for the program. If external obstacles emerge, they may help to sidestep or eliminate them, but often it is internal management where this role proves valuable. Usually the sponsor is a senior executive who meets with the program team periodically but may or may not be involved day to day.

When we profile successful executive sponsors, we don't see a functional pattern; the sponsor can come from service, sales, quality, or marketing or be a dedicated "Net Promoter" executive.

Success is more about personal characteristics than function. The essential executive choice for a program sponsor is a respected leader who has the authority and desire to make change. You would be well advised to trade internal credibility for title. The level of the individual should be appropriate to the organization's size. In a $100 million organization, it may be the CEO. In an $80 billion firm, it could be an executive one step removed from the executive staff or perhaps division president. The right answer hinges on the level of relevant authority to create change. We prefer executive sponsors with operational experience (although there are success stories to the contrary), and we like examples of companies that see this as a rotational role in career development for future top management. If this role is seen as a key post, it sends the message to the organization that the program is taken seriously.

Finally, the best executive sponsors spend time outside their own organization understanding successful strategies at other organizations. They invest in their own development and that of their program through networking, conferences, and formal or informal benchmarking exercises. This is not a hands-off role among loyalty leaders.

Business Function Owners

Ultimately the lines of business owners are responsible for driving improvements across their business functions or units based on the insights of the program. It's critical that the right representation is at the steering committee meeting from the standpoint of authority and ownership. Although the program team members can work with the owners to identify actions to create Promoters, they can't implement them. The most successful programs put clear ownership for taking action into the hands of the lines of business and are methodical in establishing goals and reviewing performance. We have found that governance models fail when they try to drive accountability and action entirely through the program team. Because this team is not empowered to take action on behalf of the lines of business, no action occurs.

The Program Team

The program team runs the infrastructure, provides education, prepares analyses, and distributes information to internal
functions so they can improve loyalty and create Promoters. The
team can sit within many different types of business units, similar
to the executive sponsor, and like the sponsor, it's more important that the team members have the right characteristics than
the right functional location.

The program team will control the resources of the program
and coordinate execution. In many cases they will also be the
analytical center, so they may be acting as an internal consultant.
They are expected to be the most knowledgeable resources in the
Net Promoter domain, up to speed with the best practices and
lessons learned from other practitioners.

It is easy to run off a list of desirable skills for this team; the
real issue is how to prioritize them when you need to make trade-
offs. Most teams are limited in their size by budget. In many organizations, the "team" is just one individual, which makes the task
of putting the skills together that much harder. In these instances,
companies cope by outsourcing the necessary skills; they may tap
another department for help or go outside to a third-party vendor.

Larger organizations typically have more resources, but run the
risk of squandering them by failing to put together the right mix
of skills. Often they use internal resources for tasks best performed
on an outsourced basis, or vice versa. We have also found many
instances where the organization fails to provide adequate budget
to support a minimal set of skills.

There are three basic skill groups that enable the program
team to drive change in the organization:

• *Line management perspective*. This doesn't sound like a skill
developed through training, and it's often not. However, if nobody
on the team has line management experience, the program risks losing credibility and traction among the very group you are relying on
to implement. In an ideal world, we would pluck someone from a

line management position with some general management exposure to run or join the team. Many successful companies (GE and Nokia, for example) see these positions (often under the quality umbrella) as staging grounds for general management skills development.

• *Data analytics skills.* We are dealing with lots of data here. More to the point, we are dealing specifically with data subject to interpretation and analysis in ways that differ from, for example, financial accounting yet may need to be linked with financial data. You might think we are referring to market research or statistical skills. Although those are useful, they often are fairly specialized skill sets, and we think it's most important that the data analysis skills here extend beyond market research skills. Financial analysis is part of the equation. Classic quality and Six Sigma skills can play a major role: you need staff that understands how to use data in a variety of management contexts. The most important skill is the ability to draw meaningful management con-clusions from data and make them understandable to everyone.

• *Process skills.* You would be well advised to have resources on the team who understands process design. You are going to be attempting to change the underlying processes of the organization, so business process knowledge will be at a premium. Experience in the world of quality is often a strong background here.

Most important, you want people on the team who are effec-tive at acting through others. They see program success as being enabled through education, ensuring engagement and providing information with an awareness of the needs of those who use the data. The right culture is a big factor in making the team work. It's easier to describe what doesn't work: staff who believe their expertise and careers are best defended by the creation of an arcane science that only they can understand.

Cross-Functional Champions

We like the idea of champions and have seen them make all the difference between success and disappointment. This is the team of people, reaching out into different parts of the organization, who can drive action in their respective groups. Champions communicate program information and data into their unit, do additional analysis, and give feedback to the program management team. They are the facilitators who ensure interdepartmental cooperation and demonstrate a highly visible stake in the success of the program. Who are they?

- They are not necessarily the management. In fact, there is a strong case to have these people more aligned with frontline employees than with management in their respective organizations.

- They are believers. First and foremost, the NPS message resonates with them at a personal and an intellectual level. They buy in emotionally and from a pragmatic perspective.

- They have credibility in their own organizations. They are perceived as successful in their roles, and their leadership in the program is seen as an implicit endorsement.

- They understand the line function they are part of. They are insiders and know how things work in the function and what the everyday challenges are.

- They work together to solve cross-functional issues and are effective at coordinating across organizational boundaries.

- They have strong internal networks they can leverage.

- They are resilient in the face of adversity and stay the course.

There is a simple test to tell if you chose the right champions. Look at the reaction of their peers to your announcement of names. Did you add or subtract from program credibility?

Sage Software selected two "loyalty champions" from each of its sixteen brands. According to Sage Software's Hal Bloom, vice president of market research, "Loyalty champions are just that: champions. They are not expected to do all the work themselves, but to challenge and motivate their business units." The champion teams at Sage comprises the various business line members who help to define which data will be meaningful to their business lines and help to interpret the data and take action. Here, they are typically project and program managers within the business units who are integrated into the day-to-day activities.

Experian's Change Agents

Experian is an example of a large, global company in the information services market with operations in sixty countries, serving both consumers and businesses. In 2003, Experian established an NPS-based loyalty program. It began with two support centers (technical and customer) and an overall relationship program. "Our biggest challenge was to create the experience of 'one' Experian," remarked Laura DeSoto, senior vice president of strategic initiatives, Credit Services Decision Analytics. "We're a huge organization with many business units that act as individual businesses or companies. However, our clients don't see us that way; their perception is that they are dealing with one company, whose individual business units work together seamlessly."

How did Experian rally the disparate groups around Net Promoter? Experian believes its success hinged on several key change management decisions:

- Establishing a loyalty program: "The Client Promise"
- Deploying forty-five internal change agents from different business units who trained and cheered on the effort
- Creating a learning map that captured and sustained the ongoing knowledge

- Holding recurring workshops, "Client Promise in Daily Work," and thereby creating a clear demonstration of the processes for making customer-centric decisions every day
- Communicating the client promise effectively
- Providing strong executive support and commitment to the customer

Experian credits its program's success, along with increased revenue, to its change agents. The forty-five change agents represented business units across the organization. These change agents helped facilitate and champion initiatives as well as help align employee actions with the Client Promise to deliver a consistent, branded customer experience to show clients a unified Experian.

Experian had to do a fair bit of resource planning to achieve these successes. Appointing change agents to take time out of their daily work to focus on driving loyalty meant getting buy-in from the change agents' managers and business function owners. A change agent might spend between 10 and 20 percent of the time focused on program governance (see Figure 3.3). (Experian change agents spent 50 percent of their time for the first six months on these efforts. The time diminished down to 10 to 20 percent after the first six months.) These change agents also undergo training, another resource for which to plan. Experian gave these champions the authority to make change happen.

General Governance Guidelines

A governance model is an important component of a successful program, but it takes work to structure and resources to do the work.

Figure 3.3 summarizes the typical roles and responsibilities of those engaged in program governance. It also provides a guideline

Role	Program Governance Responsibilities	Time
Steering committee: CEO	• Defines customer-centric culture • Focuses organization on loyalty • Delivers internal and external strategic communications	Follows cadence of business review (quarterly, biannual)
Steering committee: Executive sponsor	• Sits on the executive board, typically customer facing • Drives voice of the customer throughout organization • Maintains loyalty program visibility and accountability up to CEO, across to other executives, and down to program team and business function owners • Sets program goals, budget, and resource allocation • Escalates issues and needs • Communicates results to steering committee and organization	Follows cadence of business review (quarterly, biannual) 20% of time
Steering committee: Executives	• Executive staff: chief executive officer, chief technology officer, chief marketing officer, chief information officer, chief financial officer, and chief operating officer • Reviews, discusses, and evaluates results • Drives accountability for achieving results in respective businesses • Provides goals and business context of customer data to business function officers	Follows cadence of business review (quarterly, biannual)
Program team: Enables champions, reports to steering committee	• Manager or director level, reports to executive sponsor • Gives data to executive sponsor to support goals and drive action • Develops a program road map, sets strategies and project, manages loyalty program • Collects program requests, prioritizes, evaluates pros and cons • Defines processes (data collection and distribution, customer follow-up, root cause analysis) to help others operationalize • Provides tools, information, and best practices for business functions to act on data • Empowers and educates cross-functional champions to be advocates in their own business functions • Does not directly enact change; rather, enables others	Meets regularly 100% of time

Figure 3.3   Roles and Responsibilities of Those in Program Governance

Role	Program Governance Responsibilities	Time
Cross-functional champions: Request help from program team and provide help to business	• Typically mid- and senior-level managers, sitting within own business function • Cheerleads customer loyalty program within business function • Coordinates between program team and business function owners • Supports program team as subject matter experts who know business processes and customer needs • Receives support and education from program team • Requests help from and provides input and issue escalation to program team • Defines relevant data and their distribution process to the business • Helps business function gather, interpret, and act on data • Provides education and training to business function • Reviews program success and communicates best practices at scheduled meetings	Meets at least quarterly 10–20% of time
Business function owners: Report to steering committee, request help from program team	• Line of business operational management • Takes action to improve scores based on feedback • Holds team members accountable for customer experiences • Ensures loyalty metrics and key performance indicators are in line with program goals, targets, and employee incentives • Provides resources for cross-functional champions team and program team to enable loyalty program's success • Reports results and action plans to steering committee	Meets at least quarterly 5–10% of time

Figure 3.3 (*Continued*)

of how often teams should meet and how much time and what resources might be involved in governing a loyalty program. Use the chart as a guideline and adapt the roles, responsibilities, and meeting frequency to reflect the size, resources, and cadence of your organization.

Conclusion

In this chapter, we have discussed the factors that typically affect change management in a Net Promoter program. We have shared the challenges that prevent change. Executive engagement and sponsorship is critical to overcoming these challenges. In addition, getting employees onboard is not an easy task. Goal setting is a worthwhile exercise to align and focus the organization toward customer centricity and NPS goals. Cross-functional ownership of the customer experience, both customer facing and noncustomer facing, will aid in rolling out and maintaining a successful program. Establishing a program governance structure with cross-functional champions who are led by an executive sponsor will create organizational alignment. An effective program must consider the critical role of effective change management in driving a program's success. Change management is an art and science. Put your change management strategy together early in your program roadmap to pave the way for success.

4

Designing an Enterprise Roadmap

*Our commitment is to have customer-centric culture be a
long-term part of Experian's DNA. . . . Once the Client
Promise roadmap was built, there was real excitement
because now employees knew exactly what was expected.*
Laura DeSoto, senior vice president of strategic initiatives,
Credit Services Decision Analytics, Experian

Before embarking on a Net Promoter program, it's important
to remind yourselves what a program is and what it is not.
It is not a process you apply to your organization for a couple of
years and then toss away, and it is not an off-the-shelf solution.
Although there are common elements to any loyalty program,
each organization's program has to be designed to fit its unique
circumstances. A successful Net Promoter journey involves a
combination of people, process, and technology, supported by
a customer-centric culture.

When people read about significant gains organizations have
achieved using NPS, a common reaction is to want to dive in to
measuring NPS and start trying to reap the benefits as soon as possible. However, it rarely works that way. There are certain aspects
of a program that bear fruit relatively quickly, but the corporatewide changes take time. It is not unusual for a successful program
to take a few years to become well established and the NPS completely reliable.

In this chapter, we present some of the key elements to consider when building your program roadmap. These, together with
the Net Promoter Operating Model in Chapter One, should be
sufficient to enable you to develop your own roadmap to success.

Customer Solutions

Most programs focus on direct measurement of customer loyalty, but there are still some significant choices to consider. Let's start by identifying two types of business improvements that are driven by your Net Promoter program: operational and structural. This will help you define short-term versus long-term benefits. Then let's explore the difference between relationship and transactional measures of NPS, a frequent source of confusion in our review of existing programs.

Once we have the basics down, we will describe the relationship between these approaches and touch on other constituencies whose loyalty should be measured, such as employees, before pulling it all together into a plan.

Operational and Structural Improvements

There are essentially two dimensions of business improvements that result from a Net Promoter program: operational and structural (see Figure 4.1). Operational improvements are quick wins that are rapidly identified and resolved, usually involving tactical opportunities to improve the customer experience at the point of contact with the customer. Operational improvements typically improve loyalty one customer at a time.

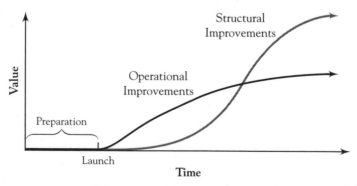

Figure 4.1   Operational Versus Structural Improvements over Time

Imagine a mail order chocolate company (our generic examples are getting more arcane) that experienced high call volume because customers were upset that the chocolates arrived after the expected due date. In this case, if a customer calls to complain about a late shipment, the service representative may immediately apologize for the delay, empathize about the inconvenience, and be empowered to expedite the shipping and offer a ten dollar coupon for a future order. The service recovery effort exceeded the customer's expectations and a possible Detractor is converted to a Promoter.

The representative took immediate steps to make a difference in a single relationship, and it paid off in terms of improved loyalty. The benefits of implementing operational improvements are that they typically take less time, involve fewer cross-team dependencies, and require fewer resources while making a positive impact.

Concurrently, organizations work on structural improvements that have a longer-term, and potentially more significant, impact on customer loyalty. These improvements typically require changes in the product, business model, or services and therefore take longer and involve more cross-functional involvement and more resources. Of course, structural improvements are specific to the circumstances of your organization. They could involve major investments in product R&D, cost structure changes, business policy changes, or any number of potentially significant investments. Structural improvements may also require gathering more data to ensure high levels of analytical support to minimize the risk of making a misguided major investment or decision.

Let's return to the example of the chocolate business. In the long term, operational improvements alone are insufficient to have an impact on a larger scale for customers. The management team may consider the potential benefits of making significant changes to their supply chain or fulfillment operations so as to improve the ability to deliver products more quickly. For example, the company conducted root cause analysis (further discussed in Chapter Six) and found that the ideal delivery time from the customer's perspective is three days shorter, and that delivery time and meeting delivery commitments have a strong correlation to loyalty and business expansion. As a result, the chocolate company targets supply chain improvements to improve delivery time, resulting in increased loyalty and growth.

Your Net Promoter program should be designed to capitalize on the characteristics of both operational and structural effects. In Figure 4.1, you can see that typically the two curves are different in their impact over time; although both are important in isolation, their interaction increases the likelihood of success. You should see an immediate impact with operational improvements, and although structural benefits take longer to emerge, short-term operational improvements will decline without addressing the structural issues. It's worth reinforcing that without operational improvement, the business may wait for long periods, potentially years, before the investments in customer experience pay off. This could test the patience of many leaders. Furthermore, operational improvements often directly drive culture change in ways we discussed in Chapter Three, through engagement with the employee base.

Structural Improvements Drive Dell's "Call Factory"

Today Dell runs a lean call center, but this was not always the case. Dick Hunter was brought in as head of consumer support to improve call center performance. In an interview with us, he shared the details of Dell's structural improvements. He faced what many other call center managers face: the trade-off between efficiency and good customer service. Hunter said,

> There was an issue with our network. We had too many sites and call queues. When I joined the team, we had 256 different call queues. I said, "You've got to be kidding me—that means that a customer gets 1 out of

256 queues." We had to evaluate the difference between call efficiency and effectiveness.

In Dell's quest to take cost out of technical support, it created a lot of small, narrowly defined call queues. Hunter explained,

> If we could get the customer to the right call queue, we would be highly efficient in solving their problem. Well, the theory was great, but the practice was not, because we couldn't get the customer to the right queue very often. In fact, we ended up having a transfer rate of 45 percent as a result. And we forced the customer to stay in the interactive voice response [IVR] mode for a long time.
>
> So we simplified the network. We reduced the number of sites, outsourced partners, and the number of queues dramatically. We simplified the IVR, and the hold time is down from seven or eight minutes to one minute. And, our transfer rate is down to 18 percent. But that whole network thing was a big deal to get fixed.

This is a prime example of a structural improvement that paid off for customer support. Dell applied sufficient resources to make structural changes to cut the queue waiting time and call transfers. To do this, it created a centralized process engineering group to make the changes. Hunter stated,

> I'm a huge proponent of lean and Six Sigma, which are staples of manufacturing. So we applied lean techniques to the call center, applied Six Sigma disciplines, and now run them like call factories. We run them with processes that people understand, can follow, and can improve on.

Relationship Versus Transactional Survey Processes

If there is one consistent area of confusion we find in the Net Promoter community, it's the difference between relationship and transactional measures of NPS. Some prefer the language *top down* for relationship and *bottom up* for transactional, but these terms may confuse others in the organization. For us, *top down* and *bottom up* refer to the actions taken by executives and frontline employees, respectively.

Transactional surveys typically measure an event with direct customer interaction, such as a support call. If we took a flight from San Francisco to London and the airline asked us about the specific flight experience, it would be measuring our feedback on a transactional basis. The survey may ask questions about the in-flight experience. The timing of the feedback would likely be dictated by the timing of the event—in this case, right after the flight had taken place. But what if the airline wanted to understand the health of its overall relationship with customers? Now, fliers may not consider themselves in a relationship if they flew with that airline just once. However, if they were frequent fliers, it would be a fair assumption that their relationship and perception of the airline transcends any one event. Their willingness to recommend is a function of numerous events that have taken place over time. In this case, a relationship measure is needed to reflect an accumulated and overall experience with the airline.

Relationship measures capture the overall perception of your business and are not related to any one specific interaction. Typically these are gathered on a periodic basis (monthly or quarterly, for example). Timing can be dictated by any number of factors, but usually within a fixed cycle so that the data is truly comparable to prior periods. There are significant benefits in being disciplined around when these periodic measurements take place and what actions will be taken based on the results.

A successful program should measure the relationship NPS on a consistent basis.

In all likelihood you will collect both relationship and transactional measures. Transactional measures, if they are significant events in driving the strength of the relationship, as in the airline example, should be a leading indicator of relationship NPS. In fact, if you don't see a lagged correlation between transactional and relationship measures, you may want to ask if the transactional touch point is meaningful. If you chose to do both types of measurements and you use the Recommend question in both instances, you will likely find different NPS results. This is logical since we might have a lower Recommend rating on the basis of the most recent flight, which was eight hours late into Heathrow, had poor movie choices, and lost our bags to boot. Nevertheless, our overall Recommend score might be higher based on the past twenty flights and long-term relationship with the airline.

Using both measurements interchangeably with the same NPS label could create confusion. "NPS" usually refers to the overall, corporate metric based on a relationship survey and "transactional NPS" refers to measurement taken of a specific event or touch point. If the customer experience is based on an accumulation of various events, use a relationship survey. If one transaction defines the relationship—for example, that interaction defines the customer's overall experience—then transactional surveys may be sufficient to gauge the health of your customer loyalty. Transactional NPS would equate to the relationship NPS in this circumstance.

Here's one final consideration. Most benchmarking is measured across the entire relationship, and a specific benchmark for a single touch point may not reveal whether your organization has successfully differentiated itself. As such, many organizations use the relationship feedback to benchmark against the competition from an end-to-end perspective.

Putting Them Together: Two Survey Types with Two Improvement Time Frames

At this point, you might be thinking that transactional measures drive operational improvement and relationship measures are about structural change. Well, yes and no. The fact is that both relationship and transactional measures can create both structural and operational changes in the business. Take a look at Figure 4.2.

Let's use an illustration of a B2B industrial manufacturing company and its view of transactional and relationship measures. The manufacturer sells big-ticket items in a complex, high-value sales cycle and has chosen to measure the relationship with each contact in all accounts every six months. This NPS provides the manufacturer, through root cause analysis, structural insights that help define longer-term improvements to its product offerings. A closed-loop follow-up on the same relationship data on a customer-by-customer basis has an immediate and operational impact through account management and sales force actions. If the customer has a question or complaint, the account manager may make an immediate, positive impact by quickly contacting the customer. Clearly this single relationship measurement has both operational and structural benefits.

	Operational: Improve Execution	Structural: Improve Business Model
Relationship Feedback	• Relationship management • Pipeline analysis • Sales and account management performance	• Competitive analysis • Brand messaging • Segmentation • Investment decisions
Transactional Feedback	• Customer recovery • Account team coaching • Performance management	• Quality improvements • Process improvements • Resource investments

Figure 4.2   Feedback Contributes to Operational and Structural Improvements

Concurrently the organization has implemented a measurement of its customer care transactions. It has a transactional measure generated across thousands of support calls, providing an almost-real-time ability to execute a remediation process on outstanding customer issues to achieve immediate operational improvements. In addition, the accumulated data over the course of the year provides a basis for root cause analysis in the customer care operation, so the organization can make longer-term investments that improve the customer experience. This is an example of a transactional system that has both operational and structural benefits.

Finally, the organization is interested in the correlation between the customer care transactions and the overall relationship to determine whether investments in customer care have a significant impact on the overall relationship. Over time, this hypothesis is confirmed by the analysis of the relationship data over a lagged period of three months. The manufacturer therefore knows that customer care is a touch point that ultimately drives loyalty and potentially repurchase or retention.

In short, to obtain a complete view of the customer experience, a Net Promoter program should monitor the individual touch points a customer has with your organization, such as a call center interaction or professional services engagement, and also measure the overall health of the relationship and the customer's perception of your ability to deliver to expectations. This combined view guides both operational and structural actions. For the most advanced programs, organizations have identified early-warning indicators in the transactional environment that will give them the insight into the impact on the overall relationship.

The Customer Corridor and Its Touch Points

You should now have an understanding of relationship versus transactional measures, or at least a good sense of how to think about your own program. Equally pertinent is an understanding of the goals of your business, the market, and your customer to help you focus on which areas to tackle first. You need to see your organization from your customer's perspective—something we call the *customer corridor*—to know what is meaningful to the customer. It provides you with the opportunity to see which changes can affect operational improvements and which can affect structural improvements. Understanding your customer's experience is critical to identifying the touch points that make the most impact on the customer and therefore focus your Net Promoter program on those areas. We discuss the customer corridor as a tool for survey design in Chapter Five, but here we can apply it as a prioritization tool.

The corridor represents your customer's overall experience with your organization. Customers don't want to see you as your internal organizational silos or as a group of business units or profit-and-loss accounts. They see you as a combination of experiences they have as they interact with your products, services, and personnel. You are one business to your customers, despite efforts to the contrary! It may require some creative thinking to gain perspective on how your customers really view you, but this exercise is important to obtaining accurate feedback.

If you map out the experiences an individual customer has with your organization, you will start to understand your organization from the customer's point of view (see Figure 4.3).

In this financial services organization example, customers may come into the corridor through marketing, advertising, or referral. As they move through the corridor, they will transact with the organization in various ways, engaging in activities such as opening a new account or applying for a mortgage. These experiences collectively begin to shape their perceptions of the organization. Some of these transactions may be more important than others in how the customer views the organization. For example, transferring assets could include criteria about whether the bank transferred the right amount, the transaction was completed in a timely fashion, and the online experience was positive. If transferring

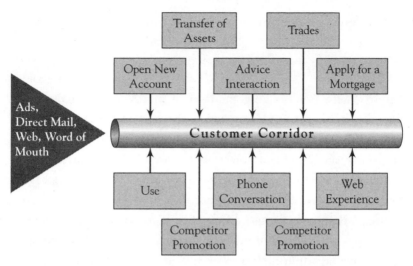

Figure 4.3   Customer Corridor of a Financial Services Organization

assets is a critical event, as it is for most people, any experience that is less than ideal could have significant impact on the overall relationship.

Putting Yourself in Your Customer's Shoes

How do organizations go about the task of defining their own customer corridor? Once defined, how are these categories prioritized? We recommend starting with a chronology that tracks the general categories of experience for a typical customer from initial awareness all the way through to repurchase. We recommend organizations make a table for each touch point and consider which specific experiences, interactions, and moments of truth matter most to your customers.

Once you've completed this exercise, you can begin to identify which of these experiences are basic to the business, also known as hygiene factors, and which could be key differentiators. Hygiene factors are items that, if missing, will be a source of dissatisfaction but are unlikely to foster loyalty because they are seen as must haves, such as sending accurate billing statements.

Key differentiators are more critical to measure, as are the key interactions that create negative experiences.

Virgin Media's Customer Corridor

Virgin Media was looking for both a metric and program that would engage and align employees. It was looking for something easy to understand that would reliably improve customer loyalty at critical touch points. In order to establish the correct infrastructure, a customer corridor (journey in Virgin Media's language) was developed by cross-functional team members (see Figure 4.4).

Sean Risebrow, Virgin Media's director of customer experience, describes the customer journey in detail. Virgin Media's approach maps transactional NPS to its processes from the customer's perspective. A typical customer journey was identified, as were the touch points along the journey. For example, a customer subscribing to cable services for the first time might call a customer service center and as the customer's account is set up, arrangements are made for an engineer to install the product. This is considered the *Join* touch point and is the first step in the customer journey. *Join* is a potential point to collect transactional feedback on the customer experience. Risebrow said, "Measuring the customer experience shortly after the event is important to capture top-of-mind details and to take action to improve customer loyalty."

Figure 4.4   Virgin Media's Customer Corridor

In addition to understanding the customer experience after the call and the engineer's visit, Virgin Media wanted to measure the entire journey. For example, it wanted to measure whether the customer's expectations were being met or exceeded as the customer moved through the journey. It could be that while a customer may be willing to recommend Virgin Media on the basis of the *Join* touch point, she may not be willing to recommend it later if promises that the customer service agent made in the initial call were not fulfilled during the installation process or if she received an incorrect billing statement.

"It is vitally important to ensure that the right end-to-end customer experience is being delivered. Therefore, all of the measures of customer experience along the journey need to be interconnected so the root cause of a problem or a delightful experience can be identified," said Risebrow. An effective way of achieving quick wins and managing change in the short term is to use a closed-loop feedback process to make operational changes that can resolve customer issues. Virgin Media has established this framework and has seen significant success not just by being able to rapidly identify root causes of NPS, but also by deploying changes at the right touch points in customer service operations, which has resulted in NPS improvements.

We were impressed by some of the rapid improvements Virgin Media saw in its NPS using this approach.

Consistent survey methodology along the journey meant that data could be compared from touch point to touch point, thus giving a single view of the customer journey. This enabled Virgin Media to prioritize actions and improvements using a stack-ranked driver analysis. For example, Get Help service at call centers was prioritized for improvement because it had low NPS compared to other groups. It was also identified that even when a customer needed a home visit by a service engineer, the key driver of the end-to-end experience was the telephone interaction with an agent. The team took action and introduced training programs into call centers with high call volumes. The survey data helped target the right improvements and transfer knowledge of best practices to the centers with high call volume that needed additional training. These call centers changed their culture, improved agent skills, and as a result have improved NPS by 10 to 20 percent within only a few months.

Virgin Media wanted to test a hypothesis that training for agents at low-scoring call centers would improve the NPS of those agents. It created a trial group of forty agents and implemented a training pilot program. The teams got together to review the data by segment, comments provided by customers, and key drivers. This approach allowed the team to extract the customer experience data that these call center agents could directly influence. Risebrow shares:

> Because NPS is measured daily at both an individual employee and individual customer level, Virgin Media was able to quickly identify the success of the trial. The score of the forty agents jumped immediately by 15 percent and stayed 15 percent ahead of the rest of the center. The teams operationalized the learnings by routing all of these call types to specially trained agents.

The journey-led design directed Virgin Media to the root cause of churn, which was not necessarily at the touch point where it was being reported by customers. It discovered that high-value customers were experiencing bill shock at the start of the relationship because their expectations during initial contact when subscribing to services were being incorrectly set or communication wasn't clear; in other words, customer expectations were not being met. Action was taken to improve communication. Since the journey is interconnected, fixing communications at the Join touch point improved the experience at the Pay touch point. Virgin Media was able to use NPS as a lead indicator of customer churn by analyzing each customer touch point and focused its improvement resources on the most important touch point from the view of the customer.

Employee Solutions

Employees interact with customers throughout the customer corridor. We know you are thinking, *Of course, employees are critical to the customer experience, and we care about employee satisfaction and loyalty!* Nevertheless, the process of integrating measurements of employee loyalty into a program is rarely done; the annual employee satisfaction survey often ranks alongside performance reviews as an exercise in frustration for all involved.

We are not going to invest more pages trying to persuade you that employee loyalty has a bearing on customer loyalty. If you want an excellent perspective on this, we recommend you read *The Service Profit Chain* (Heskett, Sasser, and Schlesinger, 1997). For us, integrating employee loyalty and customer loyalty is critical so management can invest in employee issues that strengthen customer loyalty rather than invest in those that have little or no impact. This has the effect of bringing employee loyalty out of the human resource function and right into the customer experience program.

Employee Impact

Employee surveys are designed quite differently when the goal is creating a link to customer loyalty versus measuring overall employee satisfaction. In the former case, our goals are:

- To improve business results by . . .
- Increasing customer loyalty through . . .
- Leveraging high-impact employee areas determined through comparisons of customer and employee data

Figure 4.5   Employee-to-Customer Linkage Model

Figure 4.5 shows that employee loyalty can drive improvements in customer loyalty, which can increase economic benefits to the organization. This concept is described in *The Service Profit Chain* (Heskett, Sasser, and Schlesinger, 1997).

With this framework in mind, let's get more specific. First, consider the survey. This is not a general employee health check but a broader framework by which to understand, from the employee's perspective, how to increase customer loyalty. These surveys are usually focused on key performance barriers within the typical work environment. Special emphasis is placed on responses to issues of teamwork, general communication barriers, resource constraints, role clarity, ownership, accountability, and decision-making authority. We know that employees who understand the business and customer strategy, as well as how they contribute to that strategy, are assets to improve customer loyalty.

Linking employee data with customer data has to be part of the overall program design from the outset. Having a common unit of analysis is a necessary condition to combine employee and customer data. This common unit of analysis is determined using the employee survey and can include items like the accounts employees work on, their business unit, their functional unit, and their support center. The next step is to understand customers' loyalty drivers, which will serve as the filter by which you can start to understand how to influence employee loyalty.

Organizations fascinated by the Net Promoter approach for customers have been applying a similar methodology for employees. Generally, with minor variation, organizations are asking employees, "How likely is it that you would recommend Organization X to a friend as a place to work?" Employing a similar methodology allows organizations to do a gap analysis to understand the extent to which there is a discrepancy between how employees perceive their organization and their customers' perspective.

Shifting the Organization's Culture

Although the previous discussion applied an analytical framework to understand the relationship between employee and customer, there are non-analytical methods for creating a huge shift in the organization's culture and engaging employees. As mentioned in Chapter Three, in order for Experian to turn the vision of customer-centricity into a reality, it was imperative to enable each employee to realize the impact that he or she has on clients. Laura DeSoto said,

> We needed to create a line of sight for employees, so that they could understand how they personally affect the customer experience and make it relevant and action-able. While Experian's frontline employees wanted to provide good client service, before the Client Promise initiative, there wasn't a common vision or understand-ing of what "good client service" meant. We needed to really understand what our clients wanted—their loyalty drivers. This enabled us to design and deliver an excel-lent experience under this Client Promise.

Experian invested considerable time interviewing customers to understand what drove their loyalty and repurchasing behavior to create a client promise. "It was an actual promise to our custo-mers about what an excellent experience looks like and what we would deliver," DeSoto explained. They developed touch point maps to assist in the development of a future experience and spent time in driving training and communication around the delivery of an excellent experience. The goal was to mobilize the employees around the delivery of its customer-centric model. Experian based its promise around three fundamental tenets: be easy to do business with, have execution excellence, and have information you can trust (see Figure 4.6).

They trained groups of employees through a series of six sessions called "Client Promise in Daily Work," which could run for hours. They helped each employee internalize the Client Promise message for their particular role. Change leaders were selected and were instrumental in generating enthusiasm and support for the Client Promise throughout the company. Employee participation in the company's vision enabled the improvements in customer experience. Key to Experian's success was not underestimating the effort required to gain hearts and minds within the organization and to ingrain customer centricity into the fabric of employees' daily workflow.

"Be the Reason" at Dell

Dell created an employee campaign and forum, supported by processes to encourage participation, in order to instill a customer-focused culture. Laura Bosworth is the director of global customer experience strategy and shares her experiences with Dell's "Be the Reason" campaign. Bosworth believes:

> In order to be successful, every employee needed to embrace the experience of the customers from the top down. From balancing discussions focused around revenue targets, to that of the customer, to getting customer experience into leadership training, as well as advising on bonuses and compensation structures, and other areas in human resources where we could influence teams, Dell transformed the culture and how every employee can touch an aspect of the customer journey with Dell.

Here's how the initiative evolved.

Figure 4.6   Experian's Client Promise

Listening to Employees

Dick Hunter, head of customer service, initiated a way to hear from employees. He said:

> Employees are really intelligent people who understand the inner workings of our company. I met with many tech people in one-on-one and roundtable meetings, and I asked them, "You know what you do very well. If you were in my shoes, what would you do to fix this situation and triage our customer experience?" And, you know, I got a laundry list of things to do. I asked my staff to list all the inconsistent and essentially dumb things we do. I then created a personal folder in my Outlook with the title, "Dumb Things." I categorized this list into three or four major areas that needed work. One area was around the agents themselves and the attrition rate. We needed to address this.

Dell's Campaign

The team collaborated with the corporate communications team to develop a broad campaign aimed at awareness of the customer experience and to bring that to all employees. The customer-focused cultural campaign was called, *Be the Reason Customers Choose Dell*. It had all the elements of classic campaigns: Dell had rallies, posters, and websites. The precepts are:

- Be the reason customers choose Dell.
- Be the reason customers come back to Dell.

Beyond this, Dell put in place a corporatewide system, including training and amending the human resource system to include customer experience and customer-experience-based recognition. Hunter helped create an "honorable job for employees." He said:

Attrition is typically high in call centers, and I ask the question, "Why is that?" In manufacturing I was used to attrition of 3 percent. And yet one could argue that a manufacturing job is quite a boring job compared to what a tech support agent does. I didn't understand why it wasn't a job people wanted. I feel that the tech support agent's job is the most honorable job in the company because we are helping people solve problems. . . . When a customer calls support, they're probably frustrated or want to check order status. That customer is going to now talk to someone who is going to make or break the relationship: that's a frontline agent. I felt that we needed to create the idea of an honorable job for the agents.

Dell's Employee-Based Survey

Dell added questions to the employee-based survey related to the customer experience. In fact, Michael Dell, the company's founder, even had them change the questions at the last minute, asking, "What do you think is most important for our success?" And an overwhelming number of employees responded that customer focus is what's critical to Dell's success.

Experian and Dell provide excellent examples of organizations that invest in their employees to improve customer relationships. Empowering and leveraging employees is a key element of any customer roadmap. Getting feedback from this key stakeholder is vital to understanding customer issues from the outside in and from the inside out. Next, we discuss roadmap sequencing.

Phased Versus Big Bang Approach

One of the major decisions is whether to take a phased or a "big bang" approach to rolling out a program. We have seen successful programs implemented in both ways: in stages over time and at once across the entire organization. However, the majority of circumstances seem to favor the phased approach, which offers lower risk and more flexibility.

In most cases, it's an issue of culture more than financial investments that determines how an organization might proceed. An organization with a more authoritarian culture, driven by edict, or one with a highly charismatic founding CEO who built the organization around customers, may find the big bang approach an easier option because there is no need to sell the benefits across the organization. An organization with a consensus-oriented culture may need the phased approach. Other factors that lean toward a phased rollout include existing surveys conducted using different methodologies and disparate metrics.

Many organizational cultures support action based on the demonstration of success; they are inherently risk averse and tend to look for a small group to do the trailblazing before engaging in an organization-wide initiative. Some part of the organization needs to get the wins, build the stories, and create the buzz within the organization to address a "show-me" culture. As an example, get Sales to talk about its successes and the CEO to see the benefits as a way to drive wider adoption. We have seen organizations conduct pilot programs in difficult markets or departments to prove that Net Promoter can succeed in even the most difficult environments. This gives skeptics confidence that the program team did not pick easy wins. Afterward, showcases gain buy-in. In a consensus-driven organization, the metric and program must be validated before a larger rollout can occur.

Why then even try the big bang, also known as the *revolutionary*, approach? Dramatic change can happen when the organization has customer centricity already in its DNA and will readily embrace a full-blown Net Promoter program, in which case you don't want to miss the opportunity. A loss of momentum might be a killer blow for a program in this situation, especially if leadership expects to see rapid movement. Sometimes the organization is in crisis and needs something drastic as quickly as possible.

A new CEO is brought in with a mandate for change. A big bang approach can help the organization rally around a collective sense of crisis and give the leadership team the support to make major change. Net Promoter programs can be eroded through lack of urgency. Multiple stakeholders, perhaps with a stake in the status quo, take advantage of the slow progress to undermine some radical elements that the program was founded on. The result is a watered-down version of the original idea.

Sequencing Your Roadmap

Whether you deploy a big bang or phased program, designing a thoughtful roadmap to support your approach is critical. The type of program you deploy will affect the sequence of the program and the emphasis on specific elements. For example, if the CEO gives a mandate to run a Net Promoter program, you may not need to spend as much time building a business case, gathering proof points, or requesting funding. As seen in Figure 4.7, we have created a roadmap that shows the critical elements in an order and sequence that may work for many organizations, but consider it only as a template for you to edit. The key elements of a solid roadmap follow.

Executive Engagement and Proof Points

Setting a solid executive foundation, including Net Promoter economics (Chapter Two), should be established early in the process. Skeptics will require financial proof points of increased revenue, saved accounts, and increased customer lifetime value.

Customer Strategy and Organizational Context

Build an understanding of your customer strategy (both economics and what is important in the customer corridor) and how this links to organizational culture, operating model, and management team:

- Which customers are worth investing in?
- What are the touch points that matter to them?

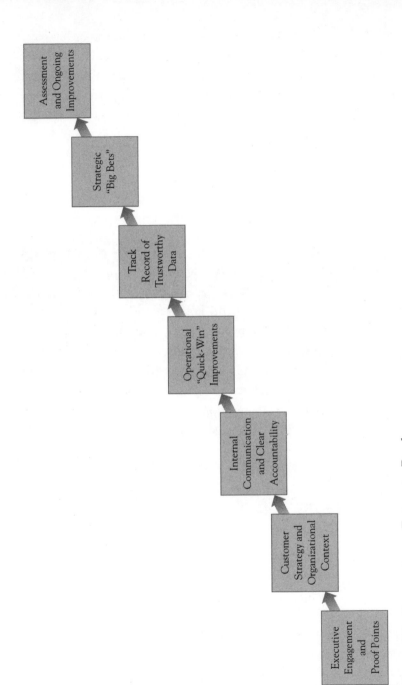

Figure 4.7 Sequencing an Enterprise Roadmap

- Which touch points hold the greatest promise for NPS improvement?

- How will the organization need to get involved and take action?

Review Chapters Two and Three for additional ideas.

Internal Communication and Clear Accountability

A closed-loop process for operational improvements requires focused communication in areas of the business that can have the most immediate impact. Ideally this communication should precede deployment of closed-loop feedback (Chapter Seven). Frontline employees need to know what to do to follow up with Detractors or Promoters. For example, which customer relationships do they own, what expectations should they set, and what actions are they empowered to take?

Operational Quick-Win Improvements

As mentioned earlier, organizations need to seek quick-win improvements as early as possible with which to illustrate success.

Track Record of Trustworthy Data

Once you have trustworthy data, you're in a position to understand the structural improvements and opportunities. Trustworthy data (see Chapter Five) and a strong program governance structure need to be in place before linking to variable compensation.

Strategic Big Bets

The executive team can use the trustworthy data to support major investments or big bets. Data analysis (see Chapter Six) provides the underlying confidence behind making structural improvements. Executive sponsors leverage their influence to ensure there's broad accountability for changing business processes or capabilities.

Assessment and Ongoing Improvements

Periodically, at key junctures, the organization and executive team should step back to:

- Assess their progress relative to key goals
- Validate return on investment on major investments
- Evaluate target setting and benchmarking initiatives
- Ensure that incentive and compensation align with goals
- Revisit their customer strategy and program status to drive ongoing improvements

These actions support product and service innovation and overall program success and transformation.

Virgin Media's Big Bang Journey

We discussed Virgin Media's touch point analysis earlier in this chapter. Now let's put that in the context of its overall roadmap.

From a business perspective, Virgin Media had a lot of change on its hands. It had been formed by the merger of three entities, each with its individual cultures, business models, and identities. The different entities were delivering varying levels of customer service using different approaches, and for an additional challenge, Virgin Media operated in a market where tenured customers were not experiencing the same attractive deals offered to new customers.

From a customer loyalty perspective, the initial NPS results varied significantly, and traditional approaches to customer satisfaction had not generated a strong alignment across management and employees. Nevertheless, Virgin Media forged ahead to prioritize the program. Let's review the steps they took.

At the outset, executive sponsors aligned on the need to improve the customer service function. As seen on the sequencing roadmap in Figure 4.7, they began the journey by tackling Executive Engagement, Proof Points, Customer Strategy, and Organizational Context. The first six months were used to secure top-down buy-in, plan a pilot, and deploy it with the goal of finding out firsthand if this new type of effort would be insightful and valuable to the business. Virgin Media assigned a small project team to help verify issues, track NPS versus the competition, map out customer touch points, and develop a roadmap. This team developed NPS proof points and linked NPS to customer lifetime value (CLV) early in the program to build confidence in their approach.

Over the following six months, Virgin Media defined its full deployment, educated and communicated across the company, and extended the program team. These actions aligned with the Internal Communication and Clear Accountability roadmap step in the process. They defined the deployment strategy, determined roles and responsibilities, and identified who, what, when, and how to deploy the program to achieve operational NPS improvements.

A clear short-term goal was quick operational wins. Risebrow said:

> One example of this was established early in the program. The training department looked at NPS by call type to see which calls were not handled well from our customers' viewpoint, and they retrained existing agents and improved induction training. All team leaders were trained on how best to work with NPS feedback and learned directly from the customer what each of their team members needed to change to improve their performance.

With some operational quick wins under its belt, the team then focused on building the trustworthiness of the data. It added relationship NPS measurement, revised surveys, worked to improve response rates, and ensured the data was truly comparable across time periods.

The final part of the journey was discovery. As the program matures, loyalty driver analysis is being used to uncover structural ways to improve the customer experience for sustained advantage in its market.

At launch, Virgin Media wanted to help focus efforts across the company. It successfully used a big bang approach, measuring from day one every single touch point so it could tune into the voice of the customer across every part of the experience. All employees, from the front line to senior management, were able to see the impact of their personal interaction and decisions on the customer experience. This whole process has helped to improve the NPS.

A note of caution with big bang programs: with all the enthusiasm, resource, and intensity, the program can easily get carried away and exhaust resources or slide into inefficiency. Some big bang programs are difficult to execute because there are many undefined program elements early in the game, so timing and sequencing of elements is more delicate and interdependent. Finally, expectations may be set so high that they are unrealistic for what is possible given the time frame, corporate culture, and market conditions.

Sage Software's Four-Phase Evolutionary Program

Laurie Schultz, senior vice president and general manager of Sage Software's Accpac and Simply Accounting groups, has been working with Net Promoter for over five years. Sage took a phased approach and rolled out Net Promoter across the organization, starting with the Sage Accpac ERP and Simply Accounting groups. Schultz said, "To truly engrain customer centricity into the heads and hearts of employees, you need to go through each of the following four steps. Depending on your organization's culture, you may go through this quickly or slowly, but to gain true organizational commitment, you need to do them all. It is important to customize the speed of implementation of the following steps to your organization's culture (risk averse or otherwise)."

Based on her experience, the creation of a Net Promoter culture within Sage's culture evolved in four phases:

1. *Reluctant organization.* In the beginning, the organization is cautious. To get any momentum, the concept must be actively led from the top. This phase is largely educational—for example, explaining what Net Promoter is. You may need to have several months of education just so people can start building a baseline of understanding, but you'll know you have accomplished it when anyone you pass in the hall can tell you what Net Promoter is. A mistake Sage looked to avoid was relegating Net Promoter down into the organization to an analyst role that didn't have the authority or credibility to drive change. Laurie Schultz believes that executive sponsorship is critical. If you are serious about Net Promoter, Schultz says, "Lead it from the top from day one." It is a lot easier for a general manager or a senior leader to get people motivated and moving.

2. *Data with volunteers.* As people gain knowledge of the "score," the organization moves toward "volunteers" who want to learn more by talking to customers. The earliest adopters or volunteers tended to live within product management and support.

3. *Targeted.* A fundamental step is to move from volunteer toward "day job." In this phase, aspects of the program became more formally enshrined with specific initiatives put in place to start "moving the needle." Participation broadened to include other functional units such as R&D and direct sales. In addition, the score itself moved from something generic to one that was segmented by customer type or product version, which enabled more effective identification and resolution of pain points.

4. *Empowered.* The ultimate phase was the formalization of goals down through the front line and the empowerment of the

employee who regularly interacts with the customer to resolve issues on the spot if possible. The day that compensation is tied to both revenues and customer experience is the day they know that they have arrived.

In this approach, Schultz believes that the fourth phase, empowered, reinforces the movement of the Net Promoter culture to the front line, where it is already pervasive across every single functional unit in the organization and people feel empowered to remove obstacles to delight customers.

Conclusion

We covered a lot of ground in this chapter. Our roadmap recommendations are to build a plan with a two- to three-year horizon that will provide timely operational improvements with longer-term structural improvements. We sought to solidify your understanding of what an enterprise roadmap contains—not only customer feedback but integration of employee feedback. We introduced the customer corridor, a way to evaluate the total customer experience. We also explored alternative sequencing (phased versus big bang) and described the path each of these approaches may follow.

We hope we have given you some tools for planning your own roadmap. Ultimately, your own analysis of customer and organizational needs will guide your judgments, sequencing decisions, and execution.

5

Building Trustworthy Data

*The worst thing we can have is a lack of confidence in the
data. So the confidence in the data was key, number one.*
Axel Haentjens, *vice president of marketing, brand and
external communications, Orange Business Services*

We have said it before: trustworthy data is the lifeblood of
your Net Promoter program. Without it, there is little hope
for creating meaningful and lasting customer-centric change in your
organization. Consider the following goals: understanding the root
cause of customer loyalty, linking loyalty to behavioral and financial outcomes, prioritizing process improvements, enabling closed-
loop customer follow-up, and creating a culture of accountability
through target setting and compensation. All of these aspects share
a dependence on trustworthy data. If employees are not convinced
that the voice of the customer has been accurately captured, forward momentum will grind to a halt. The program's validity is questioned, and employees may disregard the program and move on to
the "next big idea."

So what does "trustworthy data" mean in the context of a
loyalty program? It is not perfection or absolute certainty—criteria
that are beyond the reach of even the most resource-intensive
efforts. Customer data can render a meaningful and instructive
indicator of the true feelings and needs of customers, but all measurement has some degree of error within it. It can never be truly
perfect.

Instead, the best yardstick for whether data is trustworthy is the
extent to which employees, from the executive level through the

119

front line, are willing to make their day-to-day business decisions based on its guidance. You must ask yourself: Am I willing to determine priorities, make judgment calls, and invest time and resources according to what the data reveals? Am I willing to stake my professional reputation on the accuracy of the information?

In the recent past, loyalty programs were relatively toothless, an interesting and perhaps insightful addendum to the real drivers of business decisions but not a force in their own right. That has changed. Significant decisions, including what areas of the business to prioritize for change, how to determine the relative investment of resources, and the determination of employee compensation, are at stake. You need to be willing to make those bets on the basis of the quality of your data. In this chapter, we hear from a variety of organizations that have confronted these issues, and we will highlight the key processes and practices that will help to ensure your confidence in the credibility and trustworthiness of your customer data.

What Is Trustworthy Data?

As we have already suggested, the measure of trustworthiness is subjective. At Orange, Axel Haentjens observes, "We make sure that we have the right sample, we ask the right set of questions, and we are able to measure the results in a consistent way with a reasonable level of trust in the results. That is absolutely number one because without that, you cannot suggest to do anything."

At Experian, the same goals help to support a related need: the ability of the methodology and the results to withstand scrutiny. Laura DeSoto explains, "It is really important, because we are an information company and we have several hundred Ph.D.s and statisticians on staff. From the very beginning, we were adamant this program had to be rooted in solid data and statistics, since we're known for information and analytics."

These comments raise the common themes we hear across customers with regard to making data trustworthy: the information returned must be accurate, reliable, and relevant. The path to meeting those criteria is, in principle, simple:

- Targeting the right customers
- Asking the right questions
- Asking them at the right time

We explore each of these basic goals and the means by which they can be achieved, starting with a basic supposition: success in this endeavor is determined largely by whether you begin with a well-defined strategy for accomplishing these goals.

Creating the Strategy: Three Key Elements

In the fall of 2007, we reached out to a broad spectrum of organizations actively engaged in using Net Promoter. Our interest was in learning more about their successes, their challenges, and the practices they employed to build their programs. On the basis of the feedback these companies provided, we made an interesting discovery. Of the companies that lack a clearly defined strategy, only 23 percent were able to capture the voice of the customer in a reliable, relevant, and meaningful way. By contrast, roughly 80 percent of companies that felt that a well-defined strategy was in place also felt that they had the proper mechanisms to ensure trustworthy data. These same customers tended to be successful in the areas we identified earlier: defining and reaching the right customers, asking the right questions, and doing so at the right time.

Nearly 70 percent of successful companies have a plan in place to ensure that the depth and breadth of their customer base is represented in their program, particularly the customer segments that are critical to their business. Nearly 60 percent are able to evaluate and validate that they are asking the right questions as they link their loyalty data with operational and financial outcomes.

Two-thirds have designed their program to collect feedback in a timely fashion, including not just overall customer loyalty but the experience of their customers at critical touch points across the customer corridor through transactional surveys.

In the remainder of the chapter, we explore the most effective practices for ensuring trustworthy data, beginning with which customers you should target with your loyalty program.

The Right Customers: Measuring Who Matters

Not all customers are equal. Your business reflects this reality: you are constantly adjusting marketing, sales, product, and service strategies to target, obtain, and serve your most valuable and strategic customers. Your customer base is segmented into various categories—by financial value, region, product line, industry, and others. If your loyalty program is to be seen as credible internally, it needs to use the same customer segmentation schemes as part of its strategy for collecting and analyzing feedback.

The first step is ensuring that the customers you speak to are balanced in such a way that they represent the same mix of market segments, regions, products, and other customer segments characteristic of your general customer population. In market research, this is typically referred to as obtaining a representative sample, that is, a group of respondents who can serve as a reasonable proxy for your larger group of customers. From our perspective, this is a necessary but not sufficient condition. It lessens the risk that you will draw the wrong conclusions by listening to the wrong people, but it may not align with the long-term financial outcomes that are important to your business. Unlike other research exercises, you are trying to identify Promoters and Detractors by which you can make operational improvements. Small sample sizes prohibit this level of action taking.

The key to business outcomes is what we call "voice according to value." In essence, this means formulating a sampling strategy that ensures that you are receiving representation from key customer segments in accordance with their value to your organization. A customer whose company buys $100,000 of your products and services per year is not equal to one that buys $2 million per year. Ultimately the input of your most strategic customers should be given greater attention and greater weight in your decision-making process.

Many B2C companies use the RFM model (recency of purchase, frequency of purchase, and monetary value) to segment their customers according to value. Your sampling strategies should emphasize leveraging the feedback of your highest-value customers. This means ensuring their representation in the sample, segmenting the resulting data by value, even weighting the results to make it possible to understand and create specialized customer strategies for your most important customers. Unlike more general market research, a random sample is not your goal; targeted sampling is. It takes into account customer characteristics, buying capabilities, and other key criteria.

Some may find this perspective counterintuitive. It is important to remember that Net Promoter was born in larger part to obtain a customer feedback mechanism that would track against meaningful financial outcomes. As such, the goal is not to maximize customer experience—where all customers are treated equally—but rather to optimize it, with a keen eye on the customers who are key to the economics of your business. Your program should reflect your business, including its goals. In fact, the NPS score itself can be a powerful element of your customer segmentation. By linking loyalty data to customer characteristics and behaviors, you can better understand who your most loyal customers are and how to focus your business to maximize your growth within your high-loyalty and high-value segments.

With B2B companies, the individuals who make the purchasing decisions are not necessarily the ones who use the products or services. This adds an additional layer to the idea of customer value. First, there is the financial value of the "large C" Customer to consider, meaning the account as a whole. There is also the issue of the purchase influence of the "small c" customers within it, meaning the various individual contributors, influencers, and decision makers, which must be factored into obtaining an accurate view of the account loyalty.

Given this, the sampling and program strategies should emphasize obtaining and leveraging the feedback of high-value individuals within accounts while prioritizing the highest-value accounts across the customer base. Each account cannot be said to be represenative until a minimum number of contacts within each decision-making role described above is included, so as to more accurately reflect the total account dynamic. (These are depicted in Figure 5.1.)

This approach permits segmenting the data in multiple ways. First, it permits segmentation of accounts according to their overall financial contributions, making it possible to identify and create specialized customer strategies for your most important customers. Second, it allows segmentation by decision-making influence within and across these accounts, arming your field sales force for more effective account management information with which to create targeted strategies.

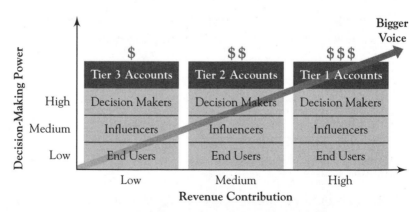

Figure 5.1   Voice According to Value by Role and Revenue

Recruiting Strategies

Frequently market researchers want to know how many respondents they need to achieve statistical significance. Although this is a consideration for your recruiting strategy, it is not the primary one. When it comes to building effective programs, we hope we have convinced you that what really matters is not how many, but who.

We suggested that your market focus (B2C or B2B) is a critical determinant in sampling strategy. It also has some consequences for recruiting strategy. For B2C businesses, it is often most practical (although not ideal) to use a sampling approach, where the goal is to obtain feedback from a targeted subset of customers. Mature B2C businesses may have a high volume of customers that make it possible to target specific customers, and segment to granular levels, without exhausting the pool of potential respondents. Talking to all customers will likely be too time and resource intensive to be practical.

A sampling approach is less well suited for B2B businesses, particularly when it comes to enterprise customers: typically large organizations comprising numerous individuals with different needs and levels of influence. The relationship between your business and the customer is more layered and more complex. Missing feedback from any level within these organizations can lead to a skewed perspective of their loyalty. That is risky given their financial impact on the business. Therefore, a census strategy, rather than a random sampling strategy, should be used to gather feedback for the largest and most strategic customer accounts. A census approach ensures that feedback from every such account is obtained and that all key roles within them are represented because every voice matters.

Sampling Considerations

After determining from whom to collect feedback for a sampling strategy, you can move on to the question of how many. It is important to collect a large enough sample to discover patterns and trends, and to draw meaningful structural and operational insights. Although any responses can be tactically useful, such as using one customer's feedback to improve their experience, it is difficult to take meaningful structural actions across an entire customer segment when sample sizes are small. You do not want to make business process change or large-scale investment decisions based on incomplete information. As a rule of thumb when using NPS, sample sizes of one hundred or greater are recommended for making comparisons among the most granular customer segments in your sampling scheme.

There are other considerations as well. You need to monitor and audit your sampling strategy to ensure a broad, balanced, and representative sample across time periods. Consistency is the key. Avoid overrepresentation or underrepresentation in any measurement to avoid skewing loyalty scores and distorting their implications. This is especially important when compensation is tied to NPS. You want the changing performance of your business, not the shifting composition of your sample, to drive the changes in the score.

When there are sample discrepancies or when sample discrepancies can't be controlled, there are a few options for separating the influences of business performance from sample composition. In other words, is an NPS change from one period to the next due to a business change or a change in the sample? Consider a business that tracks loyalty on a transactional basis across the globe. The data received on a monthly basis varies with the number of transactions, the quality of the contact data, and the types of customers answering the survey. Rather than wrestling with the issue of how to aggregate the data over time (providing one NPS score for the entire company), the business adopted a distributed approach that tracked NPS within regions over time, where sample composition was more uniform.

This approach may not work for all organizations, particularly those that wish to hold employees accountable to a single corporate NPS. Our recommendations thus far have focused on proactive planning: creating a sampling strategy that best reflects the business. If you are unable to do so, your recourse is to weight the data. Weighting is used to adjust the sample composition to better reflect the characteristics of your target mix.

Consider a B2B example in which your organization has three geographies—Africa, Asia Pacific, and Latin America—with approximately equal revenue generation. The top ten accounts in each of those regions bring in about 80 percent of the business. However, Latin America's response rate to your survey was low; you obtained feedback from only two of those ten accounts. Therefore, you have only a fifth of the normal representation of your strategic customers in Latin America. In order to balance Latin America's voice with that of the other regions, you would weight the two Latin American respondents more heavily to represent the strategic customers within that region.

The caution to this method is not receiving representative data in the first place. This can hurt the data's trustworthiness in the long run. Weighting underrepresented samples can skew and over amplify voices that are not truly in alignment with your customers' true views. For example, assume the two Latin American account responses were mostly from the influencer segment, with little to no representation of the decision makers or end users within those accounts. What now? How do you make more accurate decisions based on untrustworthy data? In the short term, weighting can help with general decision making. Nevertheless, for the long term, the best answer is to develop a program that focuses on a solid sample strategy and robust response rates. In this way, you will avoid giving too much weight to customer voice that has low business impact and giving too little weight to customer voice that has high business impact.

The Right Question: Choosing the Right Metric

NPS has proven to be a reliable measure for correlating customer loyalty with business and financial growth. That mathematical difference between Promoters and Detractors has been shown to be a reliable means of predicting subsequent revenue and profit gains. As Aon Corporation's global chief marketing and communications officer, Philip Clement, notes, "Aon selected NPS as a metric because it was 'proven' and had been growing in the public domain. There was a public record of its success." The in-depth research, data, and success stories were the proof that Aon needed to adopt NPS. For Aon, NPS is the right metric because Aon's growth, stock price, and NPS all move together. Aon uses NPS to help employees understand the issues so they can be fixed, securing its competitive advantage and improving organic growth.

However, NPS is not necessarily the right metric for every organization. The original NPS research focused on six industries and found that the metric was the best for most, but not all, of them. It was the best overall metric, but not always the optimal predictor of customer behaviors or financial outcomes. And that, of course, is important in formulating the strategy for a loyalty program. When selecting a loyalty metric, you have to determine if it is sensitive to changes in your business. You have to determine if it links to the outcomes you care about—things like the likelihood of repurchase, increased share of overall spend, or the likelihood of referral. Moreover, you have to decide if the metric you choose will work. Do all your employees understand what it's measuring and how it relates to business objectives? What kind of organizational action are you attempting to facilitate: closed-loop follow-up? operational improvements? structural improvements?

Oligopolies and companies that are in a less competitive landscape may also need to ask questions other than likelihood to recommend that will correlate more closely to business growth. This is because the likelihood-to-recommend question presumes that customers have alternatives to choose from or that referring others would not be potentially detrimental to the recommender, such as in a situation of scarce resources or potential competition. In this instance, tweaks to the question wording or an alternative metric altogether may be more aligned with outcomes you seek and, hence, more desirable.

These examples point to the importance of validating NPS for your business. Our experience suggests that three criteria will help you make that determination:

- Is the metric sensitive to changes in business performance?
- Does it link to meaningful customer and financial outcomes?
- Is it actionable at both the frontline and strategic levels?

Your answers to these should guide which loyalty metric you use within your program. Regardless of the metric, the Net Promoter Operating Model discussed in this book can be applied to drive a customer-centric culture.

Feedback to Improve Fulfillment at LEGO

LEGO is a good example of a business that adopted NPS in part for its sensitivity to changes in performance. LEGO plotted NPS against performance outcomes such as timely arrival, arrival condition, and specific product availability. In Figure 5.2, the circled areas show the sensitivity of NPS to changing levels of success within those specific performance areas. Business adjustments that led to performance changes—good and bad, with corresponding changes in customer perceptions—are clearly indicated.

Peggy Conley, director of consumer insights, recalls that LEGO investigated its packaging operation because packages shipped to households were arriving damaged. One immediate structural change was to change the packaging in an effort to ameliorate

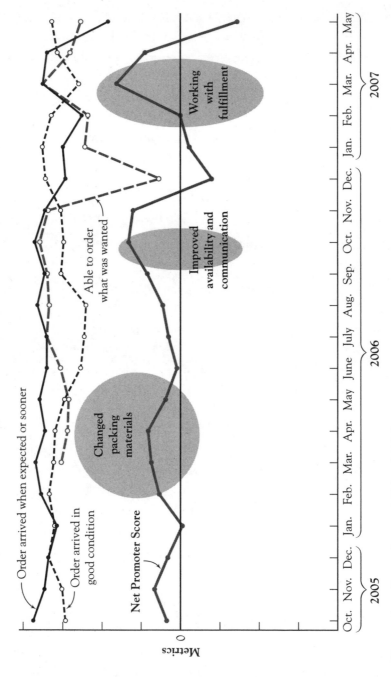

Figure 5.2 Event-Driven NPS at LEGO

the problem. Shortly after the packaging adjustments were made, orders once again began arriving in good condition, and NPS increased. In another instance, the company improved product availability and communication about availability in response to customer concerns. LEGO communicated with consumers to better inform them about the availability of older products, and NPS jumped. Today LEGO is using the loyalty driver information to work on order fulfillment. In each case, the actions taken improved NPS as measured in subsequent survey waves. NPS is a good metric for LEGO because it moves in sync with its operations.

The Right Questions: Fitting Survey Strategy to the Business

Validating your loyalty metric will take care of determining your core survey questions, but what about other questions? How much additional feedback is required to help drive action within your organization? What specific questions should you ask to gather this information? How do you balance your business needs with respect for your customer's time?

One of the core principles behind Net Promoter is respect for your customer and a philosophical bias toward shorter surveys as a mechanism for quality data capture. Some practitioners feel strongly that surveys should be limited to one or two questions; others advise asking multiple questions. There is no hard-and-fast rule around survey length; it is necessary to weigh the differences relative to your unique business needs.

Let's look at the concrete differences first. A two-question survey, with the Recommend question and one open-ended question, will produce less survey fatigue among respondents, is likely to produce higher response rates, and offers some open-ended exploratory feedback from customers. This approach lends itself to quite a bit of qualitative analysis, particularly with regard to distilling the key factors driving loyalty across groups of customers.

This qualitative review of comments can be very time and resource intensive, and the resulting conclusions are sensitive to context: for any given comment, it is often difficult to know what the customer intended to communicate without knowing the particulars of that individual and his or her relationship to your business.

A multiquestion survey, with a mix of mostly closed-ended (scale-based) questions and some open-ended comments, will produce more survey fatigue, is likely to produce lower response rates, and tends to be more directive than exploratory. The richness of the data returned is directly related to the questionnaire design. If the right performance areas are targeted, the results can yield a highly accurate picture of the relationship between specific customer experiences and overall loyalty. If critical experiences are overlooked and not included in the design, accuracy will suffer. In contrast to two-question surveys, this approach lends itself to more quantitative analysis, which requires less time and fewer resources during the analysis but more forethought and initial planning.

There are differences, too, in how root cause analysis may be applied (see Chapter Six for more discussion of analytical methods). For the two-question survey, root cause analysis depends largely on the frequency of comment themes or learning gleaned from customer follow-up. For multiquestion surveys, root cause analysis is typically based on the statistical strength of the associations between various performance questions and the loyalty metric. Figure 5.3 summarizes the approach for two questions versus multiple questions.

Bernhard Klein Wassink, senior vice president of global marketing for GE Real Estate, observes that having a strong relationship with customers helps to mitigate the effect of survey length on response rates. He observes:

> Our question count initially ranged from eighteen to twenty-six questions, but GE Corporate gave us guidance to ask only five questions. Some of Corporate's

questions had multiple parts, so we actually ended up with at least nine or ten questions. This takes our respondents roughly ten minutes to complete, which we think is a reasonable request of time commitment from our customers. It's also a fair amount of time for the business to accept, recognizing their continuing concern that we do not overburden customers with surveys. So any business professional that cares about their provider of capital will spend ten minutes with a survey company to tell you how well they are doing.

GE Real Estate's response rates vary across regions, from 20 to 30 percent to as high as 81 percent for Japan, with the norm of approximately 35 to 40 percent. The quality of the response rates is good enough to draw inferences, Klein Wassink believes. The company tends to have higher response rates where it has a smaller population of potential respondents with closer relationships to them, "so they are more than willing to speak with us," he stated.

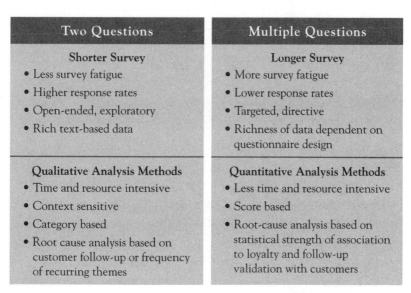

Two Questions	Multiple Questions
Shorter Survey	**Longer Survey**
• Less survey fatigue	• More survey fatigue
• Higher response rates	• Lower response rates
• Open-ended, exploratory	• Targeted, directive
• Rich text-based data	• Richness of data dependent on questionnaire design
Qualitative Analysis Methods	**Quantitative Analysis Methods**
• Time and resource intensive	• Less time and resource intensive
• Context sensitive	• Score based
• Category based	• Root-cause analysis based on statistical strength of association to loyalty and follow-up validation with customers
• Root cause analysis based on customer follow-up or frequency of recurring themes	

Figure 5.3   Two-Question Versus Multiple-Question Approaches

For example, one of the regions has twelve hundred client names and typically receives just over three hundred responses. "While this is among the lowest response rates across the regions, we do have a good sample size and the minimum number of respondents needed in each subgroup to maintain trustworthy data," Klein Wassink notes.

We find that survey length is a less-than-perfect predictor for response rates. Figure 5.4 shows a distribution of response rates across a number of B2C brands using a two-question approach in a Web-based survey. The data provide no clear correlation between survey length and response rate. For the purposes of this discussion, it is important to keep in mind that response rate is only a single factor to weigh in determining survey length. More germane are issues having to do with your business, your available resources, and your intended application of the data.

These general guidelines and considerations should help you to decide on your own approach:

- Start with your own understanding about the drivers of loyalty for your business. Multiple-question surveys, while powerful,

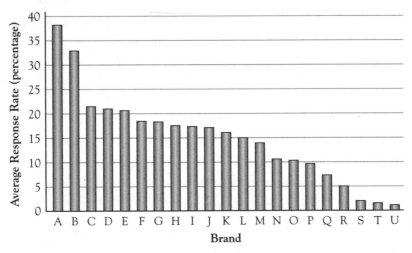

Figure 5.4   Average Response Rates with a Two-Question Approach

need to be aimed at the right performance areas to be effective. Two-question surveys can be fashioned to be more exploratory.

• How close is the relationship between your organization and the customer? As suggested in the GE example, invested customers are more likely to give their time, which permits longer surveys. Generally we recognize that B2B customers have a vested interest in the success of the product or service and therefore a higher tolerance for providing feedback.

• What resources are available to analyze the results? If you have adequate resources or if the work of interpreting the data is distributed equitably across multiple owners within the business, the time requirements for analyzing qualitative data are less of a factor. If you are limited in terms of resource, multiquestion approaches and the quantitative techniques used to analyze the data are likely to streamline your time to arrive at initial conclusions. (See Chapter Six for more detail on the various options for conducting root cause analysis.)

• How do you intend to use the data within your organization? One-to-one follow-up with customers may not require extensive information; the survey is simply a gateway (and an implicit invitation) to follow up with customers to learn more. And determining strategic investments and estimating the financial impact of planned initiatives is well served by more rigorous, data-rich approaches.

Designing a Sound Business Survey

This balance of organizational realities and business objectives tends to clarify the path forward for most. For instance, Aaron Morrison, director of customer loyalty for Misys plc, concluded, "Don't ask the customer questions that you think are important to them. Ask open-ended questions so they can tell you what is important to them." Misys's health care business is based in Raleigh, North Carolina, and the customer loyalty team established survey design fundamentals for their organization that are applicable to many businesses. Misys shares these tenets:

- Provide useful, actionable data on issues that matter to customers and employees.
- Be a good experience for your customers and employees.
- Ensure that survey questions are interpreted in the same way by every potential respondent.
- Ensure that survey questions elicit an accurate response.
- Provide consistent responses over time.

Many of these guidelines are beneficial from both the organization's and the respondent's perspective. With regard to the expectation that the survey will be a good experience for the respondent, there are a number of additional guidelines to keep in mind:

- The survey should focus on an issue, situation, or organization that the respondents care about. The questions asked should be germane to their own experiences.
- Whenever possible, avoid requesting personal or otherwise sensitive information. This communicates that you do not know the customer, and it hints at sales or marketing, even if the information is intended for an entirely different purpose, such as segmentation.
- Avoid asking questions where the answers can be found elsewhere, such as in your CRM database, because you should link your systems across the enterprise.
- Participation should confer some benefit. Customers want to know that there's something in it for them, even if these benefits are implicit (for example, that their opinion is heard and valued). Benefits may include an explicit reward of some kind, but the most motivating

reward is seeing the organization act on what they had to say.

- Surveys should respect customers' time. Don't survey the same individuals too often. We refer to this problem as "toxicity."

For additional references on survey design, we recommend, among others, *Measuring Customer Satisfaction: Survey Design, Use, and Statistical Analysis Methods* (Hayes, 1998) and *Improving Survey Questions: Design and Evaluation* (Fowler, 1995).

Writing Good Business Questions

Question design is an extension of survey design. As with survey design, much of what would be considered best practices equates to common sense:

- Questions should be concise: shorter is better than longer.
- Language should be kept simple.
- Good questions are clear and specific. Avoid words that are vague and subject to interpretation. For example, satisfaction with "technical support's ability to resolve your problem" is far better than "technical support's helpfulness."

In addition to content, question order or sequencing can have an impact on results. Some general guidelines for sequencing include:

- Keep your initial questions simple and easy to answer. The first one or two questions tend to receive the most scrutiny and create a first impression that may determine whether respondents follow through and complete the survey.

- Avoid initial questions that are difficult or personal for the same reasons.

- In multiquestion surveys, place loyalty questions prior to questions regarding specific performance areas. This will help to ensure that you capture the overall perceptions of your organization. Asking about specific performance areas prior to asking loyalty questions will tend to lead respondents to reduce the relationship to the sum of the specific topics you've highlighted, and these may or may not adequately capture the relationship as a whole.

- Group related questions, but keep the groups small.

- Place general questions before more specific ones within topic areas.

- Place overall satisfaction questions about a specific performance area before more detailed ones on the same topic.

- Place open-ended questions near the end, and don't have too many of them, with the exception of the comment question following Recommend.

- End the survey on a good note by including a thank you.

If questions are grouped in categories, they will evoke different responses than if they are distributed randomly. Although randomly presenting questions technically helps to reduce order effects—the influence that previous questions can have on the answers to subsequent ones—in practice, this makes for a poor survey experience. In designing business questions, it is more important to order content logically (for example, grouping sales, product, and support questions together in the order in which customers typically experience them) to help customers focus on the topics in a sensible way.

Sequencing Questions by Touch Point

Often mapping the survey sequence to your customer corridor, or "touch point map," is the best option. Gaining perspective on how your customers really view you is important to obtaining accurate feedback. If you map out the experiences an individual customer may have, you will start to understand your organization from the customer's point of view. As you may recall, this collection of touch points forms your customer corridor.

From a survey design perspective, one way to approach a multiquestion approach is to define each touch point along the corridor. Then map the most important factors that matter to the customer for that touch point. This mapping will form the basis for the questions you might ask. In addition, mapping the key moments of the customer corridor also corresponds to a customer lifecycle in that both are chronological. The corridor starts from initial engagement through all of the experiences along a customer lifecycle. Asking questions of your customers in this framework provides them additional business context and generally represents a better and more natural survey flow.

Defining the Customer Corridor from the Measurement Perspective

As discussed in Chapter Four, mapping out the customer corridor is an important task not only from a program roadmap perspective but also from a survey design perspective.

You might be inclined to think that most companies already know which experiences are most important to their customers, but few have taken an organized look at the variety of interactions and choices their customers face. This information usually exists in silos. For example, typically the sales department best understands the nuances of the sales experience, but it has no knowledge of all aspects of the customer's interactions with a product and its features. It takes a group of cross-functional stakeholders, working together, to obtain a truly holistic view and identify the areas that truly matter most to customers. The following Sage Software example outlines one way to define what's most important to its customers.

Sage Software's Customer Corridor

Sage Software is a leading supplier of business management software and services to 5.5 million customers worldwide. It has nearly fourteen thousand employees who advise almost 2 million customers. Its frontline people manage about thirty-two thousand customer calls every day plus a global network of twenty-five thousand resell partners and forty thousand accountants.

Here we'll describe how Sage approached the task of identifying loyalty drivers for its relationship survey for BusinessWorks, a software product providing full-function accounting for small, growing businesses. Apryl Hanson, director of partner programs, shares her experience mapping out Sage's customer corridor.

To establish a view of the customer corridor, Sage held a site-wide brainstorming meeting for all frontline employees involved in the BusinessWorks product. They were asked to volunteer a list of interactions, transactions, and other experiences across the customer lifecycle with the product. Afterward, a cross-functional group of managers met to narrow the list into key categories and then to settle on likely loyalty drivers. They began by defining the customer corridor, determining the discrete categories of experiences in chronological order from initial purchase to eventual product upgrade. Hanson observes, "It is important to gather key players across the organization to gain a holistic perspective of the customer's experiences." (See Figure 5.5.)

For each stage, the group discussed and debated which aspects of the experience were most important from a customer point of view. For most companies, this cross-functional discussion normally generates a long list of candidates: price, availability, purchase experience, partner service, and partner knowledge.

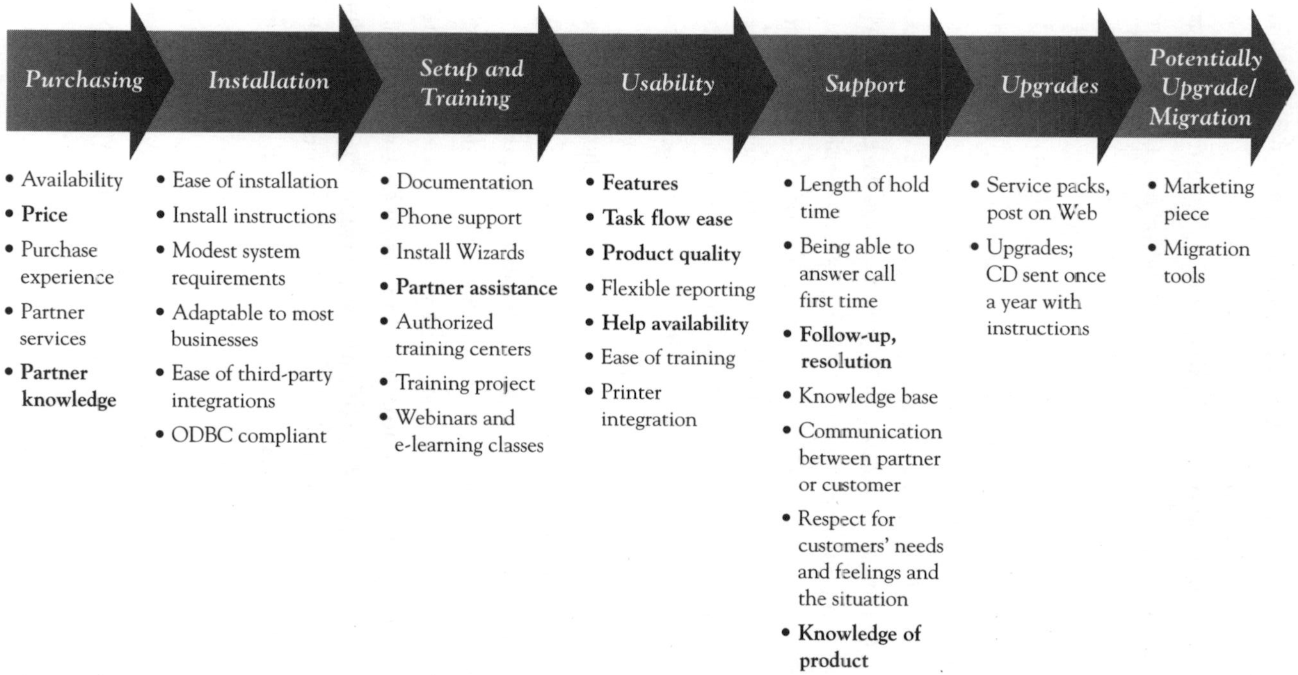

Purchasing	Installation	Setup and Training	Usability	Support	Upgrades	Potentially Upgrade/ Migration
• Availability	• Ease of installation	• Documentation	• **Features**	• Length of hold time	• Service packs, post on Web	• Marketing piece
• **Price**	• Install instructions	• Phone support	• **Task flow ease**	• Being able to answer call first time	• Upgrades; CD sent once a year with instructions	• Migration tools
• Purchase experience	• Modest system requirements	• Install Wizards	• **Product quality**	• **Follow-up, resolution**		
• Partner services	• Adaptable to most businesses	• **Partner assistance**	• Flexible reporting	• Knowledge base		
• **Partner knowledge**	• Ease of third-party integrations	• Authorized training centers	• **Help availability**	• Communication between partner or customer		
	• ODBC compliant	• Training project	• Ease of training	• Respect for customers' needs and feelings and the situation		
		• Webinars and e-learning classes	• Printer integration	• **Knowledge of product**		

Bold = Touchpoint attributes to address

Figure 5.5   The Sage Customer Corridor

Then the group concluded the workshop by systematically grading each of the attributes on importance and satisfaction. For example, they considered how important each aspect of the experience is to their customers and to what degree they are satisfied with each, and they used a 0 to 10 score (10 being best) as if they were taking a survey on these same topics themselves. The highest-scoring attributes were selected for their first relationship survey: price, partner knowledge, partner assistance, features, and ease of use, to name a few.

This exercise allowed Sage to compare its own internal perceptions to actual customer data. In its survey, Sage asked both satisfaction and importance questions for the performance attributes. When the answers were compared to the initial internal perceptions, Sage found a gap between how important certain experiences were to customers and their internal views, which permitted them to make adjustments to their survey approach and their internal key performance indicators.

Knowing what is important to customers helps tailor your ongoing survey to make it more relevant to your customers' needs. Understanding the importance gaps—internal perceptions of which performance areas are most influential versus customers' own perceptions—provides some insight into the level of alignment between your organization's activities and actual customer needs.

Taking the concept of the customer corridor one step further, an organization may consider a more detailed *customer experience mapping*. Most organizations have only a vague idea of all the potential ways they interact (or fail to interact) with their customers across the entire lifecycle. Sometimes referred to as *touch point mapping*, a more detailed documentation of customer communications, channel experiences, and other interactions can help an organization to more fully understand the depth and breadth of its relationship with current customers.

Sage undertook this challenge as well and was able to identify inadequate customer processes such as a Web portal that failed to meet expectations relative to its industry competitors, frustrating interactive voice response options, and one-size-fits-all customer treatments. Its comprehensive experience map also helped to cast a critical light on the available sources of customer data, missed opportunities for data capture, and traces where the data is stored. This information, informed by voice-of-customer data, helped to provide a foundation for understanding where gaps exist in customer communication across the lifecycle, which experiences should be improved, and which sources of data should be leveraged to create personal, more relevant customer experiences in the future.

Reviewing Your Choices

Once you have finalized your survey design, read the questionnaire again. Ask yourself for each question or attribute, "Can I make a decision or take action based on the answer to this question?" If you answer no, the question is not sufficiently business focused. Some questions may have been added as a compromise for departments that want to learn about specific items but may not be relevant for the survey. Eliminate the nice-to-know questions whose responses you cannot act on.

Determining the Right Time to Measure

Thus far, we've looked at who to measure and what to measure, but not when to measure. This question is not always one that companies think to address proactively. Many use whatever means are available or expedient for collecting customer feedback, which in many cases leads to a strategy of yoking data collection to a specific interaction. After all, it's easiest to ask customers for their feedback when they've come to you for a specific purpose (though that purpose is rarely to share their feedback) rather than to go and seek them out.

This strategy for collecting feedback is generally thought of as a transactional approach: the collection of feedback is timed so as to occur shortly after a specific interaction between the customer and your organization. This stands in contrast to relationship feedback (generally conducted on a periodic basis) using data collection strategies formulated to reach out to customers according to a pre-established schedule.

Both approaches can give you a meaningful sense of how customers perceive you. Nevertheless, these approaches are unlikely to give you the same read on the relationships. For instance, transactional approaches tend to be well suited to getting actionable input regarding your operations and execution at specific points of interaction. Because the feedback is received in close proximity to events, respondents are able to offer specific feedback about the success or failure of those experiences. Relationship surveys are less suited to collecting data that can be applied directly to process improvement and better suited for collecting general feedback that cuts across all of your customer touch points.

For these reasons, it's clear that the best time to collect data about specific transactional experiences is directly following the transaction. Customers' recollections of the event will be sharper than they would otherwise be if collected in a periodic fashion.

When to Measure NPS

In determining when to measure NPS, it is important to consider why so many businesses are excited about NPS. Most use NPS as a simple but powerful measure of the overall relationship they have with customers and as a leading indicator of growth. To meet those goals, the measurement approach must successfully meet the following criteria:

- It must successfully target the right customers.
- It must successfully capture the overall perceptions those customers have regarding their relationship with your

organization, including all key influences that shape that relationship and the decision to buy.

- It must link to meaningful financial outcomes at the corporate level.

Now let's consider which of the two alternatives under discussion—transactional or relationship data collection—is the better fit for these criteria. As with our earlier discussions, the better fit depends on your operations and business model.

The simplest and most effective way to answer that question is to start with the complexity of your business model, specifically, the breadth and diversity of the touch points you share with your customers. If yours is a low-diversity model, particularly if there is a single key transaction that tends to define the scope of the relationship you share with your customers, a transactional data collection approach may be better. Such businesses may include car rentals, travel accommodations, and ticket sales. These businesses share a common trait: the relationship is defined almost exclusively by a single transaction event. Therefore, the best opportunity to secure customer participation and the most appropriate time to measure their loyalty is following that interaction, particularly if it is infrequent or unpredictable.

In a high-diversity model, where multiple interactions define and influence the customer experience, a relationship approach is advisable. The first factor to consider in this choice is access. In both B2B and B2C businesses, certain types of customers may be interacting with specific touch points, while others may not. If you run only transactional measurements you run the risk of treating a skewed sample of respondents (for example, online shoppers) as if they were representative of the entire customer base (for example, both in-store and online shoppers). A relationship approach, which permits more precise control over the composition of the survey sample (refer to our discussion under "Sampling Considerations" earlier in the chapter) will better ensure a representative group of respondents.

The second factor to consider in a highly diverse interaction model is that of bias caused by survey timing. For businesses with diverse touch points, surveying in a transactional manner (closely following an event) is likely to skew feedback about the overall relationship according to whether the most recent experience was a success or failure. A more desirable outcome would be to survey customers after more time has passed in order for them to integrate their perspective across multiple touch points—in essence, to step back and take an overarching view of the overall relationship. A relationship approach permits respondents to weigh multiple experiences and determine which are most important. For the same reasons, it is better not to schedule relationship surveys according to specific events, such as just prior to a renewal decision or soon after delivering and installing a complex system. This feedback works best when it captures a more typical "day in the life" of your customers.

Achieving an Enterprise View

This is not to suggest that transactional and relationship surveys are mutually exclusive; in fact, they tend to be a powerful complement to one another when used in a way that capitalizes on their strengths, while minimizing their weaknesses. Consider Figure 5.6. The measurement pyramid presumes a diverse set of interactions with customers and seeks to assess loyalty and its primary drivers, from both relationship and transactional measures.

The top of the pyramid gives the big picture and the overall health of the relationship, which links to financial performance. At the top, you want to learn from customers about key areas that drive loyalty. The survey results should highlight the key items customers care most about. Then you can drill deeper into those items by conducting transactional surveys to learn how to improve those experiences.

Let's return to the financial services customer corridor (Figure 4.3) and imagine that the relationship survey reveals that transfer

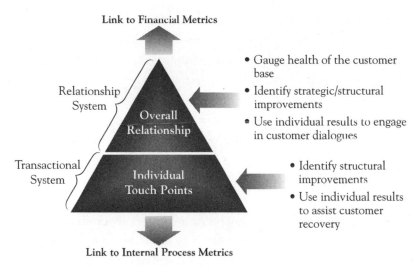

Figure 5.6   The Measurement Pyramid

of assets, advice interaction, phone conversation, and Web experience are drivers most correlated with loyalty. Therefore, at the bottom of the pyramid, measure customer sentiment for those transactions to discover gaps between customer satisfaction and your performance in order to improve those areas. The transactional feedback can go directly to the parts of the organization that oversee these customer interactions in order to make structural or operational improvements to the product, system architecture, or call center. Improving performance at these critical touch points will improve NPS and financial metrics because they are highly correlated to loyalty, as discovered in the relationship measure. Providing customers with delightful experiences during transactions will be reflected in the overall relationship NPS, which should culminate in financial growth.

Using both relationship and transactional feedback in the right context at the proper times will enable a mix of information to improve the entire business. Data collected in a relationship survey can be used to guide both strategic and customer-specific investments. At the customer level, it can be used to identify customers at risk, uncover potential opportunities for cross-sell and up-sell, and inform follow-up activities with your most strategic customers. Relationship surveys can be used to improve operational execution by helping enhance relationship management, pipeline analysis, and team performance. The data can also be aggregated to help understand systemic issues, what to fix, and how to differentiate and reposition your organization within the competitive landscape. This data is appropriate for building models that link to larger corporate financial outcomes, which helps to build business cases for planned investments.

Insights gleaned from the relationship feedback may also be useful for pinpointing moments of truth (the customer experiences that matter the most), whose contribution to loyalty makes them good candidates for measurement on an event-driven basis. An example of a moment of truth at a financial services organization would be an activity that if done incorrectly, would damage the customer experience, such as if the automatic bill pay feature did not properly pay the requested amount each month. A customer who relies on the accuracy of the bill pay feature would be upset and may be less loyal if unexpected mistakes occurred. The more detailed feedback from transactional surveys helps to supply actionable ideas that can be used to drive improvements in business processes and guide employee behaviors. In fact, transactional surveys are among the most effective for informing customer recovery plans and actions. Consider the example of transactional support surveys. Feedback returned from this mechanism can be used at the front line to monitor call center employee performance, providing feedback and identifying coaching opportunities on a timely basis. At the structural level, the same data can be used to identify opportunities for quality and process improvements, as well as guide investment decisions. For instance, customer data, when combined with operational metrics, can determine the impact of wait times and other performance variables on customer perceptions.

Clearly, both relationship and transactional approaches have their place, and both are well suited to driving action within an organization. The key consideration is to combine the feedback in a meaningful way. For most businesses, prioritizing relationship feedback to determine strategic investments and track the health of key customer segments is the best course; transactional approaches can provide more detail around operational performance and timely feedback regarding specific customer needs as they arise. Together, these approaches offer an integrated view of the customer across the enterprise and enable action both within and across the business units.

Other Considerations

We now provide material on other considerations, such as selecting a data collection channel, increasing response rates, and preventing gaming.

Choosing a Data Collection Channel

In the balance of the chapter, we'll move beyond the key questions of who, what, and when to consider a few key decision points regarding how to obtain customer feedback. The first issue to confront is how the data collection channel you choose might influence the nature of the feedback. For instance, will a question asked by a person, face-to-face, elicit the same response as the same question asked over the telephone? Will the response be the same if the phone call uses interactive voice response (IVR) instead of a live person to ask the questions? What about an e-mail-to-web questionnaire?

Ideally the answer to each of these questions would be yes. Unfortunately, the answer is more likely to be no. The data channel you select will exert its own influence on the data. You need to factor in the medium you use for data gathering when interpreting results and, if possible, settle on a consistent strategy to ensure that you can make meaningful comparisons over time. Standardizing on a single approach—whatever works best for your business in terms of access to customers—has definite advantages, because differences between segments can be attributed to performance differences rather than the influence of collection method.

However, not every customer will prefer, or even be available, using the same medium. Depending on your business, you may need to be prepared to use these four methods (phone, IVR phone, face-to-face, and Web) and possibly even paper-based surveys. You'll want to match the medium to the intended contact and to ensure, to the extent possible, that you use a single method exclusively for specific segments, but you may have to make some choices to keep within practical time and cost limitations. Here we briefly explore the benefits, costs, and biases of each of these approaches.

Figure 5.7 provides a few of the factors to consider when selecting a data collection channel: market type, access to specific customers, and trade-offs among the approaches such as bias, response rates, and accuracy.

Face-to-face interviews are best suited for relationship feedback, particularly for B2B companies, where the volume of customers may not create an overwhelming tax on the necessary resources. Interviews, including phone interviews, may also be a valuable tool to garner responses from executives or other hard-to-reach decision makers, who are typically more difficult to reach using less high-touch approaches.

One of the primary benefits of interactive approaches, both face-to-face and phone interviews, are that they permit an open-ended, exploratory approach. Interesting comments by the customer can be followed up on the spot, permitting greater insight into the customer's intended meaning and underlying cause of dissatisfaction or loyalty. (Chapter Six discusses probing for root causes.) These approaches are less susceptible to missing data (such as questions that go unanswered) because the interview will not continue until a question has been answered. However, these approaches tend to

	Face-to-Face Interview	Phone Interview	Interactive Voice Response	Web
Measurement Approach	Relationship	Relationship or transactional	Transactional	Relationship or transactional
Market	B2B	B2B or B2C	B2B or B2C	B2B or B2C
Customer type	Decision maker	All	End user	All
Benefits	Exploratory	Exploratory Active management of response rate and sample composition	Immediate	Inexpensive Accuracy of feedback Customizable
Drawbacks	Expensive Skews positive Interviewer bias	Expensive Phone access is decreasing Skews positive Interviewer bias	Low response rates	Self-selection bias Reduced access to customers who are not tech savvy

Figure 5.7   Collection Channel Comparison

be more susceptible to demand characteristics—influences within the interaction itself that may lead respondents to alter their feedback in various ways. One such potential bias has to do with interviewer bias: interviewers may subtly, even unconsciously, lead respondents in the direction of the answers they wish to hear. Respondents, meanwhile, may edit their responses so as to be more socially desirable; most customers are prone to seeing the interviewer as a representative of the organization (even when a third party collects the data) and may be less than candid in an effort to avoid offense. Relative to less interactive methods, these approaches therefore tend to result in slightly higher scores overall (Dillman , D.A., et al.). In an interesting twist, the relatively high cost of interactive approaches can lead organizations to stipulate tight time limits on the conversation, effectively destroying the biggest advantage of the approach in the first place.

Telephone IVR surveys are best used for transactional surveying and are integrated as part of a customer-precipitated phone call (many customers hang up when answering a call initiated by an automated process). It is equally appropriate for B2B and B2C, but it is most likely to capture end user contact roles because these individuals, rather than decision makers, are likely to use the transactional channels to which the data collection is tied. One benefit of this approach is its immediacy; it is possible to obtain feedback immediately following the transaction. Nevertheless, a lot of people opt out of or abandon IVR surveys, so your overall response rate may suffer.

Web survey approaches are also appropriate for relationship or transactional surveys, and they are equally at home with B2B and B2C. It can be used for all customer types and benefits from low cost, accuracy, and its ability to be customized. The key drawback is that the approach presumes a high level of comfort with computers and the Web, so it is inherently biased to tech-savvy customers. Unlike phone and face-to-face approaches, it is also more prone to self-selection biases: customers who are particularly happy or unhappy may be more motivated to participate, which may lead to a biased sample unless steps are taken to ensure a more balanced blend of participants (Taylor, 2000).

Response Rates and Gaming

No discussion of trustworthy data would be complete without some consideration of response rates that determine whether you have been successful in obtaining feedback from the customers you targeted, and gaming, which can undermine data from within. We are often asked what's a good response rate. Is it 30 percent or 60 percent or something else? It depends. Do the respondents accurately reflect your customer and business composition in order to make strategic decisions? It is important to have enough responses in a segment to draw inferences from the data that can create unique experiences. Also, from a B2B account management perspective, a good response would be to hear from decision makers, people who influence the purchasing decisions, and the people who interact frequently with the product and service in order to gain a complete picture of the account. We'll provide some guidelines to help maximize your chances of success.

Getting the Response Rate Up

Your list of targeted survey respondents is the raw material of your program; it is unrealized potential. Ideally you'd like to have every one of these customers respond to every question you pose. Realistically that is an unachievable goal; your energies should be concentrated on creating strategies that will get as many as possible to respond to maximize the response rate.

Earlier in the chapter, we considered some elements of survey design that can affect response rates—issues like survey length, as well as respondent-friendly strategies for survey content, sequencing, and customization. Here, we primarily examine what you can do from a programmatic perspective that can help increase the level of participation among customers.

The first, and most obvious, place to start is with an audit of customer databases. The quality of your contact information can play a big part in the success of your recruitment efforts, as well as resulting response rates. Do not simply depend on your current customer relationship management (CRM) database; remember that many of these databases are used for multiple purposes (for example, collecting references and identifying sales prospects). These goals do not typically produce a ready-made or complete contact list that will represent your overall customer population.

Additional steps—adding and refining data, which may require buy-in and effort from other parts of the organization—are often necessary before you can arrive at your final customer contact list. As part of the audit, make sure you have accurate and up-to-date customer information, and endeavor to minimize missing information that is critical to the targeting and segmentation goals.

When gathering contact information, align your methods to your sampling strategy. If you are a B2C organization, look for volume and coverage across and within segments. If you plan on a B2B census-type survey, look for opportunities to leverage current information (such as job title) to segment customers into end users, influencers, and decision makers. And regardless of your business, make a deliberate attempt to ensure the inclusion of all high-value customers on your contact list.

There are other ways to raise response rates. In B2C businesses, you can take advantage of key touch points, such as product registration, to identify and incorporate potential respondents into your database. If yours is a B2B business, one of the best ways to secure higher levels of participation is to engage employees in the field who can talk to customers about your loyalty program (not just the survey) and explain why their participation is important. We discuss the techniques for doing so in greater detail in Chapter Seven. Here, we simply underscore the role that sales management and field salespeople can have in increasing awareness about the purpose and importance of program participation.

Aon Corporation provides a ready example. In a recent pilot, Aon saw its response rate jump from 17 to 75 percent, an enormous improvement. Philip Clement explains how it worked:

> We needed to move from a research project to something embedded in the culture where value and impact for clients is at the heart of Aon's cultural change. It required a country or regional managing director to own it and be accountable for the program and response rate improvement. We gave iPods to people who had 100 percent client participation. This was a bi-weekly process for six weeks.

Incentives like iPods for frontline employees actively recruiting the right contacts made Aon's respondent recruitment process fun as well as competitive, and it yielded dramatic results. Appropriately incentivizing and rewarding the field can be a useful tool for securing higher response rates.

Incentives for customer participation have a different set of considerations to weigh. Although there is both empirical and anecdotal research to support the notion that incentives exert a positive influence on response rates, in our experience, the benefit within loyalty programs tends to be relatively modest—approximately a 3 to 5 percent improvement in overall response rates. When they are used, they will achieve maximum benefits to the extent that they are both relevant to customers and valued. The value need not be in absolute terms or even directly accrued to the customers. For instance, an organization may offer a twenty dollar gift certificate to a restaurant to stimulate responses, but a CEO may not find this incentive very valuable. Some companies have success using shared values with CEOs and other difficult-to-reach executives. An example is an indirect or direct contribution to a common cause, such as an environmental research fund, to encourage participation.

The potential risk to incentives goes back to our core message about obtaining feedback from the right customers. External incentives have the potential to introduce bias if they lead certain groups to overrespond, while making other groups underrespond. Take pains to ensure that your incentive strategy is in alignment with getting responses from customers you want to participate.

Solid contact and recruitment strategies will be far more effective than offering incentives. For instance, issuing polite reminders to follow through on a promised commitment to provide feedback will get as many or more people to respond in comparison to relying on incentives. Remember that incentives are intended to motivate people, but motivation also comes from within. Many customers respond simply because they wish to share their feedback and to help your business. Communicating the core goals of the program—that you wish to listen and act on customer feedback—can be incentive enough, particularly if you follow through on your promise.

Investment and Reward

The level of improvement in response rates tends to be related to the degree of effort and resources invested. A first-level approach would involve an audit of the contact list, sending targeted reminders to non-respondents, and taking minimal efforts to ensure the communications are received (for example, using standardized text in e-mail communications to avoid spam filters). At Satmetrix, we've seen improvements of 10 to 15 percent from these steps alone. With more effort, you can garner an additional boost to overall response rates of 50 percent or more. These techniques include increased internal and external communications, such as letting your own people know what's going on prior to survey collection to prepare them for recruitment tasks. Having marketing (B2C) or account teams (B2B) personally notify customers about the program ahead of time, and sending a program introduction letter to customers from an executive that explains the program goals and the steps in the process can have a positive impact on response rates. The best response rates—75 percent or better—often require rewarding internal customer owners for high-integrity contact lists and good response rates, personal follow-ups to nonrespondents, and visible action on exposed customer issues.

Thwarting Gaming Before and After

Gaming is a natural reaction to the attraction of incentives and a program that seems easy to manipulate. While you may think it can't happen within your organization, you would be mistaken.

Gaming is any action employees take that intentionally skews the data, typically for personal benefit. Gaming, once discovered, will undermine confidence in the trustworthiness of the data among your business stakeholders. It will also undermine buy-in from nongaming employees.

Programs that leverage competition and comparison are ripe for gaming, as are programs that provide compensation or incentives tied to NPS or other outcomes. Your system of incentives and rewards, designed to improve loyalty scores and therefore business growth, may inadvertently induce some employees to create false impressions of customer loyalty. Some gaming gambits occur prior to customer feedback; some are tried after the survey. To date, we have found no ways to eliminate gaming without hobbling the program. We have, however, found ways to monitor and diminish these opportunities. That, combined with a zero-tolerance policy from executives regarding gaming behaviors, is often enough to secure the data.

One popular gambit employees may try, especially in a B2B environment, is to skew results in their favor by manipulating the sample. This is a tactic deployed prior to collecting feedback. The basic goal is the same: to selectively recruit potential respondents who are expected to be predominantly positive in their feedback. Where they believe a customer may be a Passive or a Detractor, employees using this tactic will purposely misdirect e-mail notifications and invitations. Worse still would be the introduction of fictitious customers by creating new customers or altering contact information such as e-mail addresses so surveys can be redirected to the employee or their choice. Other tactics include extending the collection period to allow more positive responders to be counted and manipulating business rules to try to make likely poor scores ineligible.

The key to controlling gaming is careful oversight and auditing of customer contact lists prior to survey deployment. We've identified a four-step process that significantly helps to control this sort of gaming in a B2B context:

1. Senior management team identifies target accounts for inclusion.
2. Loyalty team managers create a sampling strategy for the selected accounts.

3. The field team reviews and appends related contact information.

4. Senior management approves target accounts and contacts.

This approach makes it much harder for any group or single employee to materially affect the composition of the sample. Although this kind of audit process is more resource intensive, it has an enormous effect on reducing gaming. Even better, integrating the respondent list with account management processes, as we discuss in Chapter Seven, provides a ready-made audit process and quality check. Klein Wassink of GE Real Estate concurs:

> We made sure to keep the survey process centralized to maintain the quality and integrity of the data. We are unequivocally convinced that keeping the program at the center has kept that data clean because we can monitor the process to prevent gaming while collecting feedback. We do a lot of audit work and checks and balances to ensure that gaming is addressed.

Another safeguard is to audit a randomly selected sample from the final e-mail distribution list to verify roles and familiarity with an organization's products and services. In this approach, questions are added to the survey to verify key pieces of customer information, such as job role, purchase influence, familiarity, or product line. Mismatches between customer responses and information from the database can help to flag potential instances of gaming.

There are opportunities for gaming even after the survey is in the field. For example, customer owners may do selective follow-up to nonrespondents, reminding only those they expect to be positive that their feedback is desired. Some unscrupulous employees may even try to influence a respondent through rewards or threats, or even, if they have access to the survey mechanism, to take the survey in place of the customer. For B2C companies, audit the feedback for outliers or patterns that seem too good to be true. For example, if one salesperson receives scores of only 9s and 10s, investigate if that salesperson is truly a superstar or if other tactics were in play.

You can protect against such tactics by providing targets and incentives regarding the number of contacts and responses, which minimizes the opportunity for selective follow-up. You can, and should, use a closed, independent survey delivery mechanism to prevent employees from tampering with responses. In addition, having management, even senior executives, participate in follow-up with customers will greatly increase the risk that employees who engage in unsavory conduct, such as attempting to influence customer responses or posing as the customer themselves, will be found out. On this last point, there is no substitute for having a zero-tolerance policy on gaming communicated by the CEO or executive sponsor. The harder you make it for someone to game your program and the more severe the penalty for doing so, the less likely gaming will threaten the trustworthiness of your data.

When we see programs that are systematically gamed, the most noticeable aspect has been that everyone pretty much knows it is gamed. It's not a secret. Consequently, the data's validity and usefulness are compromised, which undermines the program. The sad fact is that sophisticated gaming probably isn't your biggest concern; it's the design and implementation of a process where management has clearly signaled tolerance for low-quality data.

Conclusion

In this chapter, we've discussed in some detail how to ensure that your data is trustworthy—that is, accurate, reliable, and relevant. To achieve this goal, the first step is to measure who matters in order to target the right customers for your business. In almost all cases, the right customers will be those who reflect your business and growth strategy. Be sure to leverage your internal customer segmentation to define the target population for the program, and voice according to value. Ensuring that you hear from your most strategic customers should be your first priority.

Once you've targeted the right customers, take the appropriate steps to ask the right questions. Once again, your strategy should be tailored to your business. To start, it is wise to validate NPS as the metric of choice for measuring customer loyalty. Is it sensitive to changes in your business performance? Does it link to meaningful customer and financial outcomes? Is it actionable for the purposes for which you intend to use it? Your overall survey strategy should also match your business as well as your customers' experience with you. Define and leverage the customer corridor as a means for prioritizing and sequencing your survey content.

Finally, determine when to obtain feedback from your customers. If your interactions with your customers are relatively diverse, perhaps consisting of sales, product or service experience, and post sales support, consider adopting a relationship approach to measuring loyalty. This will provide the best opportunity to access the right customers and permit them to step back and consider the entire experience as a whole.

These steps, when combined with internal investments to ensure robust response rates and protect against gaming, will help make your data trustworthy and properly support your larger goal of creating meaningful, customer-centric change within your organization.

6

Determining the Root Cause of Promoters and Detractors

We view NPS as not just a metric but a holistic methodology that enables employees to listen proactively to customers, learn to understand the things that the customer liked and did not like, and then start to identify the actions that are needed to improve the experience for our customers so that we can earn their loyalty.

Andrew Clayton, *group vice president, Allianz*

No experiment is ever done in the absence of a hypothesis. The same is true for a Net Promoter program. No program begins with a clean slate and infinite possibilities; it begins with hypotheses about what drives the creation of Promoters and Detractors. The assumptions underlying these hypotheses may be part hunch, part empirical, or part allegory, but nevertheless organizations build data with a view toward learning the truth.

In this chapter, we look at common approaches for getting to the heart of what makes someone a Promoter or a Detractor. We examine the advantages and disadvantages of each approach and determine the steps needed to change the score.

It's worth mentioning that we see some programs start with an assumption that they don't need a root cause analysis process or team. It often stems from a belief that they already understand the drivers behind their NPS, so why bother? But successful programs rarely adopt this approach. Sometimes the underlying factors driving NPS are counterintuitive, or there is a significant difference between the impact you can expect as a result of resolving issues, which obviously will affect the return on your program investment. Either way, we don't see the case for making major investments or shifts in business strategy just based on gut feeling. Root cause analysis allows you to get to the drivers of loyalty and identify the opportunities to improve NPS.

Common Analytical Approaches

We focus on examining two basic approaches to understanding drivers of loyalty: *stated driver analysis* and *inferential driver analysis*. We will explore several analytical methods used for each, as well as their strengths and weaknesses, before concluding with a discussion of how your program can benefit from leveraging multiple approaches.

For stated driver analysis, we focus on root cause interviews, comment categorization, and a method used within Satmetrix called Adaptive Conversation. For inferential driver analysis, we concentrate on correlation analysis and related statistical methods such as regression and relative impact analysis.

Our purpose here is not to turn you into a statistician but to help you evaluate what analytical approach may be useful within your program and a good fit for your organization. Our focus in this chapter is uncovering the critical levers we can pull to improve customer loyalty—what we have described as the root causes or drivers of loyalty elsewhere in this book. Essentially we're asking, "What drives my NPS? What are the root causes of Promoter or Detractor behaviors?" The methods we describe are tools that can be applied to find drivers (or root causes) and devise actions that accentuate the positive and mitigate the negative.

Stated Driver Analysis

Before we dive in, a critical point of context should be considered. One of the most debated aspects of Net Promoter is the use of very short surveys (two or three questions) versus long-form survey approaches. Although we examined some of these issues in Chapter Five, we think the core of the debate concerns root cause analysis. Adopting a two-question survey versus a longer one is a decision that is often made on the basis of what kinds of analyses of the data are envisioned. Part of your survey and data design approach should be dictated by your confidence—and the confidence of your stakeholders—with what the data analysis approach will yield.

This brings up a related but sometimes overlooked point about two-question surveys: that these short-form surveys on their own won't identify root causes. The resulting NPS may help focus employees on the health of relationships with customers, and feedback may help galvanize specific follow-up efforts—but root causes, the key underlying issues that are shared across customers, require work to uncover. You need to employ a separate form of diagnosis after the survey, with the costs (including customer engagement) and benefits of that process to be weighed against those of other survey forms and root cause analysis techniques.

As we proceed, we review these techniques in some detail, discussing the data and resources required to pursue them, as well as the demands they place on organizational resources and expertise. At the end of this chapter we summarize the interaction of these techniques with survey design to enable you to create a solution that won't leave you awash with data but lacking in insight.

Root Cause Analysis

Root cause analysis is a type of problem-solving method that identifies the initial cause in a causal chain that leads to a particular outcome. The method has been introduced to many businesses through the continuous improvement movement in manufacturing and product quality, including Six Sigma and related quality management methodologies. The idea is to begin working backward from an end state (for example, Promoter or Detractor behavior) and follow a chain of causes and effects until you unveil the root, or initiating cause or causes. The motivation behind this basic analytical approach is the belief that eliminating the root cause will eliminate the chain and the end state.

Allianz, one of the world's biggest insurers, used the information from Six Sigma analysis techniques in business decisions that improved the customer experience. Andrew Clayton said:

> One of the core issues uncovered from the feedback received from Detractor customers was the lack of empathy shown to customers during the claims process. This was highlighted through the Pareto analysis that showed this issue was a core driver in Detractor feedback. We then leveraged our customer experience team with responsibility for claims to identify the root causes for this issue and the potential solutions. Clearly many solutions were identified, but we wanted to focus on the solutions with the highest payback in terms of impact balanced against the time and cost to implement. This resulted in the rollout of enterprisewide empathy skill training for claims handlers. We have already seen positive impacts on the NPS at the claims touch point and in the comments we receive from customers.

The Five Whys

One popular root cause technique is called the Five Whys. Actually, it should be called the Iterative Whys, because you may need more or fewer than five iterations to diagnose the root cause. But we think that "iterative whys" just isn't a catchy title.

If you are unfamiliar with this technique, we provide an example of this approach below. Figure 6.1 presents a graphical representation of the Five Whys' process in a fishbone diagram. These diagrams start with the effect or problem on one end and extend horizontally to the opposite root cause end. Along the way are the answers to the whys, broken down into various hypothesized

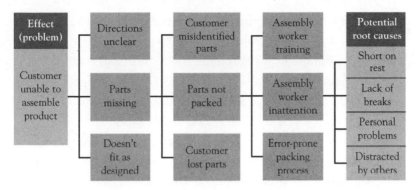

Figure 6.1   Five Whys Technique

causes and further explored until the diagram arrives at the root cause or causes.

In Figure 6.1, a customer is unable to assemble a product. The first why evokes such answers as unclear directions, missing parts, or ill-fitting parts. The next focuses on the possibility of missing parts and moves us further along to a root cause conclusion with answers like misidentified parts, parts were not packed, or the customer lost the parts. Assuming that the parts were not packed, the ultimate list of root causes are assembly worker was tired, assembly worker lacked breaks, assembly worker had personal problems, and assembly worker was distracted by others.

Example of the Five Whys Technique

One of the companies we studied manufactures retail products and uses root cause analysis to identify product and service improvements to improve its NPS. The technique depends on detailed root cause analyses of customer comments regarding their transactions. The company focuses particularly on comments from Detractors, analyzing them for opportunities to improve the customer experience. What were the real issues? Why did the customer want a callback? Was it because the wrong product was sent, installed improperly, or fell short of expectations of value? In digging deeper, our client realized that there were internal product remake issues. If the product is poorly made, the company would remake it for customers. Each customer with this experience was examined. What product did the customer buy, and which vendor shipped it? The client held weekly meetings with vendors, major suppliers, and merchandisers to discuss issues and forwarded customer comments about their products to them. At last, they discovered an issue with a particular product line, narrowed it down to a core problematic feature, and were able to fix the problem. As a result, this company moved from an average NPS of 10 percent to over 40 percent within one quarter.

As this example illustrates, root cause analysis can be used internally to develop hypotheses regarding the customer experience and potential solutions and innovations. In most cases, this work is best informed by the use of root cause interviews, embedded as part of customer follow-up activities. These interviews allow customers to clarify their experiences and help with the diagnosis of root causes. Fred Reichheld introduced this approach as a key component of Net Promoter programs in *The Ultimate Question* (2006), and more generally as a required element of studying customer interactions in *The Loyalty Effect* (2001).

To succeed with root cause interviews, organizations must include several elements in their follow-up process:

- *Train the interviewer.* The process works best when interviewers are familiar with the technique.

- *Use a team approach.* Team members should have enough knowledge of the business process to probe effectively. Individuals can bring bias to their line of questioning, so use a cross-functional team to create balance.

- *Always ask for permission prior to the interview and before getting started.* This ensures that the customer is ready to invest time in giving feedback. Be sensitive to the customer's time constraints.

- *Double-check that the customer's problem or issue has been resolved.* Confirm this before proceeding with a root cause interview.

- *Plan for a time limit.* If one customer is not able to get to the ultimate root cause, capture hypotheses and pick up the thread in another interview with similar issues.

- *Schedule internal team reviews to discuss root causes and potential solutions.* Consider changes that not only rectify problems but improve the overall customer experience.

- *Find a way to communicate back with the customers regarding actions you have taken based on their feedback.* Depending on the business model, this communication may be highly personalized or can come in the form of general customer communications that highlight examples of customer-led improvements and innovations.

Keep in mind that root cause interviews to uncover systematic patterns in the customer experience can be costly in terms of the sheer quantity of potential interviews and the challenge of maintaining a consistent process. At worst, a broadly applied root cause follow-up process can leave an organization swimming in a sea of anecdotes unless the process incorporates a way to prioritize feedback. When implemented correctly—as when the resulting feedback is reviewed internally on a regular basis to identify common customer themes—the technique has numerous advantages:

- *It is personal for customers.* The interview touches the customer directly and demonstrates through action that the organization values the customer relationship.

- *It is personal for the employee too.* There is no substitute for direct employee and customer interaction when it comes to fueling employee learning and their motivation to improve.

- *It is an open dialogue.* By its nature, this dialogue encourages creative thinking and discovery of new ideas that can drive improvement.

- *It is rich in context.* The format is excellent for understanding the entire end-to-end customer experience, including the interactions of internal functions. Studying (and telling) the complete story at an individual customer level illuminates customer needs and how those needs translate into complete experiences with the enterprise.

GE Real Estate Dives to the Root

GE Real Estate's John Godin, vice president of market research, said:

> We do deep-dive root cause interviews. We are experimenting with a couple of different things right now. One group did an actual root cause analysis using a Six Sigma quality approach. They matched up attribute data associated with specific clients who responded to the Net Promoter survey and did a root cause analysis associated with their feedback.
>
> What we are doing for next year is requesting from the field not only the list that we have asked for, which has name, phone number, address, and e-mail address, but we are also going to give them the option to add ten other pieces of information associated with that client, such as volume during 2006 to 2007, and transaction types or property asset class. This way the market research team can do root cause analysis using traditional quality tools depending on the amount of information we have.

GE Real Estate is working on ideas on how to use segmentation to better analyze what it finds. The theme derived from the most recent analyses, and that the CEO supports, is moving the Passives. The goal is to get Passives to become more active and increase their loyalty over time. The plan to achieve this goal is to apply root cause and other analyses to understand Passives better. "This way, we can better target what they need. What will it take to convert them to Promoters? So we are thinking about using loyalty segmentation as part of our root cause analysis work," explains Klein Wassink, senior vice president of global marketing.

Comment Analysis and Categorization

When organizations set out to implement Net Promoter, many contemplate how to maintain a balance between shorter surveys and the resources needed after the survey to gather the potential insight contained within a large number of open-ended comments. The questions that invariably emerge are: How can I keep up with the flow of open-ended comments that I get from my customers? How can I leverage them effectively, particularly if they represent my only available insight into the issues driving NPS?

When you ask open-ended questions, there is no limitation to how respondents may answer. They may have only a few words or detailed responses. This makes open-ended questions a potentially valuable source of driver discovery, particularly if you can find a way to structure these unstructured responses. Aaron Morrison from Misys remarks, "We asked the Recommend question and asked why customers gave us that score and what else we can do to improve. The amount of commentary we got back and the quality of the commentary was phenomenal! Customers were very open about what we are doing right and what we are doing wrong."

The most common method organizations use to structure open-ended comments is to aggregate them and then categorize by theme, examining the relative frequency of different themes to determine which may be key loyalty drivers. Comment categorization can be done manually or pursued through the help of automated software tools. With short surveys (for example, two questions), all driver analysis and follow-on inquiry begins with the respondent's comments. Even with longer-structured surveys, the open-ended comment can hold the key to customer issues and suggestions that are essential to improving the customer experience.

The good-old-fashioned way of exploring these comments is to assign internal teams to read what customers have to say. To uncover patterns and themes, typically multiple readers review and categorize the comments under one or more relevant themes. The themes may be derived at the outset of the categorization exercise or created based on preexisting categories within the organization (for example, a specific business unit or product team) or customer experience (for example, product installation, activation, or reliability).

When derived on the basis of comments themselves, readers begin by reviewing a randomly selected group of comments, noting common themes and characteristics. These become the basis of an initial categorization scheme compared across readers, refined, and finally applied to a larger data set to validate their utility. Whichever the case—starting with a list of expected criteria or deriving themes from scratch—the process must be open to accepting new categories for greatest effectiveness.

Allianz illustrates its process for categorizing comments into themes. Clayton shares:

> All customer feedback is categorized, which allows us to assess the key drivers underpinning customer dissatisfaction. We made a decision early on that we did not wish to install predefined categories across each of our businesses. Instead we wanted to encourage our businesses to use the feedback they received from their own customers to determine the categories and drivers relevant to their customer bases. The categorized feedback is used in subsequent internal workshops to identify and prioritize solutions to improve the customer experience.

Categorization enables our local customer experience teams in each of the businesses to begin to quantify the potential impact of solving the key customer issues on overall customer loyalty.

As with root cause analysis, manual categorization is inherently an interpretive process influenced by the reader's point of view. To ensure the categorization is valid, it is important to assign additional resources to check the quality of a sample of the comments or to combine manual analysis with automated techniques. The goal is to ensure that the categorization scheme is an accurate fit to the themes that customers raise and there is good agreement in how different readers or automated approaches categorize comments.

The primary advantage of comment categorization is that it permits recurring themes to be identified and segmented by product, region, and customer type. This allows organizations to move beyond one-to-one customer follow-up to produce a broader assessment of common needs shared by customer segments. Whether accomplished by employees who have conducted root cause interviews, or by applying a structured and strict categorization schema, the goal is the same: to determine what organizational actions can help raise their NPS.

There are some cautions when it comes to open-ended comments. The first is a bias toward top-of-mind issues. When invited to respond, customers do not always share feedback about the key underlying causes of their satisfaction and loyalty. That is, customers do not always step back to consider which aspects of performance are truly key; they may instead share details about a recent experience or a new concern or find themselves piqued for any reason at all. Corroborating information from other quantitative analyses from additional data or interviews is often necessary to obtain a complete picture of what truly drives customer loyalty and behavior.

Another issue is that costs for this analysis can be quite high, particularly for manual reading and categorization. While some organizations may outsource the review and categorization to third parties, what is gained may be offset by the benefits of organizational learning that comes from internal ownership of comment reviews.

Finally, it's worth noting that the frequency of occurrences for a particular comment category—the quality of the onboard meal on an airplane flight, for example—does not necessarily imply a strong correlation between that category and loyalty. Airlines know that customers are likely to complain about these creature comforts, but from experience, they also know that they are not the real criteria that customers consider in airline loyalty. Relying solely on customer comments can give the false impression you are building a good basis for action. Know the limitations of the methods you employ, and reduce your risk by corroborating your conclusions with different analytic approaches when possible.

GE Real Estate Values Verbatims

Klein Wassink and John Godin affirm that GE Real Estate has been able to learn a great deal from customer comments. Says Godin,

> We found an interesting distinction. When we look at all of the comments that we have, we see a distinct difference from what a Promoter says and how positive the comment is compared to what a Passive says. The Detractors may say, "We like your people, but your deal process really needs to improve." The next step is to use those verbatim comments and categorize them into Promoters, Passives, and Detractors and check the ranking against the underlying reason for those comments. Ultimately we would want to move Passives up to Promoters so they can become referral sources for us as opposed to bad billboards and bad press.

To increase the confidence in their conclusions, GE used NPS loyalty segmentation, other customer characteristics, and corroborating statistical analysis to identify and prioritize high-impact drivers.

Automated Tools

Some organizations turn to automated software tools to help categorize and analyze the numerous open-ended comments they receive. These tools use analytical techniques to search large volumes of text and communications to identify particular themes or patterns. As with manual categorization, the core output of these automated approaches is typically a histogram displaying the relative frequency of comment topics or themes (see Figure 6.2).

These tools reduce the labor-intensive aspects of comment analysis by using natural-language processing to extract sentiment, to categorize, and to cluster based on frequency. In addition, using automated comment analysis tools, you can include more than survey comments; you can mix in comments from other sources of text, such as e-mail and support records.

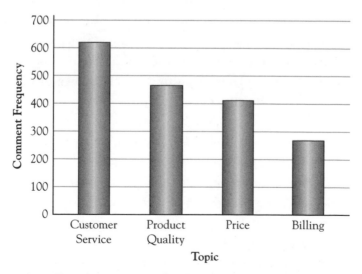

Figure 6.2   Frequency Counts for Top Comment Topics

That said, the magic of the machine is only as good as its opera-
tor. This method still requires people to review and categorize the
comments under relevant themes and key words before turning it
over to an automation tool. Just as with manual techniques, automated comment analysis does best when the categories are accurately defined. In this case, most automated analysis converges on
the best solution when provided with useful keywords or other seed
categories at the beginning of the process. In addition, these automated approaches may require very high volumes of comments in
order to make meaningful computations. While automation may
help with the laborious process of sifting through a large volume of
comments, the bigger issue is the shortcoming of an approach based
exclusively on comment frequency. The automated process does not
incorporate the importance of comments as another dimension.

Adaptive Conversation

Root cause interviews and comment categorization in the context
of a Net Promoter program are aimed at obtaining stated drivers
and arranging them in a meaningful way. In both cases, there is
considerable human effort involved for interviewing, reading, categorizing, and analyzing customer feedback. Adaptive conversations, in contrast, let your customers do some of that work for you.

The adaptive conversation is a technique that allows you to
elicit responses from a group of customers who are expressing their
own ideas and considering the ideas of others on a specific topic.
This interactive process permits customers to identify, consider,
and rank ideas without external intervention or analysis.

One of the key reasons organizations turn to automated
approaches for comment analysis is volume; combing through the
open-ended responses generated by a large number of customers is
very time-consuming. Hundreds or even thousands of unique ideas
can be expressed in a relatively short period of time. The adaptive
conversation is designed to short-cut this process, identifying the
high-priority and widely shared responses, using the customer as
arbiter. Each customer has the opportunity to volunteer ideas and

evaluate the ideas that others have proposed. In adaptive conversation, each customer:

- Contributes ideas in his or her own words
- Endorses select statements contributed by others
- Ranks the resulting statements in order of importance

The end result is a relative ranking and prioritization of customer ideas based not simply on frequency but also on average rankings of importance.

A central feature of the adaptive conversation is to obtain this ranking of ideas by an approach known as adaptive sampling, which asks each customer to evaluate a small number of selected ideas proposed by other customers. The sampling process is basically Darwinian in nature. Popular and highly ranked ideas rise to the top, and the rest go into extinction. Although all ideas get consideration, ideas that get the most scrutiny are the ones that have proven to be popular with customers during earlier stages, so they spend less time evaluating poor-quality ideas.

The primary advantage of the adaptive conversation approach is the ability to obtain prioritization directly from customers. Internal or external teams have less work to determine key or common themes. As well, it can be customized to maximize the feedback from specific customer segments. Under normal circumstances, open-ended comments can be dominated by Detractor issues: these customers are both more vocal and typically more detailed in their commentary. Promoters are more likely to give short, positive, and less diagnostic comments on an open-ended question. This technique allows Promoters to review group feedback, making it possible to gather feedback regarding the organization's strengths, not simply its weaknesses.

While the adaptive conversation technique has some unique advantages, there are also potential issues to consider. First, the process is designed for an online setting, and it requires more than three hundred participants to yield effective results, which may not fit your core demographic or the makeup of your customer base. Second, like comment analysis and categorization, it can also be biased toward top-of-mind issues. Finally, verbatim comments (with some controls) are viewed by other participants as they are rotated through the process. This public nature of the interaction is engaging for participants but can raise sensitivity in some organizations, particularly when studying and illuminating Detractor issues.

LEGO Adapts to Consumer Conversation

Let's look at LEGO Company's work with adaptive conversation. LEGO recognized that value was a loyalty driver. The company wondered how it could add more value to its relationship with parents. One idea it considered was providing parents with insight from childhood development experts in a LEGO-sponsored parent forum. The question posed was as follows:

> Suppose leading experts on child development, creativity and learning were made available to discuss your child's needs at different ages. You could discuss via "live" online chat, forum posts with answers, downloaded Podcasts on different topics, a monthly newsletter, etc. If you had the ability to set the agenda for one of these discussions with experts, what topics would you most want to discuss?

According to Timothy Kirchmann in the Consumer Insights group, LEGO Company gained significant insight from this:

> The parents were precise about the ideas floated in this adaptive conversation. It revealed parental attitudes, beliefs, and needs. And it revealed additional ways LEGO Company can engage with parents that enhance loyalty, such as connecting LEGO Play, building and interacting with bricks, with rich skills development at different ages.

LEGO Company can develop a stronger dialogue with parents. The benefits of this expanded dialogue are quite profound. Parents who realize that LEGO Play benefits their child are more likely to encourage LEGO engagement. For example, they may encourage their other kids (younger or older) to play with LEGO bricks and sets. This expanded play brings LEGO Play to a larger family-based platform, which can improve the perceptions of LEGO Company and potentially drive NPS. Lastly, engaging parents may encourage both short- and long-term product sales, which will grow LEGO Company.

LEGO Company also explored what its core constituency, children, wanted from their online environment. Figure 6.3 illustrates an adaptive conversation grid of popularity versus

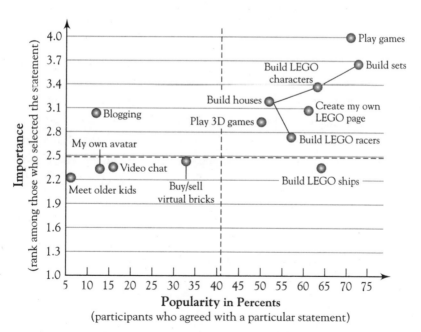

Figure 6.3   Children's Insights into the LEGO Community
Note: Sampled ideas are taken from the top sixty-four ideas. N = 307.

importance based on children's responses to the question posed. Interestingly, LEGO learned that children were interested in building with both physical and virtual bricks, an insight that it can leverage for future Web innovations to engage children more fully in that medium.

Inferential Driver Analysis

Many organizations using NPS choose to ask additional diagnostic questions beyond likelihood to recommend and an open-ended comment. These questions may cover broad themes such as reputation, value, and ease of doing business, or they may evaluate the organization's operational performance at key customer touch points such as sales, product, or support. Whatever the strategy, inferential driver analysis alone or in conjunction with an analysis of stated drivers is the method used to link the additional diagnostic questions with loyalty.

The operative term here is *inferential*. The statistical techniques we discuss here allow you to infer, based on aggregated customer ratings rather than customer statements, what aspects of customer experience are driving overall customer loyalty. Surveys that contain both loyalty and satisfaction measures are often grouped together under the rubric of a relationship approach because these surveys typically explore multiple aspects of the relationship shared between the customer and the organization. Although there is an impact to customers in the form of additional survey questions, this method is particularly well suited for identifying drivers and determining priorities within an agreed-on set of hypotheses. It is well suited to studying competitive position and performance gaps across the key touch points, at the aggregate and within customer segments.

Correlation

The most common inferential statistic for assessing the relationship between NPS and specific loyalty drivers is correlation. Correlation analysis allows you to assess the strength of association between two variables; for instance, as product satisfaction increases, does the likelihood to recommend also increase? The correlation coefficient, expressed along a continuum from -1 to $+1$, indicates the extent to which the movement of one variable moves with another:

- A correlation near 0 signifies little to no relationship at all. There is no pattern to the movement of the two scores being examined.

- A correlation near $+1$ signifies a strong positive relationship. As the score of one variable goes up, so does the score of the other variable.

- A correlation near -1 signifies a strong negative relationship. As the score of one variable goes up, the score on the other variable goes down.

Figure 6.4 provides an example of a correlation analysis. The more frequently two variables vary similarly across observations—as in the first case, which correlates product quality and recommend—the stronger the relationship between them, and the higher the calculated correlation will be. In the second case, correlating training satisfaction with recommend shows a less consistent relationship across observations, and a lower correlation value as a result. In this example, it would be safe to infer that product quality, more than training, is strongly linked to loyalty and to devote further energies to ensure that customers receive the level of product quality they expect.

Let's consider another example. Organization A operates in a market that has undergone massive change as new competitors have entered. Its strategy is to compete by differentiating the customer experience for its most profitable target segments, but its decision makers are unclear to what extent customer expectations are now driven by a new business model introduced by the competition.

Organization A's management team decides to use a relationship survey that includes the Recommend question and additional questions regarding each key aspect of the customer experience,

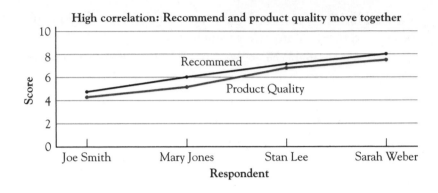

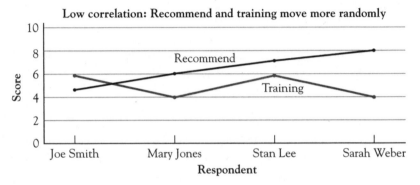

Figure 6.4   **Two Examples of Correlation Analysis**

with ratings for the importance and satisfaction for each. Analyzing the pattern of customer responses using correlation, they are able to assess the link between likelihood to recommend and each aspect of the customer experience.

The items that have the highest correlation are more likely to be true drivers of the NPS and overall loyalty. These items should be given priority in follow-up analyses, including corroboration through comment analysis and follow-up interviews. Once corroborated, areas identified as key drivers of loyalty should command greater management attention and investment in terms of pursuing improvements and innovations.

Prioritizing among key drivers can be further refined by studying the gaps between importance and satisfaction for each. Items with the highest correlation to loyalty and the largest gaps naturally rise to the top of the list in terms of corrective action, as they combine high potential for contributing to loyalty with the greatest need for improvement. Performance areas that are highly correlated to loyalty form the nucleus of experience attributes that should be considered as cornerstones for differentiation.

A common error made with this approach is to assume that correlation points to cause. Although in many cases the logical sequence of events holds true (for example, poor product and service experiences typically damage long-term loyalty,) it may not be true in all cases. For example, hot weather is known to increase crime. Hot weather is also known to increase ice cream purchases. Since both outcomes—crime and ice cream purchases—are precipitated by the same event (hot weather), the correlation between the two will tend to be high. Nevertheless, it would be erroneous to conclude that increased crime causes increased ice cream buying or that increased ice cream buying causes increased crime; the actual causal variable (temperature) has been left out. Corroborating evidence is advisable for inferential approaches in the same way it is advisable for stated driver analyses.

That said, correlation-based approaches to identifying drivers of NPS are typically sufficient to inspire action, even if you cannot establish absolute causality. This type of driver analysis is typically effective in highlighting performance domains that link to loyalty across and within customer segments and helps organizations to prioritize more quickly where to concentrate their energies.

Nevertheless, most management teams have an intuitive understanding of the items that are likely to drive loyalty. If they don't, they can start by using root cause analysis and a deeper study of open-ended comments to help guide them.

Regression Analysis

Regression analysis is similar to correlation and is in fact a correlation-based analysis. Unlike the correlations we've described thus far between two variables (for example, the relationship between product quality and loyalty, or training and loyalty), regression analysis describes the relationship between multiple "predictor" variables say, product quality, training, and phone support, and an outcome variable such as likelihood to recommend. Regression expresses both the strength and the direction of these relationships in terms of a mathematical equation. In essence, it allows you to predict how changes to one variable will affect another—for example, the extent to which improving phone support will increase overall NPS.

This feature makes regression modeling a big favorite for creating return-on-investment and linkage models between specific investments and the benefits that can be expected in terms of increased customer loyalty and related behaviors. With it, organizations can make careful bets about where to invest and which investments will yield the greatest return.

In addition to comment analysis, GE Real Estate also employs regression analysis. Klein Wassink said, "The regression analysis pointed to five things our customers told us that they need: a broad product spectrum, a deal priced and structured appropriately, ongoing relationship management, a deal delivered the way we stated up front, and a lean deal process. We can make high-impact decisions based on these drivers."

Figure 6.5 provides a simple graphical example of this type of analysis. The regression equation is displaying the relationship of the overall product quality satisfaction score and the loyalty measure. The association is relatively strong; as satisfaction with product quality increases by one scale point, the organization can expect an increase in overall likelihood to recommend of approximately three-quarters of a scale point. What remains to be determined are what issues create satisfaction with product quality and what level of investment would be necessary to increase the score in a meaningful way.

Organizations that use Six Sigma and similar process improvement programs usually include regression modeling as part of

Figure 6.5   A Regression Analysis and Its Impact

their approach for understanding NPS. Aspects of the customer experience such as customer support and product quality, which are highly correlated with NPS, serve as the predictor variables (in Figure 6.5, Product Quality Satisfaction on the x-axis), regressed against the outcome variable (in Figure 6.5, Loyalty on the y-axis). The variable Y typically represents the score on the Recommend question, which the organization has validated as a meaningful metric for its business.

The advantage of regression modeling is its suitability to build predictive models. But this is also its greatest challenge in the area of customer experience and loyalty. Unlike our example, customer experience is inherently a complex constellation of interactions, and the relationships between specific modeled variables and the outcome variable can be relatively low.

Moreover, the way that regression modeling works, the same predictor variable can be assigned a different weight—a different degree of influence—in the overall equation, depending on the order in which the variables are added to the model. Some care and expertise must be applied to the process of analyzing and interpreting the results. In addition, when two or more variables help to explain the outcome but are correlated with each other, the regression model may inaccurately report the strength of association between a single predictor and the outcome.

Let's look at an example of variables that may be highly correlated to each other. Perhaps you receive ratings of customers' product and support satisfaction, as well as ratings of sales and account management satisfaction. For most customers, product and support experiences are not distinct; they are extensions of one another. Sales and account management, meanwhile, are primarily institutional distinctions, based on internal divisions; to the customer, the core experiences (interfacing with sales staff, evaluating, negotiating, and purchasing) involved with each are nearly indistinguishable. The customer's view of the world is not neatly subdivided along an organization's internal divisions, and as a result his or her responses to satisfaction questions tend to be a piece of the overall experience and typically lead to scores that are highly correlated with one another. The promise of the regression approach—that it can provide a highly accurate model for driving priorities and investment—comes with a price, pertaining to the level of expertise and effort which is required to ensure its accuracy.

As a result, for many organizations, correlation-based approaches suffice to give management an initial sense of what is driving NPS. In fact, the two or three primary loyalty drivers identified by each approach tend to be the same in many cases. As we mentioned before, confidence in the results can be improved by gathering corroborating data from complementary sources.

Relative Impact Analysis

Relative impact analysis is another inferential approach we often use for identifying root causes. It was developed specifically to address the issue of cross-correlation among predictor variables, a particular problem for regression techniques. Assume that you find a close correlation between NPS and customer support. You also find strong correlation between NPS and on-site installation. Ideally you'd like some way to differentiate and rank the contributions of customer support and on-site installation performance to overall customer loyalty. Because these items are correlated with one another, a regression approach encounters difficulties in disambiguating their unique contributions.

Relative impact analysis was designed for this purpose. The approach was introduced by Theil and Chung (1988) and applies information-theoretic methods to a statistical procedure, averaging over orders, developed by Kruskal (1987). The outcome of the analysis assigns an independent priority to each predictor variable in the model such that the overall allocation sums to 100 percent. Using this approach enables both mathematical modeling and a clear rank-ordered view of how the selected performance variables contribute to the overall NPS.

Figure 6.6 shows the results of a relative impact analysis presented as a cascade or waterfall chart, a typical and easy-to-interpret

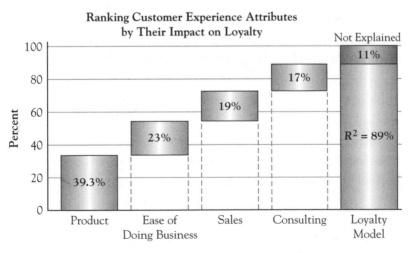

Figure 6.6   Relative Impact Analysis and How It Affects NPS

format used in many Six Sigma analyses. The interpretation of the waterfall chart is simple: any customer attribute comprising more than 20 percent of the movement in loyalty drives a large enough portion of loyalty to focus business efforts to improve the attribute in order to improve loyalty. In this example, product (satisfaction) is the obvious place to start, followed by ease of doing business, which has implications for groups involved in the sales process.

What Can We Infer?

All of the inferential driver analysis methods provide a structured and quantitative framework for studying what matters in customer experience. Their greatest strength is this quantitative underpinning, which can catalyze decision making by providing clear pointers to areas of priority and helping to solve the question, How much should I care (or invest)? Beyond identifying high-level themes and issues, these approaches can be extremely helpful in testing the value of existing key performance indicators, management hypotheses about what matters most, and determining return on investment for planned investments. These benefits may suffice to keep inferential driver analysis a viable approach despite the increased survey length and resulting temptation to focus exclusively on quantitative data rather than qualitative context.

These methods move beyond what is top-of-mind by using inferential statistics to study the patterns underlying customer responses, revealing connections that help to better understand customer behavior. But they can still be biased to the extent that the analyses themselves are focused on—and limited to—what is included in the survey design. If the survey design misses an important driver, you are at risk for misidentifying investment opportunities. For this reason and the others we explored, it's best to use a balance of quantitative and qualitative means, such as stated drivers, comments, and customer interviews, to obtain a fuller and accurate view of what matters to your customers.

Comparison of the Tools

Most organizations find that the best solutions for understanding Promoter and Detractor root causes use more than one method. You can use Figure 6.7 to help compare and select which methods are most useful for your needs and the best fit for your business. For example, if you require a method that is easily quantifiable and have limited internal resources, you may prefer using an inferential analysis approach or perhaps adaptive conversation. If you are developing a program for the first time within your organization and the primary determinant is getting employees engaged with customer feedback, you may wish to start with root cause interviews. In truth, the best programs use these different techniques selectively, as the needs and goals of their organization, and stakeholders within that organization, tend to dictate.

Absolute comparison of the strengths of these tools is useful, but what are the real trade-offs you will make in practice? Here are some guidelines.

When using short surveys with two or three questions, you won't have enough information to do driver analysis, so you are making the implicit trade-off that improved response rates and

	Root-Cause Interviews	Comment Analysis		Adaptive Conversation	Inferential Driver Analysis
		Manual	Automated		
Easy to quantify	◗	◗	◗	◖	●
Objective	◗	◐	◕	◐	◕
Scales easily	○	◗	●	●	●
Exploratory	●	◐	◐	◐	◗
Engages employee	●	◐	◗	◔	◗
Engages customer	●	◗	◗	◐	◗

Figure 6.7   Comparison of Approaches for Identifying Drivers

ease of data capture will offset the costs of postsurvey root cause analysis. Without some form of postsurvey work, you will be lacking any real insight into why NPS is what it is, and what you could do to change it. It's a frequent program error to assume that the two-question survey on its own can get you over the finish line. It won't. The most frequent solution deployed in this instance is root cause analysis as a separate process.

If you include verbatim comments in your short questionnaire (and we think you should), you will have some great data to include in your closed-loop process (see Chapter Seven) and a ton (could be, quite literally) of data. Comment categorizations techniques as they stand today do not seem to provide enough information to understand root cause. When we compare comment categorization frequencies with driver analysis, we find them lacking. It seems unwise to make strategic decisions on the basis of comment categorization alone. In our opinion, you still have to do postsurvey analysis because no shortcut exists yet. At the time of this writing, we have looked at over a dozen technology solutions, but there are no breakthroughs.

A somewhat more revolutionary approach to root cause analysis is to build a community of customers and use tools like the adaptive conversation to determine root cause. You should be seeking a big enough community to reduce bias, and that can mean thousands of members. We prefer regular root cause analysis techniques and follow-up interviews to traditional focus groups for both cost and effectiveness reasons.

If you add survey questions, they provide the opportunity to do driver analysis on the data. The biggest drawback, aside from the longer survey, is that you start with a predetermined notion of what those drivers are likely to be in order to frame the questions. In this case, techniques such as comment analysis or adaptive conversations can be used to help ensure you are not missing out on the real drivers from the customer perspective. Yes, you should start from a hypothesis, but try to find ways to ground it in customer data.

Conclusion

The right mix to determine root cause will vary depending on your situation, but the most successful approaches always have three key elements in a logical combination with your choice of survey design: a quantitative component to drive high-level prioritization, a qualitative component to discover previously unidentified customer issues and suggestions, and a mechanism for direct employee engagement with customers. Your organization is probably already using more than one of these techniques. If you have implemented a quantitative survey using inferential techniques and open-ended comments, then you have at least two items from the list. If you follow that up with root cause interviews or employee reviews of Detractor comments, add another check to your list. And if you have a systematic way of gathering Promoters together for a conversation about your business (either online or offline), then you are well on your way to identifying what exactly you should be doing to create Promoters and improve your score.

7

The Closed-Loop Process

Whether you're in Shanghai, Dubai, Mumbai, or Athy,
customers like to know they're heard.

Simon Lyons,
director of marketing & communication, Aggreko

Listening to customers and measuring NPS is not enough to make a measurable impact on business outcomes. A connection has to be made between listening and the actions you take. The closed-loop process is, in simple terms, listening to customers, acting on the data, communicating back intended actions, and validating the results through improved NPS and business outcomes. A good closed-loop process is both thorough and scalable.

The closed-loop process stands out as a differentiator for the Net Promoter approach. It's not that the process is hard to do; it's inherently simple. It takes commitment from individuals and management across the organization to follow a process for following up with customers. However, without the necessary building blocks of customer-centric DNA, trustworthy data, and strong root cause analysis, you won't be in a position to execute the closed-loop process well.

We start by offering some tips on closed-loop process design and then explore how the process works at all levels in the organization. To illustrate the process in action today, we share case studies in contact centers and B2B sales teams as specific examples of well-developed closed-loop implementations.

Defining Closed-Loop Excellence

What makes an effective closed-loop process? What gets results? When we consider the most effective examples, there are several areas that define characteristics for success.

- *Speed*. The clock is ticking. From the moment customers provide feedback, they are waiting to see what you will do. Many traditional approaches provide no response whatsoever or a response in a lagged time frame that conveys pretty much that same impression. Net Promoter leaders respond quickly; they know that time is a factor, and engaging effectively with their customers requires speed. With real-time systems in place, a follow-up response can be made in a matter of minutes, but we will provide you with guidance on how to manage the trade-off between speed and a substantive response that resolves issues.
- *Coverage*. If customers bother to provide feedback, they deserve a response. The "thank you" message at the end of the survey is a good start, but you need to provide some indication of what actions you will take based on their feedback. Follow-up can range from one-on-one meetings at the customer's office to broad-based communications in an e-mail or newsletter. You do not need to execute personal follow-up with every customer. However, you owe everyone some kind of response indicating what you've learned and what steps you are taking as a direct result of their feedback. The best programs close the loop in some fashion with all respondents, even those who didn't respond. It can be as simple as a carefully worded letter, outlining your overall learnings and the plan to address shortcomings.
- *Root cause analysis*. The closed-loop process creates another opportunity for root cause analysis and organizational learning. It provides an opportunity to engage in a deeper conversation to probe

for additional data. When you use a very short-form survey, the closed-loop follow-up process might be the only chance you have to gather root cause data. Even if you have primary root cause data from another source, here is a golden opportunity to get rich data directly from the customer. However, there are challenges to consider. Training frontline teams to capture this kind of data, let alone engage in effective root cause analysis, is difficult. You will likely discover that employees don't instinctively like to capture and document this information. Complex processes that are time-consuming will lower participation. Keep the follow-up process simple as a trade-off against the depth of data capture you might desire.

• *Initiate action.* In a perfect world, you would want your follow-up owner to resolve the customer's issues in the first conversation, but you might settle for initiating a response. This could be as simple as communicating acknowledgment and comprehension—"We hear you and understand your concerns" or using predetermined actions to address known issues identified from root cause analysis. The ideal, of course, is to provide specific solutions tailored to the customer's specific issues. This may be impractical or exact too high a price in terms of response time given that service recovery is often a goal of the follow-up actions. Complete resolution requires clear empowerment of the follow-up owners. Remember that the best closed-loop process has some call to action.

• *Governance.* The closed-loop process requires oversight to ensure that those responsible for taking action are doing so in a timely and appropriate manner. The program team will want to establish guidance on follow-up time frames and desired outcomes and guarantee they are met by monitoring activity. Some companies treat this process like a manufacturing line, checking outcomes at each stage of the process; others regard it principally as a cultural or training exercise. Regardless of your goals for this process, good governance tracks the quality of the closed-loop process and its impact on loyalty.

Designing a Closed-Loop Process

All closed-loop processes are iterative: collect feedback, make changes, get more feedback, refine changes, and so on. A basic scenario can go this way:

1. The customer responds to a survey.
2. An alert to follow up is generated based on business rules. The alert may be event driven or scheduled, depending on your program design.
3. A follow-up owner contacts the customer.
4. The issue is logged and either resolved or escalated.
5. The outcome is tracked to capture any learning.

This is not a one-size-fits-all process. Decisions about the closed-loop design depend heavily on your business, program goals, and operating environment. Details of this process differ from organization to organization.

Most approaches can be mapped along a continuum. On one end is an environment where the customer relationship is primarily driven by a transactional touch point experience. Typically in such cases, there are large numbers of existing and potential customers, and the ownership of the customer experience is distributed among multiple business functions, processes, and touch points. The airline industry is a good example of this environment.

On the other end are organizations with a direct, personal relationship with each customer. In this case, the customer base is predefined, and the revenue per interaction is high. There is typically an account or relationship management function with dedicated resources allocated to each customer. These organizations have account executives and account teams, such as large business services organizations.

In all cases, the closed-loop process should have five basic design elements:

1. Which customers should receive follow-up?
2. Who conducts the follow-up?
3. When is the follow-up most effective?
4. How is the follow-up call handled?
5. What happens after the follow-up?

Which Customers Should Receive Follow-Up?

When you ask for feedback, you create expectations that some action will take place either immediately or in the future. Asking for feedback without a closed-loop process can do more harm than good to customer loyalty. Even if you don't follow up immediately or in depth with all respondents, you will need to provide some level of feedback to all customers, even those who have not responded, to close the loop with your customer base.

Deciding which customers will receive immediate follow-up depends in part on the Net Promoter program goals. If your goal is to neutralize Detractors and you have a heavy volume, one scenario might be to begin with the most severely dissatisfied Detractors. Detractors give scores of 0 to 6 on the Recommend question, but your closed-loop efforts may be focused on those who provided the lowest scores of 0 to 3. As your process matures, you might be able to incorporate a larger set of Detractors. Some organizations run a pilot, a subset of customers based on NPS or customer segmentation, in order to better understand the volume of Detractors and to design an appropriate closed-loop process and allocate resources.

If your program goal is to optimize the overall customer experience, your follow-up may focus on all three segments: Promoters, Passives, and Detractors. This will help clarify root cause and identify differences between each of these Net Promoter segments, allowing you to design the optimal experience for each.

Brady Asia is a subsidiary of Milwaukee-based Brady Corporation that develops and markets high-performance films and identification solutions. We asked Allan Klotsche, president of Brady Asia, how follow-up alerts are handled in Brady Asia's China region:

> In China, most of our sales are direct, but alerts are not sent to frontline support people. Instead, they go directly to sales managers and the corresponding functional manager whose department was highlighted in the survey. Our action plans are geared to generating customer value. Trigger alerts from major customers are responded to with a great sense of urgency, but smaller customers are given the same respect, and we follow up because their feedback is often relevant on a larger scale.

Brady is managing B2B relationships where following up with all customers is helpful for building relationships and uncovering needs. For high-value complex relationships, the goal is to provide a complete assessment of customer relationships across the buying syndicate. You can't afford to have a Detractor who could put significant revenue at risk, and the value of any respondent in a large account, regardless of influence or decision-making power, will likely warrant follow up.

Another program goal may be to mobilize Promoters and find individuals who are likely to be good references. In this case you may set positive alerts that identify customers scoring 9 or 10 on the Recommend question. The follow-up process may include offering these Promoters special opportunities to expand their relationship with you. For example, they could be invited to join an inner circle of community members where they suggest product ideas and will be increasingly likely to provide references.

In any case, the overall program goal should be to communicate to the entire customer base that you have heard their concerns, are taking action based on their feedback, and thank them for their participation.

Who Conducts the Follow-Up?

Follow-up can be conducted by anyone in the organization, but in practice, organizations typically choose from one of the following groups, depending on the organization's structure:

- Frontline employees or the first-line manager, or both
- Frontline manager
- Account manager or account executive
- Special task force or centralized NPS team
- Executives

For your choice, you will need to evaluate goals and design the follow-up process accordingly. As in the case of customer selection, if the initial focus is on severely dissatisfied customers, the best answer may be frontline supervisors who have responsibility for issue resolution. They are typically empowered to fix customer issues, whereas frontline employees are often constrained with limited options. These supervisors obtain greater awareness of the root cause of dissatisfaction and can coach their team to continually improve the customer experience.

If the decision is made to expand the process to follow up with all Detractors, as a starting point a select group of frontline employees might be given greater decision-making authority for the task of handling the customer follow-up. This group is given guidelines for handling calls and the authority to resolve the most frequent customer complaints.

The ultimate solution is to get the engagement of all frontline employees in the process, but clearly this creates a far more significant burden on the closed-loop process and cultural training. We think it's worth it; loyalty leaders find ways to get the entire organization behind the initiative, and this is your best opportunity to do so.

When particular segments are the targets for follow up, a centralized team may be used to profile that segment further. The team must be trained in performing root cause interviews, probing for the root causes of loyalty.

In general, consider the following factors in deciding who should conduct customer follow-up:

- When direct frontline employees do the follow-up, prepare and empower them to resolve problems, which can be highly motivating. Sending them "into battle" unarmed to solve issues is not going to help customers or morale.

- First-line managers, particularly those in customer service, can hone their coaching skills by hearing first-hand about the customer experience. This can help transfer organizational learning down to the front line for widespread improvements.

- In B2B relationships, customer follow-up processes should align with relationship management practices, making account managers and account executives a good choice for follow-up.

- In some cases, executive participation is beneficial, especially for peer-to-peer follow-up. For example, if the C-level executive of a high-revenue account responds with negative feedback, a C-level individual from your organization may be the best person to respond. You may also include executives if you want to get top-down involvement and enthusiasm around the program.

- If you intend to probe deeper for the root causes of loyalty, you may use a specially trained task force or centralized team that is more senior or has longer tenure.

Allianz sees it as critical that the teams closest to the issues identified are empowered and feel accountable for taking action, and only escalate if there are issues that the immediate team cannot resolve. Andrew Clayton says:

> Allianz has developed core training programs to ensure that frontline employees are equipped with the skills and knowledge to engage in meaningful conversations with customers to probe for the reasons underpinning NPS. The key issue is not to begin our conversations thinking that we already know the problem and then just validating this with the customer. It is important that our frontline employees are able to ask open questions and probe for the core reasons that really underpin our customers' dissatisfaction. This of course requires an ability to listen; we were born with two ears and only one mouth, not the other way around. Another critical issue for conducting Detractor calls is to determine the value of the Detractor; in some cases, we assign high-value Detractors to our best or most senior people to conduct follow-up calls or visits.
>
> Clearly there will be times when there are issues, for example, process issues spanning more than one touch point that cannot be solved at a team or touch-point level; that requires escalation. Having an appropriate governance system that facilitates the escalation process is an important vehicle in identifying and solving issues that are enterprise wide.

Through customer segmentation, Allianz targets high-value Detractors and assigns its best resources to conduct the follow-up. For situations where those assigned to do follow-up are not empowered to resolve the issue, or when cross-functional involvement is necessary, you must define escalation procedures to ensure accountability for resolution.

What Is the Most Effective Time for Follow-Up?

A closed-loop process with a long delay before follow-up is ineffective. If the time between feedback and follow-up is too long, the events become disassociated in the customer's mind. From our best-practice studies, issue resolution–type follow-up activities ideally occur within forty-eight hours, particularly for Detractors. Broader communication may take longer, but typically you want to communicate within a one-quarter boundary. You can plot a curve over time suggesting that the longer you wait to take action, the lower the impact will be.

This is an important point that has implications for all aspects of program design. In customer experience management, time is not your friend. Much of the Net Promoter philosophy revolves around speed of information and response; trustworthy data and the opportunity to take action have a window of time.

Response time is inherently conditional; it will be influenced by what is feasible and what is expected. If your follow-up entails root cause interviews to determine potential issues, then forty-eight hours may be unrealistic. If face-to-face follow-up is required, it may not be possible to meet within days of the response, but making contact to schedule a follow-up meeting should occur quickly. You're being measured on responsiveness on two levels: how quickly you make contact and how quickly you resolve issues.

How Should the Follow-Up Be Handled?

The proper level of urgency, resources, and proficiency should be used. Even with a trained, experienced follow-up team, different skill levels exist. The ideal approach is to create a minimum level of proficiency and make that a qualification for your follow-up

Desired Outcomes	Follow-Up Owner	Call Handling
Neutralize Detractors	Typically frontline agent or first-line manager (or both)	Follow-up call is treated as an escalation. Primary focus is to understand the problem in order to take corrective action
Organizational learning	Typically special task force or designated team	For Detractors it is critical to address the immediate issue first. Then use root cause interview techniques to probe for more information

Figure 7.1   Aligning Actions with Desired Outcomes

team. Omitting follow-up guidance and training is a common pitfall and invariably compromises the quality of the outcome.

Figure 7.1 provides some guidelines mapped to the Net Promoter program goals.

Most organizations try to fix the customer's immediate issue before seeking more detail. The initial call is treated as an escalation, and the focus is on quickly addressing concerns and resolving the immediate issue, particularly with Detractors. After the issue has been resolved, root cause interview techniques can be used to better understand issues beneath the surface. During this process, setting appropriate expectations with the customer about next steps is important. It is better to underpromise and overdeliver. Finally, don't forget customers are doing you a favor by participating in this process. Be respectful of their time, and thank them for their participation.

What Happens After the Follow-Up?

There are two primary goals of the follow-up. The first is issue resolution: if the issue cannot be immediately resolved, it is important to define a process to route it to the appropriate owner and track the status until it is closed. The second is learning and improvement. What is discovered during the follow-up call can be shared with an individual, a team, or the entire organization for coaching and training or incorporated into product or process improvements.

In B2B organizations with high-touch relationships, account planning typically occurs after the follow-up process. An account manager may use the initial follow-up to thank the client, acknowledge feedback, probe further, and schedule a future meeting where both parties can plan a solution that will resolve open issues. With complex accounts, the account manager will often have to work cross-functionally to resolve issues. After the issue has been resolved, the account manager and the extended team can learn from the experience.

Not all problems can be resolved immediately, especially if cross-functional input is required, but customers will likely be patient as long as you are transparent and communicate a plan toward resolution. The extent of their tolerance for time depends on the nature of the relationship with the customer. In B2C environments, that patience might be measured in minutes or hours; in B2B, it could stretch to months depending on the nature of the issue and complexity of resolution. Understanding a reasonable time frame in the context of the customer is important to designing your process.

Action at All Levels

A common pitfall of some programs is to focus solely on structural improvements by investing in the initiatives identified by NPS root cause or statistical analysis. Nearly 80 percent of respondents in our best-practices database felt that closed-loop processes are needed at the operational level; about 75 percent agreed that they were also needed on a structural level in order to achieve truly effective business impact. Successful programs create a balance between both.

A successful Net Promoter program operates on multiple levels. There are three levels of engagement from the perspective of closed-loop action, and they (not surprisingly) look similar to the breakdown from previous chapters:

- Senior executives
- Management
- The front line (for example, customer-facing employees)

The closed-loop process involves all three levels, but in different ways and for different purposes (see Figure 7.2).

What happens at the front line, and the resulting customer experience, form a major part of the customer's perception of your organization. This is where you, perhaps even literally, touch the customer. Frontline employees who receive timely and context-sensitive information have an opportunity to change the customer's experience and move the NPS needle one customer at a time.

Central to the three-level framework and playing a central role in the closed-loop process is midlevel management. Management is closest to the front line, with control of and responsibility for key customer interactions. When NPS data is evaluated with other function-specific key performance indicators, managers

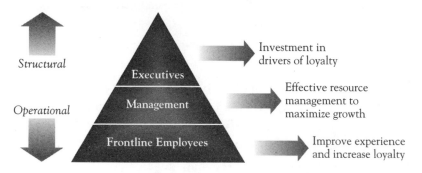

Figure 7.2   Closing-the-Loop Framework: Taking Action at All Levels

obtain an objective view of the performance of their organization. This allows them to take corrective action to improve the level of service delivered through process and policy improvements, optimize investments, and provide ongoing performance management.

The executive team gets an aggregate view of the common issues, allowing them to understand their performance relative to competitors, evaluate strategic segments, and monitor customer experience. Armed with these facts and an understanding of Net Promoter economics, the senior team can make the right customer-centric investments that optimize growth.

Closing the Loop at the Front Line

Andrew Clayton of Allianz has this to say about the importance of frontline employees:

> One of the key success factors in bringing NPS to life as part of business as usual is ensuring that frontline employees who have accountability for the day-to-day delivery of customer experience are the ones who speak to the customers, to find out the things that went well and the things that did not go so well. It is only by bringing our employees into contact (either via telephone or face to face) with customers that we can bring about the degree of day-to-day change needed to institutionalize customer experience in our day-to-day operations.

The front line can make an immediate difference in improving the customer experience. Operational data can come from transactional or relationship measures, but when the information is available to frontline employees and workflows are designed for them to take action, you will see immediate value.

Closed-loop issue resolution has the added benefit of engaging your employees in customer issues. You may think that being asked to follow up with Detractors is a negative experience, but you may be pleasantly surprised. In many instances, it's one of the most motivating and empowering acts that a customer-facing employee can do. In fact, organizations often generate new sales opportunities out of Detractor follow-up, although clearly that should be considered a by-product and not an objective.

Finally, this is a learning opportunity. The closed-loop follow-up with the front line often generates more significant insights than the original data does. It serves to corroborate and expand your employees' understanding of the customer perspective.

We would go as far as to say this: if you can implement closed-loop actions at only one level in the organization, the front line is that level.

Applying the Closed-Loop Process at the Front Line: Service and Support Center

Let's look at how organizations roll out a comprehensive closed-loop process at the front line. Following is an example of a global organization with a diversified product line that serves both consumers and large businesses. This organization decided to launch a Net Promoter program in the B2C division first, with a focus on the service and support function. The decision was driven by management's belief that their growth will be constrained until core customer experience issues are addressed. They rolled out the program in stages and modified decisions over time while reacting to changing conditions, opportunities, and new findings.

In this scenario, NPS was below the industry's benchmark, and management needed to better understand customer support issues and identify corrective actions. Because they were unsure of Detractor volume, the initial closed-loop process focused on the most dissatisfied: a Recommend score of 3 or below. Customers who respond with this score receive a call from an employee empowered to resolve the issue. The callback process is integrated into the existing customer service escalation process.

Management used the root cause of the NPS results to drive key improvement initiatives in customer service. Although the NPS is still below the industry benchmark, the results after six months suggest that the number of low-scoring Detractors has been reduced dramatically.

After tracking NPS progress, the customer service group now decides to expand the follow-up to all Detractors. To give the program more visibility and engage the front line, the customer service leadership team increases its program investment and adds follow-up with a target percentage of Promoters. Promoter follow-up comments are published to inspire the front line and used in coaching and training.

Meanwhile, the organization's senior management has reviewed the data at an aggregate level and has identified a target segment of customers who tend to replace products at three times the rate of the average customer. They decide to evaluate NPS feedback from that segment to identify Promoter and Detractor root causes. A closed-loop process is launched for all of that segment's respondents in order to better understand their needs.

One year after the launch, the organization sees the value of the initial program and extends closed-loop processes to its B2B division, focused on the organization's most valuable accounts. The closed-loop process for these key accounts is integrated into the existing strategic account management process with the goal of establishing an ongoing dialogue to improve and expand the key account relationships. As a result, all survey respondents receive a follow-up call (the dollar value of every respondent is high enough to justify the investment).

This example illustrates the underlying factors that should influence your closed-loop process design:

- Balance follow-up costs with potential business benefit.
- Start with a simple process and expand.
- Listen to Detractors to fix problems.

- Listen to Promoters to evaluate customer experience.

- Listen to Passives to find out what would move them to become Promoters.

- Review feedback at an aggregate level to look for patterns across segments, and target follow-up to improve relationships within specific customer segments.

- In B2B environments with highly complex relationships, use follow-up to improve and expand account relationships.

Sage's Simply Accounting Gets Personal

A prime example of a company that understands the power of customer follow-up at the front line is Sage, with its Simply Accounting division. Simply Accounting has posted huge gains: its NPS has increased from 30 to 50 percent—a twenty-point gain and an increase of 66 percent. In an interview, Laurie Schultz said, "It took a couple of years for us to witness that kind of payoff, and you can imagine here, three years later, the fact that we've increased—almost doubled—our NPS is very gratifying for the organization. One key learning we've had is that to move the needle, you need to make things personal."

Schultz shares one of the initiatives it used to "get personal": the Discovery Team:

> As the NPS program became more formally enshrined in our organization, we felt it was important that we deepen our follow-through with customers who had taken the time to send us their feedback through an in-product survey. On average, we receive over fourteen thousand responses a year to this survey, of which 10 percent are from Detractors (0–6) and another 5 percent from customers who wanted a follow-up call.

We took the philosophy that if you ask someone to "leave you a message," you better be prepared to return their call. Considering that we take over half a million calls a year anyway, it was only a very small investment for us to make the commitment to call every one of these 15 percent of customers responding to our survey.

The role of our Discovery Team (within the customer service organization) is to personally call 100 percent of Detractors and other defined alerts and to resolve their issues on the spot where possible. After doing this for one year, we've witnessed an amazing result: of the Detractors called, 25 percent were converted to Promoters, and another third to Passives just due to the phone call alone. The key learning is that the secret sauce in all of this is to make it personal. This has also had the side benefit of making those employees on the Discovery team very proud, and when we have our quarterly meetings, we showcase them and their accomplishments. It's a badge of honor.

Applying the Closed-Loop Process at the Front Line: Account Management

In B2B environments, incorporating a closed-loop process for strategic accounts and channel partner relationships will improve both individual and account-level relationships. Business rules will influence closed-loop design decisions in account management processes. As with service and support representatives, account managers will review feedback and follow up with customers shortly after, but the rules for which customers receive a follow-up and how the follow-up occurs may differ. Follow-up conversations should be part of an existing account management process with the added benefit of using the customer's feedback in the process.

One goal for Net Promoter account management programs is to use responses to understand the customer's perspective of their relationship with you and to use follow-up as an opportunity to improve those relationships. Although "alerts" may be set for Detractors who will receive immediate follow-up, account managers may also follow up with all respondents, and sometimes nonrespondents, because it allows them an opportunity for building relationships. Another goal may be to follow up with Promoters to identify additional opportunities, ask for referrals, request participation in a reference program, or include them in a special community to provide input into product and service innovation.

In B2B account relationships, not all respondents are the same. Let's look at one way organizations disseminate Net Promoter information to account managers in a meaningful way. Figure 7.3 shows a mapping of the type and level of relationships within an account and their resulting Net Promoter categorization. This chart shows the score for each individual in the account, segmented by decision making and influence power.

A detailed view of a response from each individual in the account is a critical input for an effective account management process because this information can quickly provide insight into the effects of NPS on buying decisions. As seen in the chart, the decision maker is a Detractor with scores of 0 to 6, while end users have more Promoters (9 to 10). Account managers don't want to be blind-sided by a Detractor who is also a decision maker or influencer, especially when pursuing contract renewal or up-sell opportunities. Account managers review the scores and additional feedback to determine what actions to take to improve the overall account relationship. The sales organization can use this information to understand account health and the potential for up-sell or cross-sell opportunities. Finally, it is important to also review nonrespondents. What does the lack of response reveal in terms of the health of the relationship? Is it because the nonrespondent

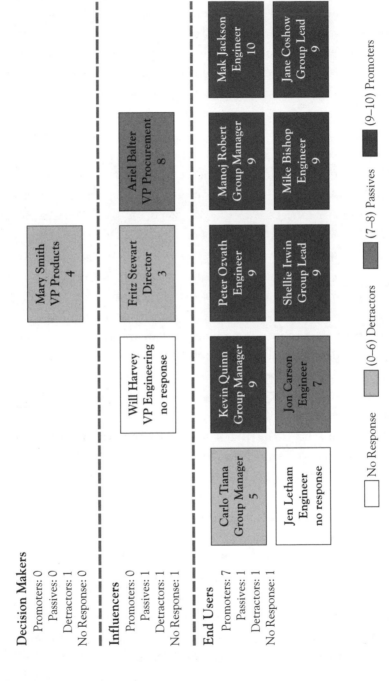

Decision Makers
Promoters: 0
Passives: 0
Detractors: 1
No Response: 0

Influencers
Promoters: 0
Passives: 1
Detractors: 1
No Response: 1

End Users
Promoters: 7
Passives: 1
Detractors: 1
No Response: 1

Mary Smith
VP Products
4

Ariel Balter
VP Procurement
8

Fritz Stewart
Director
3

Will Harvey
VP Engineering
no response

Mak Jackson
Engineer
10

Jane Coshow
Group Lead
9

Manoj Robert
Group Manager
9

Mike Bishop
Engineer
9

Peter Ozvath
Engineer
9

Shellie Irwin
Group Lead
9

Kevin Quinn
Group Manager
9

Jon Carson
Engineer
7

Carlo Tiana
Group Manager
5

Jen Letham
Engineer
no response

☐ No Response   ☐ (0–6) Detractors   ☐ (7–8) Passives   ☐ (9–10) Promoters

Figure 7.3   Account Team: Mapping Account Relationships

has a weak relationship with the account manager? Is the nonrespondent from a particular role or key customer segment?

Strategic account management tools such as the account influence chart must be integrated into the employee's workflow to be useful. For example, if the field uses a customer relationship management (CRM) system for managing contacts and opportunities, this information should be integrated into the CRM system. Presenting information in a way in which employees can easily understand and take action helps facilitate the closed-loop process.

In our experience, account-level relationship mapping that incorporates the Net Promoter scores has many aspects, including these:

- *Building a quality data set.* One of the key insights from account relationship data is the response or nonresponse from key players. Did we select the right people? A management review process of selecting the proper mix of decision makers, influencers, and end users per account, as well as during ongoing account reviews, significantly improves the data quality. It will be hard for the sales team to game the program if they are reviewing their respondent data as part of the standard account review process.
- *Surprises.* We are not suggesting that the NPS data is better than the judgment of the account team; what's interesting to see is when the views differ. The sales team sometimes perceives Promoters as Detractors prior to obtaining independent data, and vice versa. Data that differs from the assessment of the sales team is a call to action.
- *Trends at the individual level.* What does it tell you when a prior Promoter becomes a Detractor or doesn't reply anymore? Changes in scores for individuals are valuable to explore directly. Nonresponse is still a call to action. And of course, seeing Detractors convert to Promoters is highly motivating for the account team.

• *Bringing NPS into an existing process.* We have extolled the virtue of integrating Net Promoter into existing processes. Account planning and review is typically a critical process in account management, and using NPS as a temperature check for individuals within an account will help with development of an effective account development plan. As such, it's the perfect opportunity to make the NPS part of the regular rhythm of account management.

We think account-level relationship mapping is one of the most effective tools in the Net Promoter tool kit, yet it's not used as commonly as we had hoped. The principal reason organizations fail to adopt this process is said to be poor-quality data, weak adoption of their customer relationship management systems, and resistance from the sales organizations. However, it is not more work than good account management practices. The added benefit is that feedback can be used by the sales or account representative to engage in a dialogue with key customers on how to improve the overall relationship outside the context of a sales pursuit or issue resolution. When it works, both the sales team and sales management benefit through improved customer relationships and pipeline growth.

Aggreko's Net Promoter Toolbox

Aggreko highlights how it has communicated account recovery stories from the field to motivate account manager participation and increase visibility around loyalty initiatives. Simon Lyons noted:

> Client issues arise more regularly than we might wish; however, we have excellent account recoveries primarily because we can react very quickly. We also actively capture any success stories about account recoveries and get them back out to the business because they need to be reassured that NPS is not a stick with which to beat

them. In other words, it gives the salespeople the hard facts for them to recognize that sales may be down but those customers are also delighted. This allows the field sales teams to say, "Hold on, be patient; the customer is delighted, and the account *will* recover." By looking at NPS as measurable data, it transforms NPS into a usable tool for their betterment and strength.

Aggreko has put together the necessary tools for the sales team, including recorded Webinars detailing the Net Promoter approach. It developed a Net Promoter toolbox that puts all the data a salesperson would need in a single location. Management made open communication and transparency a basic tenet of the program. "In the beginning," Rupert Soames told us:

> I would say that management teams did not want to give transparency to the figures that show how they were running their operations on a day-to-day basis. They were suspicious of why we would want to see the customer relationship scores. One way we turned people who were suspicious into absolute converts was to tell them the good news about NPS: that managers who give their figures to me get the great fortune of understanding their business better and getting my support. If I went in and said, "It's really good news that the CEO can see everything that you're doing to help customers," the program would not have been welcomed. Instead, I told them, "Really good news! I've got a tool that gives you reports that help you see what your salespeople and service engineers are doing and what is actually happening in accounts."

Managers quickly supported the effort. Transparency was the key. Aggreko uncovered the core insight here: people love having more information about their own business. Although they are often less keen on giving transparency further up the line to their bosses, they do value the data so they can improve their own businesses.

Case Study: BearingPoint Closes the Loop at the Account Level

We encapsulate this section on closing the loop at the front line with a case study of B2B strategic account management. BearingPoint represents a good six-step process. Cheryl Gutierrez, senior manager of client experience management, and her team, Yesenia Mendez and Monique Libier, share their successful process (see Figure 7.4).

Step 2
Meet with clients to gain
commitment to participate

Step 1
Select clients to survey.
Use 3 × 3 model

Step 3
Send survey
notification to the
client by e-mail

**Client
Satisfaction
Program**

Step 6
Individual account plans:
created, implemented,
reviewed, and updated;
close the loop

Step 4
Account action
session

Step 5
Meet with clients:
review results, action plans

Figure 7.4   BearingPoint's Closed-Loop Process at the Account Level

BearingPoint's Carrot

Cheryl Gutierrez told us how important frontline involvement is to the process and how BearingPoint gets its sales organization to use the Net Promoter program:

> Getting the field to buy in is critical. Show them what's in it for them. This is where educating the field on the benefits of a strategic account approach is important. Make sure the program and processes are relevant to the field. For instance, we highlight potential revenue, revenue protection, and lead generation in the education sessions. On the first slide of our presentation, we show the revenue at risk, and it is in bold and red writing to get the field engaged.

BearingPoint tries to find the right balance between positive and negative reinforcement, says Gutierrez:

> The strategic account management program is a case for the carrot and the stick. The carrot is that using the program will generate revenue, and the stick is that program involvement is mandatory. Recently participation has jumped up, and the culture is shifting. We've seen benefits of both carrots and sticks.

Step 1: Selecting the Respondents

While this step seems easy enough, how management chooses to select the sample affects the interpretation of the results.

One team started with the focus of building a census among their largest account, mostly composed of executive and project-level team members. They had a large sample of key players across the account; once the results came back, they had about 24 percent Promoters, 60 percent Passives, and 16 percent Detractors.

When analyzing the health of the account by comparing the NPS in relation to the pipeline and bookings, the account did not fall in the quadrant expected. This account behaved differently from the others of its segment in that the chief information officer (CIO) had the sole power to decide future purchase decisions. This example demonstrates that in complex B2B relationships, who gets measured and how you interpret results does matter.

Step 2: Positioning the Program

Positioning the program correctly with the client sets the stage for the rest of the process. If the team takes the time to explain the program the client is more likely to provide feedback. More often than not, clients want to know how much time they will be investing and what they are getting in return. Account representatives need to position their intent and the benefits to the client, set expectations for what they will be doing with the feedback, ask for participation, and explain the next steps.

It proved important that teams position *the program*, and not the survey, with the clients. The survey is just the tool used to gather the data; the true value of the program is in what you do once their feedback is collected.

In the case of BearingPoint, it was important to position the program face-to-face as a first option, providing another opportunity to have a meaningful conversation. BearingPoint learned that showing the potential return on investment of their clients' time was effective. Similarly, the team made an appointment in advance of the results so that the client committed to both complete the survey and review the results.

According to Yesenia Mendez, operations manager, Latin America, team members said that after they met with the client to discuss the results, the client was more at ease. Some even became Promoters almost overnight from just that meeting because they appreciated that the team created a plan to address their concerns and followed through with it.

Step 3: Survey Notification and Follow-Up

Mendez said that once the program rolled out, BearingPoint would check back with the client to ensure the person had received the survey. They wanted to use the opportunity to gauge the client's willingness to complete the survey, making sure to thank him or her for the time investment and stressing the importance of the program.

Once the client receives notice of the survey, BearingPoint provides two additional automatic reminders in a five-week period. "Use face-to-face or verbal reminders as much as possible, and use caution with e-mail so that it doesn't seem like spamming," Mendez advises. Automatic reminders were coordinated with the team's own personal reminders so that the client didn't feel bombarded. In the long run, high levels of client communication paid off, with response rates exceeding 60 percent.

Stage 4: Results Review and Action Planning

BearingPoint reviewed the data at two levels: account team and segment leadership. Most teams chose to create a one- or two-page slide addressing the concerns and how they expected to resolve them. They would set a time frame around which they would communicate the plan of action with the client, yet another opportunity to create an open channel of communication.

Stage 5: From Action Plan to Account Plan

Once the client follow-up was complete, BearingPoint took the action items developed for each account from the survey and included them in its overall account development plan. "This allows us to maintain an ongoing plan of action and be more proactive in addressing our client's needs and preferences. Basically it allows us to establish a framework from which we can continually assess and address the status of our client relationships," Gutierrez explained.

Stage 6: Closing the Loop with the Client

Closing the loop with the client is the most important part of the process. This was the time when meetings were scheduled with clients to review the account development plan. Depending on the team's approach and the size of the account, BearingPoint would segment the results and close the loop in different ways. Some teams opted for addressing the overall concerns of the account with each client, while others preferred to address individual concerns one-on-one. The approach used was driven by the client's comfort with a given approach.

"Clients wanted to know that BearingPoint was listening to their concerns, that their concerns were our concerns, and that we would act on their feedback accordingly. Chances are that once you meet with the client, the conversation will lead to all kinds of topics," Monique Libier observes. "So be prepared."

It is not unusual for organizations to uncover new business opportunities during the account-level closed-loop process. Often customers are impressed with the commitment to improve and will invite the account team to address additional business needs, resulting in new sales opportunities.

Closing the Loop at the Management Level

"Management" refers to leaders of each business function (for example, sales, service, support, and product) or, in some business models, the leaders of individual business divisions. This level of management is responsible for driving performance within its area of responsibility to deliver on the overall corporate strategy (see Figure 7.2).

Closed-loop processes for managers enable them to optimize the customer experience within a specific functional area or business unit, as well as identify opportunity to improve the experience across functions. To begin, the functional leader must understand the impact the function has on the enterprise-level NPS (for example, service and support's overall role in moving the relationship NPS, not just executing against issue resolution within their function). This insight should be a direct result of the root cause analysis discussed in Chapter Six.

Taking action at the management level involves incorporating NPS into management's rhythm and ongoing reporting. Most often customer information is integrated into quarterly operations reviews, where investment decisions are made. The goal is to review operational and financial performance in the light of its impact on the customer.

Brady Corporation provides a good example of a tightly aligned management-level process. At the senior management level, creating and developing a base of loyal customers is an integrated part of the annual planning process. Throughout the year, customer feedback is collected at a variety of touch points and analyzed in the context of operational data; then each business function identifies initiatives and areas for improvement. On a quarterly basis, the management team and leaders from each functional group meet to review progress against customer loyalty initiatives. These sessions provide visibility to the entire team of the actions taken and results achieved within each functional area, achieving alignment.

Customer Service and Support Management-Level Application

Although usually thought of as one customer touch point, customer service is one of the most critical areas from the customer's point of view. The customer service function for the customer can represent a way to solve a product issue, a service experience, and a perception of how easy that organization is to do business with. If your analysis found that the customer service experience is the most important driver of loyalty and that you are not meeting expectations, this becomes an obvious area of focus for remediation.

Let's suppose you are running the call center operations, a major touch point for your customers' overall experience. You will likely want to understand performance across your various locations. The ranking in Figure 7.5 might represent your scores by location.

First, you see that all of your call centers are not performing equally. This may be due to something systemic (how all call centers were set up to operate) or local (something specific to that particular call center). You feel gratified because Atlanta seems to be performing well. You have an example within your organization that can be used for internal benchmarking, as well as give you the ability to recognize good performance and foster competition across centers. You may review your transactional data and find that the most important driver of customer satisfaction is first call resolution. Further analysis of call handling data reveals that a couple of groups of customer service representatives are responsible

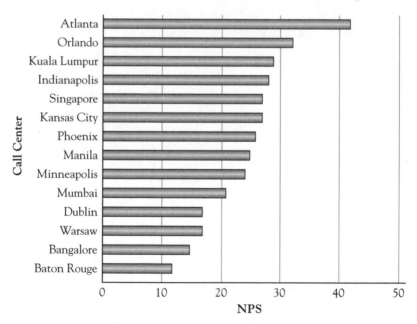

Figure 7.5   Stack Ranking NPS by Call Center

for a higher-than-average rate of open calls after first contact. You can focus coaching and training at these groups to improve their performance, which will likely improve your NPS.

To better optimize your operation, you map NPS data with other metrics to determine the investments required for structural improvement. This could include things such as call handle times, the cost per call, and employee retention metrics. All of these, combined with customers' feedback, will give you additional insight and ability to take action that could have large-scale impact.

Management should close the loop internally by communicating operational wins that occurred because of actions taken, sharing lessons learned across the organization, and identifying structural changes based on feedback to improve the overall operations performance.

B2B Strategic Accounts Management-Level Application

Within a B2B sales organization, individual customer accounts have significant impact on overall financial results. Reviewing account-level NPS in the light of revenue contribution and account-level revenue helps the functional management team to focus resources on strategic defense activities (high-value accounts with low NPS) and growth opportunities (low-value, high-NPS accounts). An example can be seen in Figure 7.6.

For each quadrant, you might make different decisions. For example, you would consider accounts that look like A to be model accounts—those that are performing optimally from both a loyalty and a financial standpoint. Identify and communicate the best practices of these teams. For Accounts B and C, you might want to optimize your investments, but these decisions could differ. For account B, you might be overinvesting at the moment, but you may be able to make this up over time through up-sell opportunities. Accounts like C have significant revenue

---

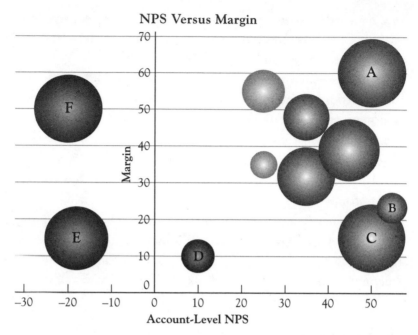

Figure 7.6 NPS Versus Margin for Top Accounts
Note: Bubble size refers to estimated account revenue.

but poorer margins due to resource requirements to support the account; however, they may serve as a good reference.

Accounts D, E, and F, are all on the low end for NPS. However, you may make different decisions based on the financial context. Account F is an immediate "fix" account: resources should be invested and the root cause of the negative perception investigated. For account E, with low margin but significant revenue, you might consider whether to continue the investment in this account. Account D, at a marginal NPS and low margin and revenue, may not fit with your product and service offerings. In this instance, you may divest this account after understanding more about the issues.

While we have used individual accounts, margin, and revenue for this financial linkage analysis, it's worth pointing out that you could use this same approach for evaluating customer segments, revenue, pipeline, or other operational metrics, such as call handling time, to prioritize investment.

The closed-loop process for the functional leader is to ensure customer feedback is integrated into regular management process, decisions are made in the context of customer impact, and communications regarding improvement initiatives are made to customers and employees. It is also important that functional leaders work across organizational silos to evaluate the interdependencies of each function on the end-to-end customer experience.

Closing the Loop at the Executive Level

The executive level has two primary responsibilities in the closed-loop process:

1) Identify structural issues and investment needs;
2) Communicate feedback and intended actions to employees and customers.

The executive team's charter is to apply resources to initiatives that have the most impact on loyalty. This requires strategic segmentation to define which customers are most valuable and understand their loyalty drivers. For example, through review of loyalty drivers and root cause analysis, LEGO discovered that its packaging led to many customer issues, so it changed its packaging. That's a top-down action that a frontline employee cannot do.

Communication to customers as well as employees is also an essential element of the executive closed-loop process. Employees want to know the results of the survey and that the actions they are taking, especially at the front line, are making a positive contribution to the customer experience. Meanwhile, customers want to know that their time and feedback were valued and that the organization is taking action based on the results.

Executives are accountable for closing the loop by making strategic customer-centric decisions based on loyalty feedback and communicating those decisions to customers and employees.

Customer-Centric Decision Making

It is the executive level's responsibility to set direction and fund the appropriate business function or business unit to deliver on the customer experience strategy. The executive level may decide to deliver a differentiated experience for specific customer segments and provide resources and direction for the various business functions to deliver that experience. The executive needs to provide a top-down perspective that guides the business units and frontline efforts into a cohesive effort aligned with corporate objectives and loyalty improvements. Where unbridled business unit efforts could lead to overemphasis in lower-priority areas or customer segments, guidance from the executive level is crucial to maintaining the right balance. It is here, based on even more strategic data analysis, that corporate positioning and messaging are inspired.

Allianz applies segmentation to optimize its follow-up practices. Clayton states:

> In our program setup, a key factor was to ensure that feedback is captured from critical segments. Normally such segments fall into those with high current or high potential business value. I am not saying that we should ignore feedback from other segments, but from our perspective, we need some way to prioritize the actions we take. Clearly it is important to get the balance right to ensure we make effective trade-off decisions—choices that focus on the cost of implementing solutions versus the value of the customers affected. The guiding principle is that customers need to be treated equitably but not

necessarily equally in terms of how we deal with their feedback and the actions or initiatives implemented.

In addition to the one-to-one follow-up process you should design a broad communication strategy to customers, employees, and partner organizations. This may be through e-mail, newsletters, or your website. Consistent communication of your focus for improving loyalty will support your quest to build a customer-centric DNA and increase customer and employee confidence, resulting in improved NPS.

A core component of the executive level closed-loop process is communications to both employees and customers. Employees should be kept in the loop about what the feedback reveals and the resultant structural changes. Also, executives should celebrate exceptional employees who have delivered a superior customer experience, successfully closed the loop, and made contributions to the business. Externally, customers expect to hear back from your organization after they have invested their time and thoughts.

Every customer deserves some level of follow-up. As part of your commitment to customers, communicating what you heard, what you have done, what you are considering doing, and expressing deep thanks is an important final step in closing the loop. This action signals to customers that you are serious about your intent to listen, learn, and improve their experience based on their input. This step will increase the likelihood of future participation and create an ongoing dialogue with customers.

A culture of customer-centricity and large-scale competitive differentiation cannot take root without a closed-loop process at this highest level. Executives must make investment decisions in the context of customer feedback and communicate these decisions clearly to customers and employees. It is this consistent commitment to customer-centric decision making and closed-loop communication that shapes the program in ways that make both employees and customers come away feeling that it's a win-win situation.

Accountability at All Three Levels

Net Promoter programs work well when the front line, management, and executives are all engaged in the closed-loop process, with each level focusing on its role in the overall scheme. A program governance structure helps ensure that all levels are following up with the appropriate audiences.

High-level metrics and resolution sharing are the most effective technique for tracking progress of follow-up actions. The best programs track time to issue closure, conduct verification exercises with customers to ensure issues are truly closed, and monitor the health of the overall program and system in executing the closed-loop process. If you don't know what's happening at each stage of the cycle, you may be disappointed by the quality of the interaction.

Cognos's Gold Standard

We interviewed Dan Beer at IBM Cognos, a company that sells performance management (PM) solutions to large businesses. He shared his thoughts on why the closed-loop process is important at all levels for improvement:

> We want to integrate customer-centric decision making into our DNA. And the way we plan to get there in a year is to have an internal customer success portal where every single employee within Cognos can view aggregated customer feedback and satisfaction results, along with the action items that every department is doing on behalf of improving those scores. Accessibility and transparency of actions and results is key.
>
> So a gold standard for management around the field-facing customer would be following up with specific action items and tracking deliverables in the back end of what we are doing in every part of the business to move these scores forward. That is the vision of where we want to be.

Customer feedback and tracking actions taken at the front line in a database will feed into the information that managers need to optimize their departments. Managers along with the program team help define the closed-loop process.

There needs to be a gold standard in the field that says specifically what people do in this process. The gold standard provides guidance: When do you close the loop? What triggers do you get? When do you get them? When do you call? What do you say? How do you increase the participation rate by soliciting customers to participate?

Managers will spot trends from the feedback that bubbles up and can share that information cross-functionally in order for departments to make improvements across multiple customer touch points.

Every group has some feedback they are getting from our Net Promoter surveys, and we are trying to roll that all up on a regular reporting basis. It would say what we have done with the feedback our customers say is not working. It is not just support; it is also product issues, how are we not engaging the sales relationship cycle, what the customers are not feeling they are getting from us. Of course, NPS will be the benchmark of whether we are or aren't.

Beer believes that some of the key elements in this process are frequent communication and relevance at the executive level:

Keeping information first and foremost in people's minds and tied to something relevant such as business performance is critical. Communication on why we are doing it, why it is good, and what the results are is important. In my mind, it is the relentless communication at the most senior levels of all the departments, where they reach out

and embrace customer loyalty, that creates the environment for people under them to also do so. This type of
information needs to be shared at all levels; otherwise, it
fades away into irrelevancy. Cognos is trying to establish a
regular drumbeat or cadence of information sharing at the
most senior levels of all the departments and a cadence of
communication throughout the company, so it becomes
something we measure our company on.

Conclusion

We started this chapter with an assertion that a closed-loop
process is a key differentiator in the Net Promoter program.
More than that, we believe it's the essential element in building
customer-centric DNA within the organization: the process that
connects employees with customers in a direct fashion.

Closed-loop process design differs according to your program
goals and resources, but it is important to remember that you
should close the loop with every customer and that employees at
all levels have responsibility. An effective closed-loop process bal-
ances the most desirable attributes found in the best program with
practical implementation. The ability to use this process to discover root cause and an opportunity for service recovery and issue
resolution is balanced with the need for speed, recognizing that
the customer is expecting a response to their feedback. Employee
enthusiasm for the opportunity to resolve customer issues can be
diminished if the closed-loop process seems too complicated and
onerous. The best programs find ways to combine event-driven
follow-up with communication to all customers who respond, as
well as those who don't.

Significant innovation continues to take place around executing the closed-loop process. The examples and case studies in this
chapter should provide some inspiration and practical guidance to
build a process that works for your organization.

8

Setting Realistic Targets and Improvement Strategies

I would caution people not to focus as much on the raw NPS when comparing country to country but to look at how quickly each country is improving on prior performance. As leaders, our greatest contribution is setting the expectation for improvement and putting the right management team in place to make it happen.

Allan Klotsche, president, Brady Asia

How high should your organization reach when setting improvement goals for your Net Promoter program? If you set them too high, you risk demoralizing your people by pushing success out of reach. If you set them too low, you risk having the organization become complacent.

In this chapter, we look at how to set realistic targets in the context of competitive benchmarks, market, and cultural differences and how these targets affect organizational behavior. We then examine how to use these benchmarks to develop a roadmap that encourages continuous improvement and discuss how to apply loyalty to performance management.

Relative Performance

There are three basic approaches to benchmarking your business's performance, and all focus on relative, not absolute, performance. The first is to evaluate your performance relative to the industry and to your specific competitors. As you will see, Net Promoter scores differ across industries, so much so that what is considered leading performance in one may be poor performance in another. Although industry comparisons are valuable, your key competitors are likely to be a subset of the larger industry. It is important to understand your NPS relative to this competitive set to differentiate your brand and gain market share. The second is to evaluate your performance in the context of cultural influences. Research has shown that Net Promoter scores differ by region and even by country within a region. Understanding the impact of cultural differences can help isolate true performance issues from cultural response biases. Finally, some of the best performance metrics are internal, such as benchmarking the relative performance of business units, product lines, and support centers in comparison to one another. These internal comparisons can provide a realistic barometer of current and potential performance for your organization.

Performance Relative to Competitors

Every organization wants to know how it is performing relative to other companies within its industry, relative to specific competitors, and relative to world-class companies. By now you understand there are tangible benefits to increasing Promoters and decreasing Detractors. Inevitably the question is asked: How good is our NPS? Benchmarking provides a relative measure by which to evaluate your NPS. It also helps set the bar for future performance and define your NPS goals in order to achieve growth.

Approaches to Gathering Competitive Benchmarks

There are three prototypical approaches to gathering competitive benchmarks. Each has its trade-offs in terms of cost and comprehensiveness. The easiest approach is to add questions to your survey comparing your organization or product with that of your competition. Although this has the advantage of simplicity and is cost-efficient, the sample is constrained to respondents who have an experience with your brand and a competitive brand. If your customers do not have experience with a competitor, they cannot provide an accurate view of your true competitive performance. Furthermore, it's probable that you will see bias from your own customers; after all, they did choose you as a vendor. Typically you can expect a positive bias, where your performance will be elevated and that of your competitors depressed relative to what a true external benchmark might yield. This approach does not offer insight into your competitors' performance from customers whom you have been unable to attract. It is most useful as an indicator of the comparative competitive performance relative to key competitors.

Another approach is to obtain a vertical-sector benchmark. These are typically prepared by a third party using contacts gathered from customers within an industry. This approach offers a more balanced view in that the sample would include respondents who have a current relationship with you and your competitors. Since these studies are completed once and sold to many organizations, they are more cost-effective than custom research. But these reports may be difficult to obtain and may not provide the granularity you desire.

The third option is to hire a third party to develop a custom study in your market segment (both your own customers and those of your competitors). This will provide a much more comprehensive view across your addressable market, but at a higher cost. When choosing this option, remember that the quality of the results is directly proportional to the quality of the sample.

Most organizations we meet are keen to benchmark themselves against specific competitors on specific attributes, often down to the geographical region. The practical problem is cost versus detail; there is no inexpensive solution to highly customized and difficult-to-obtain data. We do think, however, that organizations can apply the 80/20 rule and get close enough to determine which quartile they fall into without breaking the bank.

Industry Variation

In our years of research, we have found that industries are likely
to have widely differing benchmarks and quite different standards
for success. Put another way, the NPS at which you are likely to
enjoy leadership (and hence superior growth) varies considerably by industry, as does the number of companies that achieve
an NPS worthy of loyalty leadership. For example, in the highly
competitive world of luxury hotel chains, only a very high NPS
will provide an organization with any real competitive advantage.
In other industries, the levels of customer loyalty are so low that
a score of zero may represent a winning proposition. Segmenting
our own database by industry, we found significant differences in
the scores across numerous industries, including telecommunications, financial services, Internet, and technology. The best score
for telecom companies was below the average for technology companies, and the average score for telecoms was about the same as
the lowest score for financial services companies (see Figure 8.1).

Overall we find that NPS tends to correlate with the degree of
involvement that customers have with a product or service. Mass
market brands tend to produce less loyalty and advocacy overall
than boutique brands. Industries made up of organizations that
lack brand power or emotional attachment to their products and
services (they lack an "affinity" brand) tend to be characterized by
low NPS. What appears to be a universal truth is that organizations that excel in their markets have an NPS that is considerably higher than their industry and geography averages, even if
the absolute score is not high.

GE Real Estate's Competitive Benchmarks

John Godin at GE Real Estate shares his company's method for
competitive benchmarking:

> We actually ask five competitive questions. We ask
> people to rate us on the questions, and we ask them if

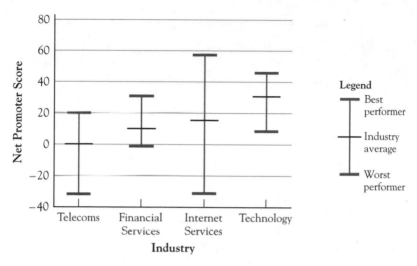

Figure 8.1   Net Promoter Scores by Industry

Source: The data comes from the 2007 Satmetrix Cross-Cultural Benchmark database of survey responses collected between July 1, 2006, and June 30, 2007. Twenty eight companies are represented, totaling about 330,000 survey responses across the globe.

they have a primary provider other than GE Real Estate. If so, then we ask them the same NPS question about that primary provider. We use that as a litmus test—even though a business group's score may have gone up fifteen points year over year, if their competitor score goes up twenty to twenty-five points over the same period, then our team is at a disadvantage. We actually rank each group as being at parity, being ahead, or being below the competition. It shows that you have got a lot of work to do to match or exceed the competition.

Bernard Klein Wassink adds:

The second mechanism we use is to then follow up in selected cases where the action plan requires that we dig deeper. For example, we found in our North American equity business that cycle time was an issue and we were behind the competition . . . . We dug into the cycle time issue, and not only did we get more granular data down to exactly how cycle time was defined by the market, but also how individual competitors performed and what they did to perform at those levels . . . . NPS is related to our general marketplace reputation or brand, and we complement that score with awareness and impression surveying to track reputation.

Cultural Differences

Customers within different cultures answer the Recommend question differently, which makes cultural influence an important factor to consider in evaluating regional performance. In some cases, differences in cultural influence can give a false impression; for example, it may appear that loyalty within one country may be higher than in another country, but cultural influences on customer responses may give the impression that the reverse is the case.

We did an analysis of our data based on geographical differences and found that scores of countries and regions are considerably different from each other (see Figure 8.2). There are several reasons for these NPS fluctuations. Mendez and Libier, who have managed several regions at BearingPoint, offer a possible reason. Mendez said: "One difference might be that in Latin America, the client expresses more often that they are doing business with the person, not the company. In these cases, it seems they are valuing the qualities and trustworthiness of the person they are doing business with as high or even above those of the company."

The cultural benchmark scores enable us to develop averages and maximum and minimum score ranges that can be used to better understand cultural response biases and create a meaningful context in which to interpret scores from various countries and regions.

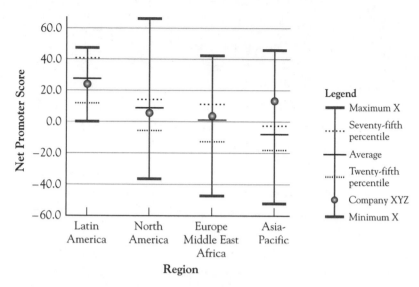

Figure 8.2   Variation in NPS by Region

Source: 2007 Satmetrix Cross-Cultural Benchmark Database of twenty-eight large, leading companies' B2B Relationship surveys from July 1, 2006, to June 30 2007, with approximately 330,000 responses across 184 countries.

It is important to keep in mind that cultural differences are not the only explanation for the variations in loyalty scores across regions. You must also consider the competitive environment in each market, your distribution strategy, and your ability to execute equally well in locations that are farther away from your headquarters or sphere of geographical influence. The fact that scores are typically lower or higher in specific regions may speak to differences in cultural styles, but these differences may also be driven by underlying differences in business strategy, execution, and leadership.

This is an important distinction when determining whether you should apply regional weights to NPS targets to equalize performance across regions. This is a tempting proposition based on the widespread acknowledgment that there are cultural variations in survey responses. But these adjustments can be self-defeating if they mask performance gaps by mistakenly attributing all observed differences to cultural bias. In our experience, organizations tend to take one of the following approaches:

- Establish an absolute score across all geographies as a basic tenet of the organization's strategy. Take the view that cultural differences are dwarfed in comparison with execution errors.
- Establish local baselines and targets at a regional level, and charge those groups with improvement from the baseline rather than absolute targets.

In either case, while it is interesting to do cross-regional comparisons, it's dangerous to do them simplistically. This is particularly true when evaluating performance and setting goals. In this context, it is wise to set local targets based on current performance within specific regions and countries or global targets using incremental growth (for example, a 5 percent increase in NPS) that can be applied to local scores. Both approaches help to avoid rewarding or penalizing specific regions for scores that have more to do with cultural influence than actual performance differences.

Brady Corporation and Goal Setting

Allan Klotsche's goal-setting efforts for Brady Asia are a good example of how to approach setting targets in a global environment and how to avoid common pitfalls: "We set individual goals by country and subregion with no intention to have each country compete against one another for the highest NPS. There's always a little bit of a tendency to do that, but what we really focus on is the slope of the improvement curves. We set different goals by country based on our expectations for improvement."

The start of this process was a challenge for Brady because it lacked a baseline for individual countries and initially set expectations around North American scores, which was not representative across the various countries. "Fortunately, we didn't tie compensation to the NPS too quickly," said Klotsche. "It took two years to get the right benchmarks down to a country level."

Klotsche likens the goal-setting approach within Brady to Six Sigma improvement programs: "Clearly, we expect a larger improvement for sites having lower Net Promoter scores than those with higher NPS."

We routinely suggest that organizations not compare their various NPS results on an absolute basis but rather on a relative basis, and Klotsche agrees: "We definitely share the data across regions because we want them to learn from each other, but what we've found to be most valuable is the improvement they made from last year to this year. That is more of a realistic expectation to have across businesses than the actual score itself."

Brady found that two country teams embraced the program: Australia and China. These two countries could not be more different, yet their response to setting goals was similar and aggressive. Brady attributes this to strong leadership in those regions. With regard to China, Klotsche shared:

> It took them five quarters to really accept this program, and a few hits to a bonus plan where they weren't as focused as they should have been. Within the last year, they've really embraced and begun to constructively use the feedback from our customers. Once the value of the Net Promoter program and the supporting data was clearly understood, it has become woven into the fabric of how they manage the business.

Setting Realistic Goals

Tracking and evaluating customer loyalty is insufficient if this work does not inspire appropriate behavioral change within your organization. To encourage and motivate employees to adopt customer-centric behaviors, meaningful and achievable targets must be set and progress against those goals measured and reinforced.

The first step in establishing meaningful targets is to create a loyalty program infrastructure that can support them. We mean a program that:

- Builds trustworthy data
- Establishes baseline and tracks over time
- Maintains organizational alignment
- Keeps data in context
- Aligns with desired behavior

These activities are not achieved overnight. Keep in mind that it takes time for your program to gain stability. As your program develops, your scores may fluctuate in unpredictable ways. It is possible to set targets under these conditions, but you risk not knowing whether you can achieve them. It is better to wait and set meaningful, defensible, and stable targets than rush in and risk undermining the credibility of the targets and the overall program.

Internal Comparisons

One approach to evaluating performance is to compare NPS across business units, functions, or branches by stack-ranking results. This has a twofold purpose: it identifies business units that achieve high scores, which can serve as a model for best practices, and it unveils business strategies and processes to target for improvement.

Organizations such as retailers with hundreds of stores distributed nationally may find significant differences in NPS on a store-by-store basis. A national average should be calculated, but it's important to use it appropriately.

One approach for establishing positive change is to rank each store's scores and establish quartiles (see Figure 8.3). From this

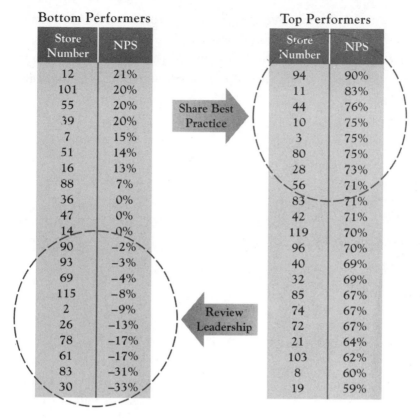

Figure 8.3   Stack Ranking by Performance

analysis, you can identify the highest-performing stores where you can learn best practices and the lowest-performing stores to target improvement. Also, stack ranking can be a good method to foster competition. If a given business unit is ranked seventieth out of eighty business units, it encourages them to want to move out of the bottom quartile. According to Simon Lyons from Aggreko, "The numbers themselves are designed to make internal competition very strong. So you have areas performing well or worse on profits, and you have areas performing well or worse on NPS, and that drives their thinking." Comparing your department's performance with your colleague's will increase internal competition and, the hope is, drive overall performance improvements.

There is a counterargument. Stack ranking across incompara-
ble business units will likely yield frustration rather than a positive
outcome. Even geographical comparisons are risky if the nature of
the business is significantly different between the different units.
Nevertheless, the data can provide guidance on where to look for
improvements in NPS.

Allan Klotsche created an Asian leadership team consisting of
the five regional profit and loss leaders plus the functional leaders
in the region. He said, "Once per quarter, the team shares best
practices, creating a blend of both cooperation and competition.
We are constantly trying to make improvements from where we
are today to where our customers expect us to be in the future."
Ideally organizations benefit from both team cooperation and
competition.

Goals and Organizational Learning

Let's first think about some of the organizational reasons for setting goals and targets. You may want to have a goal that defines
the relative success of your program objectives; for instance,
many organizations use the metric to provide a baseline measure of their customer centricity. Targets and goals provide a
framework to prioritize corporate activities (the drivers of the
metric are typically the areas of focus for the organization). Most
important, it is the behavioral aspects of your organization that
you are trying to shift, so targets and goals should motivate management and staff to improve and innovate, as we discussed in
Chapter Three. The metric creates a common vocabulary and
framework by which to focus the organization in the areas that
matter most to customers. However, sometimes you need to get
underneath the metric to capture the real learning from your
customer feedback.

As an example, we recently participated in a review in which
an account manager identified a challenge in her account NPS
data. She had invited a number of new customers to take the

survey, and this group had responded with scores of 5 on the Recommend question. When follow-up calls were conducted, the most common reason cited was that they had insufficient experience to form a judgment. "A 5 equals neutral, right?" The account manager fell short of her NPS goal because of the number of Detractors. Leaving aside the score, the early impressions were still valuable as a learning opportunity, and the manager obtained useful data that helped her to develop deeper relationships. Gathering that data was valuable but damaging to the metric. The point is this: in some situations, you may be forced to balance NPS targets and organizational learning.

Compensation

Many organizations make a mistake by connecting NPS to compensation before their program has reached the appropriate level of maturity. Even programs that have existed for the better part of a decade could prove to be immature; it's not time but level of integration of customer feedback that defines maturity. Other programs suffer from the misperception that customer loyalty is owned solely by the program team chartered with running the program, such that the broader organization is not responsible for changing its behavior to affect the corporate target. Finally, many organizations have not staffed the program appropriately to reach a level of maturity. The net result is that years of measurement go by with little if any improvements.

If you believe your organization is ready to tie compensation to NPS, you will need to consider what compensation strategy is most likely to motivate the right behaviors. No single approach exists in setting NPS goals and corresponding compensation. Various methods are appropriate, depending on the information available, the organizational structure, corporate culture, program maturity, and business strategy. We have found that the integration of NPS into performance goals and variable compensation tends to evolve. As such, the status and efficacy of the program should be evaluated on a regular basis, with a corresponding evolution of the compensation structure. The following issues should be considered when implementing an appropriate performance-based improvement program:

- How long will it take to establish a baseline?
- Who should participate in the compensation program?
- Should compensation be based on the outcome of a single metric or a combination of metrics?
- At what levels of the organization should targets be set?
- What percentage of variable compensation should it affect?
- What is an appropriate time frame for improvement?
- What is the appropriate methodology for determining realistic but challenging improvement goals?

Establishing Baseline Performance

The first step in setting performance targets is to establish a trustworthy metric by which to tie compensation. Before choosing a baseline value, collect feedback over an extended period of time to establish the normal amount of movement inherent in the Net Promoter score specific to your business and customers. As we discussed in Chapter Five, a baseline measure needs to comprise statistically robust sample sizes and adequately represent your key segments.

Participation in the Compensation Program

It is sometimes argued that only employees who work directly with customers should have a component of their variable compensation driven by customer feedback. However, because most industries now operate in fiercely competitive, service-driven environments, we typically recommend that if you decide to tie compensation to NPS, all employees should have some component of their variable compensation determined by customer feedback metrics. Noncustomer-facing employees with logistics, product innovation, or product manufacturing roles can benefit from having their work ethic and processes at least partially driven by customer loyalty goals. An inclusive approach encourages all employees to focus on creating customer success and dispels the mistaken perception that just one department owns customer satisfaction and loyalty.

Suhail Khan, senior director at FileNet (now IBM Enterprise Content Management) discusses how they chose to roll out compensation:

> For us, it was critical to support what we were really trying to do, which was to improve relationships with our clients. Our approach to tying compensation included the whole company. The senior executive team had their compensation tied to an overall loyalty score, agreed upon by the CEO and his staff.

In this division of IBM, the remainder of the employee base had their targets based on their specific roles to ensure that all employees understood that what they did every day at their jobs had a direct impact on customers. "Management business objectives turned into customer loyalty objectives," said Khan, "and so began the strategic transformation of our company.

A Single Metric or a Combination

The next phase involves selecting the appropriate combination of high-level indicators and detailed functional attributes that measure specific areas of performance. In general, particularly for the latter, it is best to focus goals on those performance areas considered to be in the span of control of the targeted employees. For instance, in most organizations, frontline employees do not have control or influence over the corporate Net Promoter score in the same way that executives might. As such, organizations may consider setting goals based on measuring specific touch points and aligning the touch point performance with the corresponding employee group. However, we recommend this only when the business fully understands the impact these touch points have on NPS. There is no sense in focusing employee energies on matters that are within their purview but unlikely to have an impact on loyalty. When selecting these attributes, make sure that they influence NPS and align with the overall strategy of your business. Once you do, tying compensation to achievement of those attributes can support your initiatives.

In other instances, companies tie a smaller percentage of the variable compensation to a corporate NPS score, and a larger percentage to the touch point. This distribution reinforces that NPS is important for everyone; however, what is within employees' immediate control is also relevant.

Because executives and senior management have areas of responsibility that are strategic and expansive, they should be held responsible for meeting performance targets on overall measures of customer loyalty such as the Net Promoter score. Customer feedback metrics may be considered and integrated if they measure progress made on a key business strategy, such as improving product quality. Depending on your organization's culture and goals, ties to compensation can be equally as effective if they are based on a single metric such as NPS or a combination of metrics.

Compensation and Level of Employee

It is important to ensure that the analysis used for setting compensation goals is not too remote from individuals. In an organization of thousands of employees, setting improvement goals from a single corporate score may not be sufficiently motivating for employees. They may not understand the score, or they may not believe that they can affect it in a meaningful way. The need to make metrics more direct should be balanced with two other considerations:

- *Overall business strategy.* Setting separate functional or regional targets must be aligned with larger business targets, such as operating more seamlessly as a global organization or developing a cross-functional view of the customer, to avoid potential conflicts.

- *Sample size.* By imposing more granular goals, the available sample sizes for each metric calculated will be reduced, which may have an impact on the calculation of statistically significant improvement goals.

Align goals with desired behavior. For example, many sales organizations set response rate goals for their teams in order to build trustworthy data. We have seen these programs be very effective when the measurement program is well established, the response rates are defensible, and there are tried and tested ways of ensuring the sales team does not inappropriately bias the data collection. Using highly granular measures can be particularly effective at aligning employee behavior in a business-to-business setting, where very small numbers of respondents can have an enormous impact on retention and growth.

A similar approach is being adopted in many service organizations, where the performance of customer service representatives is evaluated based on the cases they manage. These programs are able to support more granular targets for these reasons:

- The volume of possible survey incidents is high, so it is often possible to calculate statistically significant goals on a quarterly, semiannual, or annual basis.

- Systems are in place to measure the total volume and nature of transactions and ensure the survey results reflect reality, thus managing any potential bias in the results.

- For managers, compensation typically takes a similar form as described previously for frontline employees. At the executive level, it is most common to tie compensation at the corporate NPS. Whichever level is appropriate for your organization, it is still imperative that you have built on a foundation of trustworthy data.

The linkage between feedback and variable compensation tends to vary according to the circumstances of each industry and organization. In general, the percentage of total compensation that is affected will be tailored to the role of the employee, with customer-facing roles having a larger component of total compensation subject to loyalty improvement goals. For this reason, variable compensation often comprises a larger component of total compensation for sales staff, senior management, and executives. Certainly all employees should be encouraged to take responsibility for successfully managing the customer experience, but it makes intuitive sense that a larger percentage of this group's total compensation is affected by customer loyalty because they are most directly involved with the customer.

The actual weight given to customer loyalty measures needs to be meaningful enough to encourage the desired customer-focused behavior. We consider 10 percent of variable compensation to be an appropriate minimum level. We have also seen successful programs evolve to a point where 30 percent or more of variable compensation is being affected by these metrics.

Enrique Salem discusses Symantec's view of this complex topic: "A lot of companies wrestle with the issue around compensation. I think the answer tends to depend to some extent on what works in the culture in which you've built," he told us. Symantec wanted to make sure that it kept the compensation system as simple as possible. Beyond compensation, those in senior management were quick to recognize that there would be a disconnect if employees saw that the executives were not modeling the ideal behavior:

> While compensation is interesting, it is also important
> to model how I act and what I talk about when I am in
> a meeting. So I think it is easy to say, "Well, we will just
> change the compensation and all things will be good."
> But quite frankly, I think it is more important that the
> executives have to model the behaviors they expect in
> the rest of the organization. In my opinion, compensa-
> tion is interesting, but what matters are the behaviors.

Demonstrable behavior ultimately sets the tone because compensation is a blunt tool that can cause as many problems as it
can cure. If you don't have that demonstrable behavior and you
don't have the culture right, compensation is not going to solve
your problems for you.

Improvement Time Frames and Rhythm

When setting performance targets, an organization must decide on
a time frame for achieving desired customer loyalty targets, as well
as the path for measuring progress for time periods in between.
Most organizations set targets on an annual basis, with progress
toward the goal evaluated quarterly as part of the standard business reporting. For certain functional areas, such as customer
service, there may be an opportunity to set shorter-term improvement goals using ongoing transactional measurement. In general,
the time frame needs to relate to the change cycle. If it will take
you twelve months to make the changes required to improve the
performance of a product line, your estimated time to improvement will be vastly different from that required to coach a contact
center employee.

NPS goals should also align with your organization's natural
reporting rhythm. NPS targets reported annually will create dis-
cordant communication challenges if most other metrics are
reported quarterly. Ultimately your goal is to have targets for NPS

given equal weight and importance relative to other corporate metrics. Your data must be trustworthy and of sufficient sample size and stability to reflect true customer perceptions. Any holes in your sampling strategy across segments and subgroups (roles, region, account type, customer segment) could create sampling and response bias, leading your target-setting effort to be based on incomplete data.

The Methodology for Setting Targets

Many organizations are interested in the best practices for the target-setting process for NPS, specifically the numerical approach used for creating sensible goals for future NPS performance. We recommend a multitiered process that takes a variety of factors into account:

- *Historical NPS data.* Our process starts with trend analysis to establish an upper and lower bound around the corporate NPS over time. This trending exercise helps to create a growth rate expectation based on past performance. Understanding historical trends will help in establishing realistic yet improvement-oriented targets.
- *Reasonable improvement rates.* We have been collecting loyalty scores on an annual basis for a variety of organizations over the past six years. This database of approximately 300,000 customers (both B2B and B2C) from the telecommunications, high technology, Internet services, and financial services industries has allowed us to understand the extent to which organizations are likely to see improvements in their NPS year over year. One of our observations is that the NPS a given organization has at the outset tends to dictate the possibilities for their NPS growth rate. Generally companies that start out at the lower ends of the NPS range have larger potential opportunities for improvement than those at the top of the range (see Figure 8.4 as a general example

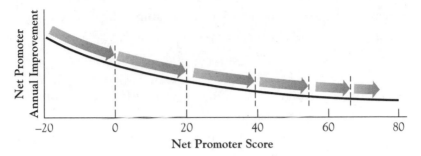

Figure 8.4   Illustration of Improvement Potential by NPS Range

of this concept). From a target-setting perspective, the data, when aggregated, helps to determine feasible growth targets based on what other companies with similar scores are able to achieve.

• *Cross-cultural benchmarks*. Cultural considerations can influence the scores. These cultural influences can affect the target-setting process, so applying cultural benchmarks can help to establish a local context on which to base country or regional targets.

• *Weighted growth information*. Target setting needs to be fluid and flexible to take into account the changing business environment. Different business units or regions may increase at different rates due to business expectations. For example, if Asia Pacific is the largest growth region, target setting will need to take into account the cultural influence and the growth expectations of this region relative to others. With this in mind, trying to project your improvement targets by two or three years would mean overlaying the expected growth to 'weight' those faster-growing segments in alignment with their growth potential.

• *Significant improvement test*. Many companies want to set preliminary targets based on statistically significant change year over year. Some rate of change in the metric may prove to be simply noise or part of the margin of error, and management wants to ensure moving beyond that threshold. Although significance should not be the only consideration, most companies wish to ensure that the targets they set are meaningfully different from the current state of performance.

_____

Using these techniques can provide you with a realistic target. However, it's important to remember that the competitive market pays no heed to statistically significant improvements or reasonableness of goals. Ultimately organizations need to establish goals that align with their competitive circumstances and determine what it will take to get to a position of primacy in their market in a time frame that is consistent with their growth objectives. There is little point in congratulating yourself on executing against stretch goals if your competition has pulled further ahead over the same period. Relative success, in a competitive context, is the ultimate measure.

Conclusion

By implementing an NPS performance-based program that aims for increasing customer loyalty, organizations can begin the journey toward continuous improvement. In general, however, the process for setting performance goals is not an exact science. Many variables come into play, including the natural tension that exists between the need to set realistic targets and the value of setting targets high enough to ensure that staff and stakeholders will stretch to meet them. When setting performance goals, remember that all targets should be based on a careful analysis of what is realistic to achieve given the information and resources available, balanced against the needs of the corporation to compete effectively.

Your success in setting realistic goals and improvement strategies also depends on meeting certain preconditions within your larger program. First, you must ensure that the data you collect is trustworthy, relevant, consistent, and reliable. Second, your program must be aligned with the rest of the organization. Target and goal setting can succeed in motivating behavior only if the program involves the whole organization and is seen as relevant to every employee.

When these conditions are met, establish your performance baseline as a means for measuring progress or regression against your goals. Your targets need to balance an understanding of how you compare with competitors, where you stand with your industry's benchmarks as a backdrop, and how to normalize your performance in the face of cultural differences. Finally, if you tie NPS to compensation, be careful to consider timing, level of employee, and the maturity of your program to help ensure that you derive an equitable compensation structure that is truly linked to the customer and drives the desired behavior.

Innovation Drives Transformation

We create Elationships.

Diana Dykstra, president and CEO,
San Francisco Fire Credit Union

"Elated relationships," or "elationships," are what market leaders like San Francisco Fire Credit Union, with an NPS of 75 percent, are trying to create for each customer. The company has not used traditional means to succeed; it spends nothing on direct marketing and grows at double the industry rate. The organization made a strategic decision not to invest in additional branch offices with ATMs. Instead, it took the overhead cost savings of over half a million dollars and used it to waive ATM fees worldwide, regardless of machine. Customers can conveniently withdraw from their accounts wherever they are, which would delight any banking customer. This win-win solution helped seed positive word of mouth, costing the company nothing. Moreover, the credit union rewards employees for going above and beyond to address customer needs and ensures they are empowered to thrill customers. Diana Dykstra said, "Our employees ARE our business; if they are Detractors, we breed Detractors." Demonstrating this focus on employees, they not only measure customer loyalty but also measure employee loyalty. About three years ago, the credit union's employee NPS was around −20 percent, and today, it has soared to roughly 65 percent, and corporate NPS climbed from 52 percent to 75 percent. Dykstra is so customer focused that she includes her own e-mail address for members to "Ask Diana," and she responds to inquiries late into the night. Leading by example and focusing on employee and customer success, Dykstra has helped transform employee and customer loyalty with San Francisco Fire Credit Union.

Many of the organizations running successful Net Promoter programs see both internal and external transformation as well as product, service, and process innovation. Innovation encompasses introducing something new, improving a process, or changing established policies, products, or services that creates a new dimension of performance. Transformation occurs throughout various aspects of a business: people (employee engagement, partner alignment, and customer community involvement), products (innovations and additional product lines), and processes (increased channel and workflow efficiencies). Innovation in these areas typically fuels profitable growth and expansion opportunities and may pave the way for transformation.

Many companies start their Net Promoter programs from a defensive perspective: solving an immediate perceived problem with the business. In other cases, companies have moved beyond remediation to create transformative outcomes and break new ground. They have gone beyond defense to offense. This chapter focuses on ideas, techniques, and approaches to enable innovation and transformation. These progressive approaches include technology-enabled transformation, process innovation, online communities, and activating NetWorked Promoters. We provide case studies with thoughts on where we see leading organizations applying some of these ideas. We hope you will be inspired by these success stories and glean ideas to infuse your business.

Technology Enables Transformation

We are shameless technocrats. Although we made a conscious decision not to make technology the focus of this book, we felt that we would be doing a disservice if we did not mention its importance. Technology innovation permeates all aspects of business. From the days of e-business to today's Internet-enabled consumer-generated media, technology continues to change the way we do business. Net Promoter programs are no different. Those who find ways to leverage technology to improve their program's success and innovate around the customer experience will achieve greater success than those who do not.

The technology choices that organizations make play a major role in their long-term success. A Net Promoter program involves a lot of coordinated actions, data gathering and analysis, reporting, and information distribution. This cannot be a manual process or a stand-alone application but must be integrated into the infrastructure that runs your business. Integrating customer feedback with financial data, and customer relationship management systems (CRM), along with online communication vehicles such as corporate websites and blogs, is necessary to run businesses effectively.

In this section, we focus on how technology can enable a holistic view of the customer across the lifecycle as opposed to a silo of information disconnected from day-to-day business operations. We share how technology helps to organize and consolidate information to provide opportunities for product, process, and experience transformation that drive NPS improvement. Technology plays a major role in integrating the elements of the Net Promoter operating model, such as Enterprise Roadmap, Trustworthy Data, Root Cause Analysis, and Action and Accountability.

Enterprise Roadmap

As discussed in Chapter Four, developing an enterprise roadmap requires an understanding of the moments of truth in the customer experience. Collecting data using both relationship and transactional systems will provide a deeper understanding of your customers' experiences across events and time. Technology should help automate your program by collecting experience data in real-time and disseminating information to the right people at the right time. By automating the process of data collection and distribution, organizations can spend more time focusing on customer needs rather than inefficiencies caused by lack of technology infrastructure.

Trustworthy Data

A flexible and secure system is needed to support data quality, collection, and reporting throughout the organization. Good sample management ensures less NPS volatility due to poor sample quality (for example, e-mail bounces and balanced and represented segments). Data collection mechanisms should be flexible, allowing you to collect customer data in a way most convenient to your customers. Integration with mobile devices, voice response, online communities, and e-mail to web are a few of the most popular ways to automate the data collection process. Making the process fit into the natural interaction customers have with your business is critical to building trustworthy data.

Your data management system should allow integration of customer demographic information, roles, and segmentation with your loyalty data. It should allow real-time reporting on response rates to enable employees to recruit customer participation. It must be secure. This information, the lifeblood of your organization, contains sensitive information on customers and their likelihood to continue to purchase. You must ensure you have the proper security and authentication to protect this information.

A robust enterprise technology solution enables program and data governance to ensure trustworthy data that drives critical business decisions.

Root Cause Analysis

A flexible technology infrastructure enables a variety of analytics to uncover the root causes of loyalty and dissatisfaction. Technology solutions that incorporate driver analysis and performance gaps, and capture the results of root cause interviews accelerate the decision processes needed to improve NPS. The technology infrastructure should be able to stack-rank NPS by business unit, geography, product line, or agent; analyze data from multiple viewpoints; and categorize comments to enable further insight into the drivers of loyalty.

Action and Accountability

We believe getting the right information to the right people at the right time is critical for operational success. Often companies fail to achieve success due to time lapses in responding to customer feedback. Real-time information creates a sense of urgency. Your technology infrastructure should evaluate the business rules for action and distribute information as an "alert" through e-mail or CRM integration to support immediate action. Since action is highly distributed, management reporting is required to provide oversight into the actions of the organizations, ensuring accountability across every corner of the business.

Innovation and Transformation

By monitoring the customer experience at critical moments and measuring the ongoing loyalty of your customers, you will get the information you need to build a customer-centric DNA. Your technology infrastructure should allow you to identify and communicate with customer segments in a way that continuously improves the customer experience, increasing loyalty and driving positive word of mouth.

Anyone can use a calculator to calculate the score. However, successful Net Promoter programs follow an organizational discipline for integrating customer data into the daily workflow of the business as customer centricity becomes ingrained in the organization's DNA. The Net Promoter discipline is an iterative process, and a sound system infrastructure that automates the process will help you run your program with ease and success. In 1949, John Von Neumann said, "It would appear that we have reached the limits of what it is possible to achieve with computer technology, although one should be careful with such statements, as they tend to sound pretty silly in five years." We encourage you to be on the lookout for burgeoning technologies that can facilitate data collection, analysis, and distribution in ways that enable you to reach your goals.

Operational Improvements and Innovation

Transformation of your business can occur through operational improvements. With many companies implementing Six Sigma–based approaches, we found that process and operations often present opportunities for advantage and can help differentiate organizations from the competition. The GE Consumer and Industrial division applies a "Lean" Six Sigma approach to its business to eliminate "waste," or "non-value-add" activities, which results in improved, more efficient operations that impact loyalty drivers. Master Black Belt Vivian Hairston Blade shared her experiences implementing NPS and Lean at GE and finds that Lean and Six Sigma work effectively together in combination to drive Net Promoter outcomes. Lean reduces customer cycle time by attacking waste in the process, while Six Sigma reduces customer cycle time by attacking defects, rework, and variation. As much as 95 percent of the elapsed time experienced by a customer in a process can be "non-value-add."

According to Blade, "NPS is not about managing the score . . . NPS is about how we improve customers' experiences." At GE, the CEO drives NPS from the top down and thinks of NPS and Lean Six Sigma as complementary to driving organic growth. GE uses a simple and straightforward framework of "listening, acting, and measuring" in order to improve customer experiences. Customer feedback obtained using Net Promoter programs drives prioritized investments in process improvements using Lean principles. NPS-driven actions are focused in two buckets: tactical (action plans per customer with a three- to six-month follow-up) and strategic (systemic fixes, such as customer-facing processes). An important part of NPS and Lean is measuring the results of your actions against key customer metrics, including cycle times versus customer expectations and customers' growth. Understand your stakeholders' experiences and moments of truth to determine where resources should be applied to meet and exceed their expectations.

Ascension Health: Operational Improvements Create Ideal Patient Care

Health care is not always perceived as an industry that is driven by innovation, operational efficiency, or customer centricity. That's why the pioneering practices at Ascension Health and a top-performing hospital in Kokomo, Indiana, stood out for us to share as a case study.

Ascension Health, the nation's largest Catholic nonprofit health system in the United States, operating in twenty states with $12 billion in revenues, has been fostering hospital best practices that have been transformative for physicians, nurses, and staff, as well as patients. We were impressed by the stories that Peggy Kurusz, director of research and development at Ascension Health, and Mary Ellen Griffin, executive director of support services of St. Joseph Hospital, shared. They discussed how their organization uses NPS to focus attention on the patient experience.

Ascension Health has three strategic initiatives:

- Health care that works (in other words, 100 percent satisfaction)
- Health care that is safe (for example, no preventable deaths or injuries)
- Health care that leaves no one behind (for example, every person can have access to a medical home)

Ascension Health spoke with clients and found a variety of areas that made their experience exceptional: the hospital's reputation and quality, administrative efficiency, comfortable environment, and emotional and spiritual support. Meeting these expectations on a consistent basis was challenging. Ascension Health found that on average, nurses spent only twenty minutes of every hour on patient care; the majority of time was consumed by administrative work, teaching activities, and other inefficiencies. To improve the patient experience, they wanted to increase the time nurses spent with patients. Also, because there were many hospitals in the network, there were disparate patient satisfaction surveys being used, with some seven hundred different questions around patient satisfaction.

In an attempt to transform their stakeholders' experiences, Ascension Health employed the adaptive design technique, modeled on Toyota's production line process improvement methodology. It is different from other approaches because it focuses on problem solving at the front line. It is accomplished by watching a process, understanding interactions, and engaging the front line to determine root causes and potential improvements.

"Many hospitals do not reach operational efficiency, like you might see in high-tech companies," says Griffin. "Adaptive design gets us the operational efficiency we need to differentiate for a better experience. We want to create 'ideal patient care'—exactly what patients need, where and when they need it, customized individually, and immediately responsive. We want to create a safe place physically, emotionally, spiritually, and professionally, without waste and inefficiencies."

Ascension employs two types of problem solving: first-order problem solving, which focuses on fixing a particular problem but results in inefficiencies and workarounds, and second-order problem solving, which seeks the root cause of the problem and involves staff to identify solutions to prevent the problem from recurring. Ascension focused on second-order problem solving because it wanted to know why something was not getting done correctly the first time. Griffin states, "Adaptive design begins with observation and literally drawing on a piece of paper how the employees do their work. We call this "drawing an A3," which is the description of an eleven- by seventeen-inch piece of copier paper on which we draw. We do a lot of drawing! You have to be a humble learner with no judgment. Just observe what the staff are doing. We ask, 'How do you know to do that?' rather than 'Why do you do that?'" (See Figure 9.1.)

Ascension Health looked at three primary things:

- Pathways: Where people travel and move in order to do their work

- Connections: To whom the nurse talked and what he or she talked about

- In which activities nurses participated and how much time they spent problem solving

It turned out that nurses spent the majority of time putting out fires and not much face time with patients.

They walked us through one of their issues: the patient had to wait for a specimen cup. "This was a big problem because our patients need them when they need them. The process for restocking specimen cups was too complex for new employees, caused nurses to hunt for supplies, and generated inventory inefficiencies," said Griffin.

Why were no specimen cups available on the floor? Mainly because it was difficult for the materials staff to know what supplies were needed because there was no clear signal to restock; consequently, the nursing staff on the patient floor would run out of supplies. In order to get the patient what he or she needed immediately, nurses would run to another floor and take supplies out of the supply closet. But this process was completely invisible

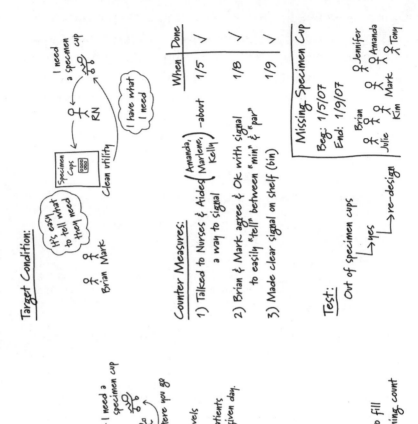

Figure 9.1 A3 Drawing: Problem with Specimen Cups

to the materials staff, who didn't know that the nursing staff was running out of supplies. Instead of the nursing staff calling materials staff in the middle of the night when no one was there, the nursing staff was first-order problem solving. Nurses were doing what was best for the material services associate but not what was best for patients. According to Griffin,

> The improvement to our operations happened after we mapped out the pathways. If the bins for specimen cups were empty, then nurses simply picked up the bin and put it on a different table. Then, materials would easily see the empty bin, take it, and fill it every day versus every other day, as had traditionally been done. After discovering the root causes using adaptive design, the team eliminated inventory outages and reduced total time spent restocking by 50 percent. Better yet, this increased nursing time with patients, which improves patient relationships as well as nurses' satisfaction.
>
> We are developing our people, and these process improvement exercises have given associates a sense of empowerment. Today, staff are reporting more and more problems because they see that senior management is listening, and issues are getting resolved. If senior leaders did not change the way that they worked, then why would anyone else change the way they work?

The transformation occurred across Ascension Health's entire organization (associates, physicians) as well as outside the organization (patients, materials vendors), and the product delivered (health care that works, is safe, and that leaves no one behind) is greatly enhanced. Associate satisfaction scores jumped from 68 percent during the fourth quarter of fiscal year 2006 to 82.8 percent in the fourth quarter of fiscal year 2007. The physician score to the question about "overall satisfaction with my hospital" climbed from 97 percent in 2006 to a perfect satisfaction score of 100 percent in 2007 and NPS is high: 67 percent.

The key lesson for us was the importance of understanding the impact that poor processes had on patients and frontline workers and making the appropriate changes. We can all learn from Ascension Health's concept of "humble learning" and engaging the front line in problem solving. Frontline employee engagement can transform both internal and external experiences. Improving processes and engaging people can turn an ordinary hospital visit into an exceptional one.

Developing Brand-Focused Communities

Community is quite the buzzword in the marketing world today. What is community and why is it important? In this section we refer to a community as an online web environment where organizations or brands create an active and ongoing dialogue with key segments, analyze member input, prioritize and act on feedback, and close the loop with community members. The growth of the Internet and social networks has created this vehicle to dialogue with customers about products and services, shifting market investments from traditional advertising to interactive engagement models including brand-based communities.

Developing vibrant customer communities is becoming increasingly important for brand differentiation and competitive advantage. eBay, with a quarter of a billion users, has built a community around its global trading platform. It began this journey with a foundation of community values to create an open and honest environment, one of the key ingredients for success. The vice president of marketing is a huge advocate of community building. Kip Knight had this to say: "Community matters at eBay because it is a strategic differentiator; it builds loyalty, drives customer retention, and keeps members actively engaged. eBay's online community is one of our biggest assets, and we want to keep it vibrant for everyone. We have to maintain the balance of an open community with sufficient safeguards and rules."

eBay created community development programs to collect customer feedback. Knight went on to say, "You must have a lot of courage to invite your customers in and let them share anything they want because they may share negative feedback. However, giving customers a voice in an open forum is a valuable asset." eBay used outreach vehicles such as member workshops, blogs, forums, town hall meetings, and personal calls. It also created a forum for customers to share feedback, the Voices Member Input Program, which started in 1999. It is an ongoing advisory group selected to provide qualitative input on policies, projects, and critical decisions to help eBay take the most informed action. Knight wants to continue the Voices community to receive customer feedback that will improve eBay's relationships, business decisions, and overall growth.

Brand-Based Communities

The incredible growth of social networking services such as MySpace, LinkedIn, and Facebook has changed the landscape for you and your customers. Customers are increasingly interconnected, using a converging array of communications and collaboration technologies such as Internet, mobile, SMS, MMS, e-mail, blogs, and social networking services that are linked and ubiquitous in social and business life. We can leverage these new technologies that are quickly becoming mainstream to learn from and communicate with customers through a vast array of channels.

Online brand-based communities provide an opportunity for brand managers to embrace and engage with their best customers. They offer a place where users can interact with the brand and with one another. These are different from social networking sites, where the primary goal for users is to connect with other users based on off-line connections and common interests. The goal of brand-based communities is to engage customers in a way that improves the relationship, creates better products and services, and activates word of mouth.

This market is so fast paced that by the time you read this book, some of our comments may be obsolete. Large-scale social networks put millions of people from multiple demographics and geographies into communities of aligned interest. That interest could be a product or service, or just the opportunity to go to a special restaurant that evening. People seek communities that share their passion for a topic, and our bet is that they will join and leave many different communities during their lifetime. Some are designed to be transient in nature (support for a presidential candidate; a group for young mothers), while others aspire to stay with you for life. The landscape is incredibly fluid. This section applies and expands on social networking concepts to create vibrant brand-based communities.

Brand communities extend the peer-to-peer engagement model to allow community members to interact with the brand. Membership is valued by the community members because they have an opportunity to influence improvements in products and services with which they have a strong affinity. Successful communities work hard to continuously find ways to provide members with unique benefits of value such as early access to new products. The value to the brand is twofold. First, insight is gained from feedback from your most passionate customers. Second, increased loyalty results; by building long-term relationships through demonstrated listening, you can increase word of mouth for the participants who could prove to be the most vocal brand promoters.

Promoters who are brand enthusiasts will be more than happy to interact with your organization on a personal level by giving feedback. Some of the strongest brands in terms of passionate customers and brand affinity (Apple, Harley Davidson, Starbucks) have direct touch points with the customer through stores, dealerships, and events. An online community can augment these experiences by creating a touch point that is based on listening to customers and not selling to them. This becomes even more important for brands delivered through a channel intermediary. When the only interaction the customer has with the brand is the product itself, it becomes very difficult for the customer to engage with the brand; the online community therefore becomes a critical point of interaction.

This format of listening to the customer to gain brand feedback is different from that of an online panel or focus group, where the interaction typically ends there or after the coupon, discount, or other incentive is exchanged for their participation. Communities create a feedback mechanism but the difference is that they allow the creation of an ongoing relationship and typically attract brand advocates, not just people in search of a coupon. This relationship isn't based on paying people for what they think; instead it's based on an opportunity to engage with the brand that they love and to make it better together.

Identifying brand advocates who want to engage with you is the easier part of the relationship. By leveraging the touch points you already have (websites, customer support, packaging, point of sale, advertising), you create many opportunities to invite customers to participate. The challenge that organizations usually run into is remembering to close the loop by sharing the learning and telling or showing community members how you have used their input to improve the brand experience. The Intuit story described later in this chapter is a great example of closing the loop with customers and illustrates one of the main reasons its Inner Circle community is so strong.

We have shown that referrals from Promoters are critical to business growth. What's most exciting about word-of-mouth opportunities with communities is the win-win opportunity they offer. There are two ways to generate word of mouth are feeding and seeding. Feeding word of mouth is an overt call to action for people to talk about your product or service. This is done through asking members to talk about the brand; giving them coupons, discounts, or product samples to share with friends; or other blatant attempts to get people talking. Feeding isn't necessarily a bad way to generate word of mouth, but it can be expensive (if coupons or samples are involved), and, more important, it's not sustainable over time.

In contrast, seeding creates experiences or opportunities that make people want to talk about your brand. Giving your Promoters sneak peeks or prerelease samples that others outside the community cannot access provides them with social currency. The ability to talk about unique information can be more appealing than a coupon or discount to this target group. In a sense, you are thanking your best customers with access or information that becomes social currency that they "cash in" with friends and colleagues by talking about your brand. That's the win-win and the seed for an organic and powerful form of word of mouth.

LEGO's Communities

The rise of brand-based online communities can be seen at companies like LEGO and Intuit. Brand-based communities give better return on product investment and marketing dollars. LEGO is a successful example. In previous chapters, you read that LEGO developed user communities, including the kids' Inner Circle, around 7,000 members. Although they see the community as an asset that provides customer feedback for operational improvements and product innovation, customers also value the community because they can voice their opinions, learn from others, and receive benefits. It engages members by a specific segment that may want a different type of product than what LEGO had previously offered.

LEGO engaged community members to provide feedback into product development and created the Star Wars Imperial Star Destroyer. The toy was marketed to and through the community, with astronomical success: the annual production run was sold out in just five weeks, and the toy achieved ten times return on the product investment in eighteen months. To date, this has been the most successful and profitable product LEGO has ever developed. On top of that success, a product created to cater to the same segment, the Santa Fe F7 locomotive, sold out in two weeks. The common theme is that LEGO listened to customer needs, engaged members in requirements and market testing, took action on the feedback, and activated word of mouth. This was a win-win strategy for innovating products and improving customer engagement and loyalty.

Creating an online community is only the first step. As your program advances, identifying segments within the community and working with each segment uniquely will enable more opportunities to cultivate loyalty. The Imperial Star Destroyer was created by identifying a niche segment that wanted a larger building experience: LEGO also identified highly influential trendsetters in the community who were effective in spreading positive word of mouth. Offering no incentives, these influencers recruited children to LEGO Club, and the number of kids doubled through a natural effect of word of mouth.

How can organizations build brand across communities, brands, and segments? We discuss the next generation of community development strategy and share the advanced techniques of market leaders like Intuit to leverage specific segments.

Intuit's Inner Circle Collaboration

Intuit is an outstanding example of a company that has created a virtuous loyalty cycle. This company provides software for accounting, personal finance, and tax preparation with well-known brands such as Quicken, QuickBooks, and TurboTax. It has transformed a specific group of TurboTax product users known as the "Inner Circle" into what are effectively loyal product development teammates. From their feedback, Intuit's internal product development teams are able to continuously create innovative and more usable products based on valuable customer feedback. In addition, employees are inspired to find new ways to treat this special segment in ways that matter to the community and increase loyalty. For customers, the Inner Circle is "a place to share your insights and see the results." Intuit created this symbiotic relationship by empowering community members to participate in product development, which in turn increased word of mouth and customer retention.

The Inner Circle is one of the biggest assets to Intuit's product and marketing teams. In essence, product and marketing managers can get answers to their questions quickly. How many firms would want to be able to turn to their customer for immediate product help? Intrigued, we turned to Christine Morrison, the product manager of customer relationships, who runs the Inner Circle, to ask how Intuit put together a "product development team" of over thirteen thousand ready, willing, and able voluntary participants. Morrison shared the highlights:

> When we first started engaging with customers, we asked TurboTax customers to sign up as beta testers, and two thousand people signed up. We grew this community from two thousand to over thirteen thousand in four years! We believe they answered the call because we do what most companies don't even think of doing: we give these self-identified, voluntary customers early access to products and a greater voice in product and marketing development.
>
> Through community surveys, we learned more about customer segments, specifically who within the Inner Circle were the most influential ones. Originally we considered flying some of these customers in to meet our general manager, but the numbers got too big. Instead, we decided to host local events, which were easier for us to handle and easier for customers to attend. We held local member appreciation events and invited everyone in the area. We had fun with the

event: drink champagne, take pictures, post the pictures to a blog, do product demos, and send everyone home with a free copy of TurboTax. We set up tours where customers shake hands with people making the product, where their feedback is going. Members love it.

Another Inner Circle event was the Town Hall Meeting. At the session, Intuit's general manager and senior staff worked in-person alongside the hand-picked Inner Circle members and made product decisions and resolved design issues on the spot. It was incredible!

If we don't know why customers are not using product features, we ask the Inner Circle members for help. Let's say our product managers are wondering if a button should be on the left or right side of the screen. With the Inner Circle, they can literally get the answer almost immediately from a thousand people. That's instant gratification from the people who matter most. Our product managers are wowed. Before the Inner Circle, they might have guessed to put the button on the left, but they could not quantify their hunches or validate them. The Inner Circle takes the guesswork out of building changes into our product and marketing efforts.

I will share two examples of design issues that were resolved through our community. Last year, users who received an error message saw a pop-up window with a button called "More info." If they clicked on the button, they'd go to a screen that would help them troubleshoot the error. The problem? No one clicked on the button, and we weren't sure why. The team knew we needed a new label for the button, but they weren't sure what it should be. To find out, I took a screen shot of the button and put it on the blog and asked what we should rename the button. After about seventy-two hours, we had dozens of responses from the community. The team reviewed the responses and blended two of the responses and renamed the button "Click for Solution." Here is the blog posting that shows the steps we took to close the loop with customers:

We Need Your Help!

December 27, 2006 03:15 PM | by cmorrison

We need your help! We have a quick question we'd like the customer perspective on. To respond, please just reply in the comments. We'd love to get responses from as many members as we can over the next week.

Here's the situation: This year, when users hit an error message in the product, we can link them to the support site article that gives you **troubleshooting information on what to do to resolve the problem.**

The issue? People who reach the error message don't seem to be clicking the "More Info" button. **What would be a better label for this button?**

Looking forward to your response,

Christine Morrison
Manager, TurboTax Inner Circle

———————

January 5, 2007 03:12 PM | by christine_morrison

UPDATE FROM CHRISTINE MORRISON:

You guys made me proud . . . thanks for all the great ideas! We don't need to collect any more; the team is considering the many options you provided.

The team is down to the top 5 ideas they like:
Troubleshoot error
Solution
Troubleshoot Info
Solution Option
Fix it Myself

I'll let you know when they choose a winner.

Christine Morrison

Manager, TurboTax Inner Circle

January 11, 2007 09:35 AM I by christine_morrison

FINAL UPDATE from Christine:

The team has decided to go with "Click for Solution," a combination of several ideas. Thanks again for all your quick help!

Christine Morrison

Morrison continued:

Another example of how our customers help with product development is a sheet with tax filing instructions that people could print out to help with the filing process. The original printout was difficult to read and needed better spacing and breaks, but would take valuable engineering time to fix. We sent the question to our Inner Circle with an example of the proposed layout. An amazing one thousand people responded overnight and overwhelmingly in favor of the new design at 84 percent! This allowed Intuit to stop internal debate about the instruction sheet layout and proceed with improvements that would add value to customers. We also saw a drop in call volume after the change.

We are world-class listeners—that's how we create more Promoters. We listen and make changes on valuable customer feedback. For example, last year we had some data that implied Promoters and Detractors sign up for different reasons. In response, we customized the Inner Circle website to optimize relevant information according to whether members were Promoters or Detractors. For example, our Promoter website contained

information about beta testing and social interaction—
things Detractors weren't as interested in. Meanwhile,
Detractors typically want to see what issues have arisen
and how they have been fixed. We moved the needle
six points with this group of members within the same
season, based solely on their level of engagement with
Intuit.

Who speaks up on our behalf? The people we have
the closest relationships with. We've noticed that
those customers we have the closest relationships with
are more likely to actively "stick up for us" on our forums
and blog comments. We have seen a link between
engaged Inner Circle members and an increased NPS.
Our next steps are to harness the momentum we have
and expand the group. We're also interested in finding
ways to map the help they give us with a corresponding increase in Net Promoter score. We know the Inner
Circle is a powerful asset and want to continue to serve
them as they serve us.

Morrison's story illustrates how Intuit has innovated product
design by using feedback from its special segment of Promoters.
Inner circle feedback influences both product designers and the
Web community. The story also reveals the untapped potential of
positive word of mouth. Intuit's next step is to leverage this loyal
and vocal Promoter group to amplify word of mouth throughout
the larger customer base and create a groundswell of Promoters.
We look forward to hearing a great number of success stories in
the near future.

Identifying NetWorked Promoters

In Chapter Two, we discussed the role that NPS plays in predicting word-of-mouth behaviors. In that discussion, we focused

on two behaviors most commonly linked with profitability and growth—buying and referral—and demonstrated the robust relationship between NPS and each behavior for a variety of industries. Furthermore, we examined how referral economics, which quantify the business that is gained (or lost) as a function of word of mouth, exerts a significant influence over total customer worth.

Our findings regarding the central role word of mouth plays in customer purchase decisions is strongly supported by research literature. Consumers often seek recommendations from others when making purchasing decisions about many types of products or services, and consider information gleaned from others to be more trustworthy than advertising or other sources. In fact, approximately 80 percent of consumers cite other people as the most trustworthy source for purchase decisions (Forrester, 2004; GfK Roper Consulting, 2006; Nielsen Company, 2007; Vizu Corporation, 2007). As well, the incidence of seeking out opinions on the Web is on the rise; a poll conducted by Vizu Corporation found that approximately 75 percent of U.S. consumers consider it "very" or "extremely" important to use customer reviews as part of their purchase process. As a result, word of mouth has a huge impact, positive or negative, on an organization's success.

With the recent increase in interest in the impact of word of mouth, there has been a corresponding increase in explorations of how this peer-to-peer information is exchanged. One of the most influential treatments of this topic comes from Malcolm Gladwell, author of The Tipping Point (2000), Gladwell uses a combination of social science research and business anecdotes to identify three distinct roles in the propagation of customer preferences: Mavens, Salesmen, and Connectors. While the mechanisms and model for communication are still debated, the key idea is that different types of individuals may have different roles and differing levels of influence on others. It is little surprise, then, that organizations that have come to embrace word of mouth as a marketing tool have begun to consider the question of *who* to target as part of their campaigns.

Which customers have the greatest potential for evangelizing on behalf of your brand, for influencing the purchase decisions of others? This is the question that leads us to the concept of what we call "NetWorked Promoters." As the name implies, these individuals are Promoters in the classic sense based on their NPS, yet they are differentiated in the network effect they offer. In the research reviewed in Chapter Two, we demonstrated that Promoters are the nexus of positive word of mouth: they are the individuals most likely to recommend your products and services. The link between Promoters and word of mouth is not perfect because one's stated likelihood to recommend is not a guarantee of actual referral behavior. As such, even Promoters are differentiated in terms of their potential to influence others on your behalf. If this is the case, how can you identify that segment of Promoters who exert the greatest influence on potential customers?

What's Special About NetWorked Promoters?

NetWorked Promoters in many ways are the ideal customers from a marketing perspective. They are a proxy for your sales force, sharing their positive experiences and referring others to your business. We've identified the following key elements that make them successful in this endeavor:

- Their likelihood to recommend your products and services
- Their connection to a social network of others like themselves
- Their actual referral behavior

These dimensions are independent of one another—for example, a particular customer may be quite enthusiastic about a particular organization or industry but nevertheless have limited reach in that he or she has relatively few opportunities to interact with others on that topic. However, when the dimensions converge, the confluence yields a special category of NetWorked Promoters. The key identifying features of NetWorked Promoters can be broken down along the two primary dimensions of the name: Is this customer a networker (connected to others) and a Promoter (likely to recommend your products and services to others)?

Networkers

We all know people who are the resource for everyone within our social circle on a particular topic. Most of us also have one or more friends or acquaintances who are tireless social gadflies who occupy the center of our extended social network and seem to know everyone. Individuals with these characteristics are well positioned to reach a broad audience with their opinions.

There are several possible approaches to measuring the extent to which someone is a "networker." Most simply, it can be estimated based on the size of a customer's social network relative to others, something that can be assessed with a few simple questions (for example, the Affective Communication Test developed by Howard Friedman). It could be based on customer self-assessment or it may even be assessed indirectly—for example, tracking of actual referral behaviors, nomination by others, and engagement and participation of individuals within a community over time. The goal is the same: to converge on customers who are positioned to share their opinions about you with the greatest number of potential new customers.

Promoters

An individual's response to the Recommend question is a measure of *potential* word of mouth rather than the realization of that potential. As we noted in our review of the Net Promoter word-of-mouth economic framework (Chapter Two), of the Promoters in the computer hardware industry, approximately three-quarters report that they made a positive referral in the previous year. Although being a Promoter is strongly predictive of referral behavior, it is not a guarantee.

For this reason, NetWorked Promoters are an extension of the traditional definition of a Promoter. These individuals, for a variety of reasons, tend to follow through on the inclination to share their positive experiences with greater frequency than other Promoters. Contributors to this tendency may be individual personality characteristics, level of personal engagement and involvement with your products and services, and, of course, passion for your organization or product itself—the cornerstone of the NPS measurement.

Targeting your NetWorked Promoters, those who will promote your products and services, are inclined to share their experiences with others, and have a ready network of potential customers to receive their message, can have an enormous long-term positive impact on growth.

Harnessing Word of Mouth

Organizations interested in assessing and harnessing the power of word of mouth are faced with the following key challenges:

- Identifying customers who are likely to say positive things about the brand
- Identifying customers who have a greater opportunity to talk to and influence others
- Understanding what these key customers like to talk about, and why
- Assessing the impact of the word-of-mouth behaviors of these key customers
- Identifying opportunities to leverage and amplify the influence that these key customers have on others

This presumes that the overarching goal is to find individuals who are natural drivers of word of mouth for your products and services. On the other hand, the advertising world offers an alternate school of thought that equates word-of-mouth behavior with buzz. Typically this approach seeks to influence potential customers directly through television, advertising, online, or even paid advocacy in an effort to create interest and momentum around specific products and services. In the context of Net Promoter, we think such efforts place the cart before the horse; as practitioners of Net Promoter programs are aware, creating a compelling customer experience *first* is the key. Once this has been accomplished, customer loyalty and its benefits, including positive word of mouth, will follow.

Marketing messages alone will not create the conditions for organic growth; it is the alignment between the brand promise and the actual customer experience that fuels positive word of mouth and growth. Once under way, this dynamic—a compelling customer experience that drives loyalty, loyal customers who tell others, and indoctrinating new loyal customers—creates an ongoing growth engine or promotional spiral.

Activating NetWorked Promoters

Organizations have had success with a Net Promoter program strategy of targeting NetWorked Promoters to maximize the impact on future growth. They typically start by setting corporate, program, and business unit goals and then work on segmentation and customer treatment strategies to create unique benefits for this group. Through profiling and segmentation, they find NetWorked Promoters who can influence others by spreading positive word of mouth more quickly and more broadly than average customers.

Some business-to-consumer (B2C) organizations have created online communities during the product and service registration process by collecting customer interests, size of social network, and likelihood to influence others. By combining inputs from other technology sources such as CRM systems with demographic information, website log-in frequency, past feedback provided, buying and spending habits, and referrals, organizations can triangulate which customers have been the most engaged and then rate these customers based on their level of influence. At this point, calculating the value of an "average" customer against a NetWorked Promoter will provide a tangible basis for creating different treatment levels, rewards, and benefits for the most influential segments with the greatest sphere of influence. After running a campaign with NetWorked Promoters, track their behaviors over time to get a more concrete understanding of their reach, buying patterns, and word-of-mouth referral impact to the business. Do their purchase, referral, and brand engagement behaviors as well as NPS increase? This type of analysis will provide proof points as you build your business for future engagements.

Brand affinity is equally as important for business-to-business organizations. For example, Marketing often manages a customer reference program. Traditionally, Marketing works with customers by asking their participation in speaking engagements, case studies, press releases, and sales references. This activity may be complemented by building communities for Promoters, allowing you to leverage their extensive network, naturally spreading word of mouth within their network. NetWorked Promoter attributes that show their potential sphere of influence may include the number of LinkedIn business contacts, the number and breadth of speaking engagements performed annually, their associations and memberships, their organization brand value, and softer factors such as their credibility in the industry, personality, and ability to articulate their affinity to your brand.

NetWorked Promoter Summary

Tailoring marketing efforts to NetWorked Promoters extends the Net Promoter approach by focusing your efforts on those that can have the greatest impact on your business. Launching a proactive referral program, creating and encouraging community (online involvement, advocacy events), providing content and tools to seed promotion (inside scoop), and empowering involvement in product design, problem solving, and new product launches, are ways to develop your community. Engage customers by bringing them into partnership and by leveraging the word of mouth of your most influential advocates. Mass marketing is no longer an effective way to reach customers. Instead, identifying customer segments, creating brand advocates, activating NetWorked Promoters, and partnering with this special group will help strengthen your brand, develop innovative products, and transform your business to set you apart from competitors.

Conclusion

In this chapter, we explored the leading edge of innovation around customer experience and its subsequent impact on organizations' performance. We admire those who break new ground. So many organizations choose to follow rather than lead, driven by the belief that there is safety to be found by avoiding risk; not so among Net Promoter leaders.

By now, the benefits of focusing your organization on building a customer-centric DNA should be clear. We have shared several stories we found in our research of what world-class companies are doing to transform their organization and build competitive differentiation. These activities increase value for your business through increased loyalty resulting in positive word of mouth and profitable growth.

We hope that in this chapter, as in the rest of the book, you are inspired by the innovations of these organizations to go beyond just building a great Net Promoter program to transformations in customer experience.

Resources: Interviews Conducted

Aggreko. Headquartered in Glasgow, Scotland, Aggreko specializes in the rental of portable power generation, air compression, and temperature control equipment. With over $1 billion in sales and 121 locations in thirty-one countries, Aggreko rentals help clients save money while solving problems and reducing risk. An intense focus on their customers' experience has helped Aggreko become the market leader in its focused market. http://www.aggreko.com/.

Rupert Soames, CEO

Simon Lyons, director of marketing & communication

Allianz. One of the world's biggest insurers, Allianz SE offers a range of insurance products and services—including life, health, and property and casualty coverage for individuals and businesses—through some one hundred subsidiaries and affiliates operating around the globe. www.allianz.com.

Andrew Clayton, group vice president

Aon. Aon is a leading global provider of risk management service, insurance and reinsurance brokerage, and human capital consulting. The company offers these services through its three business units: Aon Risk Services, Aon Re Global, and Aon Consulting. www.aon.com.

  Phil Clement, global chief marketing and communications officer

---

Ascension Health. Ascension Health is the nation's largest Catholic, nonprofit health system with more than ten thousand associates and health facilities in twenty states and Washington, D.C. It serves patients through a network of hospitals and related health facilities providing acute care services; long-term care; community health services; and psychiatric, rehabilitation, and residential care. www.ascensionhealth.org.

  Peggy Kurusz, director of research and development
  Mary Ellen Griffin, executive director of support services

BearingPoint Management and Technology Consultants. With over $3 billion in revenue and 17,500 employees, BearingPoint Inc. is a leading consulting firm with operations in over sixty countries worldwide. The U.S. government accounts for approximately 30 percent of sales for BearingPoint, while its private sector operations provide solutions to many of the world's leading companies in industries such as communications, financial services, and technology. www.bearingpoint.com.

  Cheryl Gutierrez, senior manager, client experience management
  Monique Libier, director of sales operations, commercial services, Americas

Yesenia Mendez, manager, client experience management, CS North America and Latin America

---

Brady Corporation. Headquartered in Milwaukee, Wisconsin, Brady is a global leader in industrial identification and specialty materials. With $1.3 billion in sales and eight thousand employees, Brady products include high-performance labels, wire markers, safety signs, industrial printing systems, specialty materials, and people identification products. www.bradycorp.com.

Allan J. Klotsche, president, Brady Asia

Dell. Dell Inc. is the world's largest direct-sale computer vendor, with products ranging from desktop and notebook PCs to network servers, workstations, and storage systems. The Dell approach of direct-sale, built-to-order machines has allowed it to grow to over $57 billion in annual revenue and eighty thousand employees. www.dell.com.

Laura Bosworth, director, global customer experience strategy

Dick Hunter, vice president of Global Consumer Support

---

eBay. Online auctioneer eBay is a cyberforum for selling more than fifty thousand categories of merchandise, from Beanie Babies to fine antiques, hosting about 300,000 online stores worldwide. www.ebay.com.

Kip Knight, vice president of marketing

Experian. Experian Group Limited, headquartered in Dublin, Ireland, is one of the world's leading information services companies.

With over 15,500 employees and $3.8 billion in annual revenue, Experian provides information to businesses and consumers to make informed commercial and financial decisions. www.experiangroup. com.

> Laura DeSoto, senior vice president, strategic initiatives, Credit Services Decision Analytics
>
> Julia Fegel, senior manager, client experience

GE. General Electric Company (GE) operates as a technology, media, and financial services company worldwide. The company was founded in 1892 and is based in Fairfield, Connecticut. www.ge.com.

> Vivian Hairston Blade, marketing, GE consumer and industrial

---

GE Real Estate. GE Real Estate, part of General Electric Commercial Finance division, manages around $72 billion in assets and employs two thousand professionals in thirty-one countries around the world. Its holdings include retail, industrial, and office properties. The focus on helping customers achieve success often requires custom-tailored solutions and technological innovation. www.gerealestate.com.

> John Godin, vice president, market research
>
> Bernhard Klein Wassink, senior vice president, global marketing

---

IBM Cognos. IBM Cognos (formerly Cognos Incorporated), based in Ottawa, Ontario, makes business intelligence and performance management software. Founded in 1969, it employed almost thirty-five hundred people and served more than twenty-three thousand customers in over 135 countries. In January 2008, Cognos was acquired by www.Cognos.com.

Dan Beer, associate vice president, global support programs and renewal

_____

IBM Enterprise Content Management, formerly FileNet. Acquired by IBM in 2006, this is a market leader of software for content management and corporate network solutions. It employs over sixteen hundred professionals with the goal of helping its business customers make effective and efficient decisions. www .filenet.com.

Suhail Khan, program director of worldwide customer loyalty program

_____

Intuit. Intuit Inc., located in Mountain View, California, is an industry leader in software for accounting, personal finance, and tax preparation. With $2.7 billion in sales and over seventy-five hundred employees, Intuit's product line is well known for its quality and ease of use with software such as Quicken, QuickBooks, and TurboTax. www.intuit.com.

Christine Morrison, product manager, customer relationships

_____

LEGO. The LEGO Group is a privately held, family-owned company, based in Billund, Denmark. It was founded in 1932 and today is one of the world's leading manufacturers of play materials for children, employing approximately forty-five hundred people globally. www.LEGO.com.

Conny Kalcher, vice president of consumer experiences

Peggy Conley, director of consumer insights, LEGO Company

Timothy Kirchmann, manager, CED consumer insights

Misys. Misys Healthcare Systems, based in Raleigh, North Carolina, is part of the U.K.-based Misys plc. It serves over 100,000 physicians and other caregivers with the tools they need to succeed in the constantly changing health care industry. www.misyshealthcare.com.

Aaron Morrison, director of customer loyalty

Orange Business Services. Orange Business Services helps connect companies around the world with its expansive network operations. Its offerings include global Internet protocol services, virtual private networks, and information technology services. Orange has a large list of multinational clients that benefit from its innovative technology and expanding professional services offerings including consulting and project management services. www.mnc.orange-business.com.

Axel Haentjens, vice president of marketing, brand and external communications

---

Sage Software. Sage Software is the North American business of U.K.-based Sage Group plc and provides small and medium-size businesses with software tools. With over $650 million in annual revenue and eight thousand employees, Sage Software offers products for every aspect of business management, including accounting, customer relationship management, and human resources. www.sagesoftware.com.

Hal Bloom, vice president, market research

Laurie Schultz, senior vice president and general manager, Sage Accpac and Simply Accounting

---

San Francisco Fire Credit Union. San Francisco Fire Credit Union of San Francisco has 20,947 members and assets of $429 million. The credit union, opened in 1959, has fifty-seven full-time employees and three part-time employees, or 361 members per employee, compared to a national average of 462. www.sffirecu.org.

Diana Dykstra, CEO/president

Symantec. Symantec Corporation, headquartered in Cupertino, California, has over $5.2 billion in annual sales and employs over seventeen thousand professionals operating in forty countries. As a leading provider of content and network security software to businesses and consumers, Symantec aims to "protect the integrity and unimpeded flow of the world's information." www.symantec.com.

John W. Thompson, chairman and CEO

Aisling Hassell, vice president of customer experience and online

Enrique Salem, chief operating officer

TD Canada Trust. The Toronto-Dominion Bank and its subsidiaries are collectively known as TD Bank Financial Group. TD Bank Financial Group is the seventh largest bank in North America by branches and serves approximately 17 million customers in four key businesses operating in a number of locations in key financial centers around the globe. www.tdcanadatrust.com.

Larry Hyett, vice president, retail sales and customer experience

---

Virgin Media. Launched in 2007, Virgin Media is the result of the merger between two cable companies, Telewest and NTL, and the addition of the highly successful Virgin Mobile brand. Together they now offer four of the most popular communication services: TV, broadband, fixed-line phone, and mobile. www.virginmedia.com.

Neil Berkett, CEO

Sean Risebrow, director of customer experience

References

Anderson, N. H. "Averaging Versus Adding as a Stimulus-Combination Rule in Impression Formation." *Journal of Personality and Social Psychology*, 1965, *2*, 1–9.

Arndt, J. "Role of Product-Related Conversations in the Diffusion of a New Product." *Journal of Marketing Research*, 1967, *4*(29), 1–295.

Dillman, D. A., Phelps, G., Tortora, R. D., Swift, K., Kohrell, J., and Berck, J. "Response Rate and Measurement Differences in Mixed Mode Surveys Using Mail, Telephone, Interactive Voice Response and the Internet," The American Association for Public Opinion Research (AAPOR) 56th Annual Conference, 2001.

Dillon, W. R., and Weinberger, M. G. The Effects of Unfavorable Product Rating." *Advances in Consumer Research*, 1980, *7*, 528–532.

Forrester Research. 2004. http://www.forrester.com/rb/research.

Fowler, F. J., Jr. *Improving Survey Questions: Design and Evaluation*. Thousand Oaks, Calif.: Sage, 1995.

Friedman, H. "Understanding and Assessing Nonverbal Expressiveness: Affective Communication Test." *Journal of Personality and Social Psychology*, 1980, *39*, 333–351.

GfK Roper Consulting. 2006. http://www.gfk.com/north_america/index.en.html.

Gladwell, M. *The Tipping Point*. New York: Little, Brown, 2000.

Hayes, B. *Measuring Customer Satisfaction: Survey Design, Use, and Statistical Analysis Methods*. Milwaukee, Wis.: American Society for Quality, 1998.

Herr, P. M., Kardes, F. R., and Kim, J. "Effects of Word of Mouth and Product-Attribute Information on Persuasion: An Accessibility-Diagnosticity Perspective." *Journal of Consumer Research*, 1991, *17*, 454–462.

Heskett, James L., Sasser, W. Earl, and Schlesinger, Leonard A. *The Service Profit Chain: How Leading Companies Link Profit and Growth to Loyalty, Satisfaction, and Value*. New York: Free Press, 1997.

Kroloff, G. "At Home and Abroad: Weighing In." *Public Relations Journal*, Oct. 1988, p. 8.

Kruskal, W. "Relative Importance by Averaging over Orderings." *American Statistician*, 1987, *41*, 6–10.

Laczniak, R. N., DeCarlo, T. E., and Ramaswami, S. N. "Consumers' Responses to Negative Word of Mouth Communication: An Attribution Theory Perspective." *Journal of Consumer Psychology*, 2001, *11*(1), 57–73.

Levitt, S. D., and Dubner, S. J. *Freakonomics*. New York: HarperCollins, 2006.

Mizerski, R. W. "An Attribution Explanation of the Disproportionate Influence of Unfavorable Information." *Journal of Consumer Research*, 1982, 9(3), 301–310.

Nielsen Company. Word-of-Mouth the Most Powerful Selling Tool: Nielsen Global Survey 2007. http://www.nielsen.com/media/2007/pr_071001.html.

Reichheld, F. *Loyalty Rules! How Today's Leaders Build Lasting Relationships*. Boston: Harvard Business School Press, 2001.

Reichheld, F. "The One Number You Need to Grow." *Harvard Business Review*, Dec. 2003, pp. 46–54.

Reichheld, F. *The Ultimate Question: Driving Good Profits and True Growth*. Boston: Harvard Business School Press, 2006.

Reichheld, F., and Teal, T. *The Loyalty Effect: The Hidden Force Behind Growth, Profits, and Lasting Value*. Boston: Harvard Business School Press, 1996.

Richey, M., Koenigs, R., Richey, H., and Fortin, R. "Negative Salience in Impressions of Character: Effects of Unequal Proportions of Positive and Negative Information." *Journal of Social Psychology*, 1975, *97*, 233–241.

Taylor, H. "Does Internet Research Work? Comparing Online Survey Results with Telephone Surveys." *International Journal of Market Research*, 2000, *42*(1), 51–63.

Theil, H., and Chung, C.-F. "Information Theoretic Measures of Fit for Univariate and Multivariate Linear Regressions." *American Statistician*, 1988, *42*(4), 249–252.

Vizu Corporation. 2007. http://answers.vizu.com/solutions/pr/pdf/Online-Holiday-Shopping-Market-Research.pdf.

Wilson, W. R., and Peterson, R. "Some Limits on the Potency of Word of Mouth Information." *Advances in Consumer Research*, 1989, *16*(1), 23–29.

Acknowledgments

We start by thanking all the organizations that have contributed their time and thought leadership toward examples and case studies. In particular, we thank our colleagues and friends at Aggreko, Allianz, Ascension Health, BearingPoint, Brady, Dell, Experian, GE Real Estate, IBM, Intuit, LEGO, Sage Software, Symantec, and Virgin Media for all the rich experiences they shared for the in-depth case studies. This is a book about successful cases and examples, and it would be pretty thin without these organizations and the folks who lead them.

Many of our colleagues at Satmetrix worked hard to make this book a reality. Thanks to John Abraham for his efforts to bring together leaders who contributed to the Net Promoter certification course and the book, as well as driver analysis work. Thanks to Emilia Brad for her insights on closed-loop process, Glenn Donovan for editing assistance, Martin Green for his program roadmap expertise, David Hankin for customer value calculation, Kevin Otsuka for cross-cultural benchmark research, Anita Tulsiani for input on the Dell case study, and Kevin Knowles for information on gaming.

A special mention to four individuals for their long hours of work and great ideas: "Dr. Know"—Vince Nowinski—our principal methodologist, made significant inroads in word-of-mouth research, as well as drafting and editing several chapters. If you understand any of the technical work in the book, it is probably due to Vince. Deb Eastman, our CMO, who not only provided conceptual insights but also contributed content to several chapters and helped edit the book. Raj Dhillon provided behind-the-scenes coordination and support for the project. Finally, a special thanks to Amy S. Cheng, our business consultant and project manager, who coordinated this gargantuan effort, provided ideas during brainstorming, assisted with contributor interviews, drafted and edited chapter content throughout the book, and managed grumpy authors.

The Authors

Laura L. Brooks, Ph.D., is widely regarded, along with Fred Reichheld, as the co-developer of the Net Promoter Score. Years of research, collection of *recommend* scores to the Net Promoter question (How likely is it that you would recommend Company X to a friend or colleague?), and understanding follow-on purchase behavior across multiple industries led Brooks and Reichheld to discover the power of Net Promoter. Since the publication of Reichheld's seminal article on Net Promoter in *Harvard Business Review* in 2003, Brooks has worked with leading companies to create effective Net Promoter programs. As a consultant and practitioner, she has extensive experience in advising organizations in the areas of employee opinion surveys, organizational development, customer satisfaction, management development, team building, quality, job evaluation, and designing compensation strategies.

Before joining Satmetrix as vice president of research and business consulting, she worked as a project director and manager for several consulting firms that specialized in statistical and psychological tools for measuring customer satisfaction and employee performance. Brooks has published on inter-rater reliability and validity in behavioral research methods in computers and also has participated in the survey-specific portion of the Malcolm

Baldrige Award. She holds a Ph.D. in industrial/organizational psychology from Rice University and a B.S. in psychology from Duke University.

Richard Owen arrived in the United States from Great Britain to attend graduate school at the MIT Sloan School of Management after several years as a management consultant with KPMG. Pure luck and lack of work opportunities led him to join a struggling Dell Computer Corporation in 1992, where his greatest hope was that the company would survive longer than his work visa. Things turned out ever so slightly better than expected. During eight years at Dell, he had the opportunity to participate in the reengineering of the company's supply chain and the launch of numerous international businesses, and he found himself as a vice president and general manager in Dell Japan. In the late 1990s he was responsible for Dell's Internet business worldwide and saw it grow to 50 percent of the company's total revenue.

Owen left Dell in 2000 and moved to California to head up AvantGo, a mobile technology company that he took public on the Nasdaq market and that was subsequently sold to Sybase. He joined Satmetrix, a technology and services company in California, in 2003 as CEO. Owen has a bachelor's degree in mathematics and economics from the University of Nottingham, England, and lives in California with his wife, Susan, and son, Alex.

Index